SHAMANIC QUEST
FOR THE SPIRIT OF
SALVIA

SHAMANIC QUEST
FOR THE SPIRIT OF
SALVIA

**The Divinatory, Visionary,
and Healing Powers
of the Sage of the Seers**

ROSS HEAVEN

Park Street Press
Rochester, Vermont • Toronto, Canada

Park Street Press
One Park Street
Rochester, Vermont 05767
www.ParkStPress.com

Park Street Press is a division of Inner Traditions International

Note to reader: The information provided in this book is for educational, historical, and cultural interest only and should not be construed as advocacy for the use of Salvia or other hallucinogens. Neither the author nor the publisher assume any responsibility for physical, psychological, legal, or other consequences arising from these substances.

Library of Congress Cataloging-in-Publication Data
Heaven, Ross.
  Shamanic quest for the spirit of Salvia : the divinatory, visionary, and healing powers of the sage of the seers / Ross Heaven.
     pages cm
  Includes bibliographical references and index.
  ISBN 978-1-62055-000-7 (pbk.) — ISBN 978-1-62055-148-6 (e-book)
  1. Shamanism. 2. Salvia—Miscellanea. 3. Salvia—Therapeutic use. I. Title.
  BF1623.P5H435 2013
  616.89'166—dc23

                                                                    2012047603

Printed and bound in the United States

10 9 8 7 6 5 4 3

Text design by Brian Boynton and layout by Priscilla Baker
This book was typeset in Garamond Premier Pro with Trajan, Gill Sans, and Legacy Sans used as display typefaces

Plates 1–4 paintings and plate 5 photograph by Ross Heaven.
Plates 6–8 and 10, and the illustration on page ii by Bruce Rimell, from his forthcoming publication *Salviaspace: Images from the Heartscape of Xca Maria* (www.biroz.net/salvia) used by permission.
Plates 9 and 11 by Yvonne McGillivray, www.creatrixx.org, used by permission.

To send correspondence to the author of this book, mail a first-class letter to the author c/o Inner Traditions • Bear & Company, One Park Street, Rochester, VT 05767, and we will forward the communication, or contact the author directly at **www.thefourgates.org**.

This is for the Sarah I knew in a different dream.
Fuma y agua. Amor para siempre.
And for Bodge in this one.

*Also for J. D. Arthur for beginnings. For what was found
and lost in Spain and Peru. For Jon Graham for support.
For my children and Indie. With thanks to Darryl,
Bobby, Tania, Emily, Suzie, Teertha, and Suzanne
for new possibilities. It's been emotional.*

CONTENTS

Salvia divinorum . . . *is definitely one of the plants which will shape the next few decades of the new millennium. . . .*

TERENCE MCKENNA

Salvia provides access to parts of the psyche that are normally out of reach. For this reason people often learn a lot about themselves during Salvia trips. . . .

DANIEL SIEBERT

Salvia did not fulfill any of my personal philosophical predispositions but rather, devastated them. The touchstones that had served to define my concept of reality have had to be discarded and a completely new set of reference points installed. . . . Salvia forced me to re-examine an entire complex of perceptions and assumptions that under normal circumstances would have been immune from such scrutiny. . . .

J. D. ARTHUR

*With your feet in the air and your head on the ground,
    try this trick and spin it.
Your head will collapse but there's nothing in it.
And you'll ask yourself: Where is my mind?
Way out in the water, see it swimming.*

PIXIES

Voyager (Bruce Rimell)

This image reminds me of the visions experienced by my wife, in Peru and then in Spain, of a "reality annihilation machine" of sorts: a multileveled conveyor belt holding various landscapes and slices of reality, worked by an overseer (in her case, a "blue god" of some kind): "like rolls of living wallpaper." Bruce's art conjures the same feeling, but in reverse: of realities unwinding and coming into being, a process again overseen by an entity of some sort. The similarities are striking from two people who have never met, shared experiences, or were even known to each other. The key difference—whether we see our realities as beginning or ending may say more about our own patterns and processes than it does about the nature of "reality" (whatever that means) or the spirit of Salvia.

BEFORE WE START DREAMING TOGETHER . . .

The Origin and Purpose of This Book

Few have heard of it
Fewer know what it looks like
Fewer still have ever met the sagely ally

DALE PENDELL, *PHARMAKO/POEIA*

A little over three years ago now I embarked on a shamanic quest to find the spirit of *Salvia divinorum*. Salvia is a power plant, a teacher and ally, which has long been used by the shamans of Mexico for healing and divination, but I had hardly worked with it before. So why the interest? There were a few reasons.

First, I have studied extensively with San Pedro, the visionary mescaline cactus of Peru, which is my own ally, and during my journeys with it, it suggested that I also get to know Salvia as the two plants had much in common. I had gone to Peru for several months to begin serious work with San Pedro, and it was as part of this that my Salvia explorations began.

Second, I was then co-owner of a plant medicine retreat center in the Amazon rain forest where we offered ayahuasca and sometimes San Pedro to participants to help with their healing, and I wanted to see if Salvia (a plant that also has a reputation as a profound healer) could become part of our program and an ally to others.

Third, Salvia is developing an unfortunate reputation in the West as a "dangerous recreational drug," and there is a (misguided and ill-informed) moral outcry by the media to have it banned. I understood the plant as a sacred shamanic medicine and was sad to see it belittled like this and its healing potential denied as a result of media panics and bandwagon politics. The same thing has happened since at least the 1960s with many of the useful psychedelics that aid our understanding of the self and the world we live in: LSD, DMT, mescaline. In America, Australia, and parts of Europe ayahuasca was also being targeted, "magic mushrooms" had been declared illegal, cannabis was moved from one "drug" class to another and back again. Even common herbs were being considered for an off-limits status unless you were a medical professional and "properly qualified" to administer them (which would theoretically make even giving a friend a cup of chamomile tea illegal unless you have trained first as a doctor).[1] We were back in the days of the witch hunts, and I wanted in some way to redress the balance, to show the potential of Salvia to heal.

I wasn't enamored with the idea of any teacher plant being used solely and soullessly for recreational kicks by ill-prepared teenagers (which is pretty much still how Salvia is presented on forums like YouTube) but there was no body of literature on the shamanic applications of Salvia and, in the absence of guidance, people with a need for healing (or at least to escape the mundane world and reconnect with their spirits) will always experiment for (and on) themselves. I thought that by doing this research I might be able to offer some of the advice that was missing on how to work with the plant in pursuit of the self.

There were one or two books on Salvia, which were a useful introduction, but none of them looked at shamanic work with the plant or its uses in healing, and most of them stemmed from the personal accounts of solo explorers. As J. D. Arthur, the author of one of these books, remarks, "My attempts to chronicle my own experiences presuppose [a] subjective interpretation. I have no idea if the experiences of others might parallel my own or be of a radically different nature."[2] Daniel Siebert, an early pioneer of Salvia (see the next chapter) adds that "although it does seem to have a lot of potential, the use of Salvia as a therapeutic tool has barely been studied at all."[3] It was time for a book based on more than single-person reports so that wider and more objective conclusions might be drawn about the nature of Salvia and its applications for healing.

My final reason for undertaking this project was less noble, more personal, but it was important to me at the time. I was in love with a woman who loved Salvia, and I wanted to share a journey with her. She should really have written this book—I wish she had—but that is a different story (and I will tell you some of it later).

It all hinged though on meeting The Shepherdess, as Salvia is called by the shamans of Mexico: connecting with its spirit so its teachings could be heard; and this became my quest. The search for the spirit of Salvia would turn out to be quite an adventure, entailing shamanic ceremonies in Peru and Spain, work with participants and clients over the course of more than two years, a tragic love affair, and an encounter with a promiscuous nun before I finally met The Shepherdess and was clear on what she has to tell us. The result is this book, the first shamanic study of diviner's sage and its ways of healing. I hope you find it useful.

The work continues with you. The tragic love affair is not compulsory (the nun may be) and in my experience is best avoided.

1

SALVIA DIVINORUM, THE SHEPHERDESS

An Introduction to Diviner's Sage (The Shepherdess),

Its Shamanic Uses, and Its Contemporary

Form, Salvinorin A

If I have a sick person during the season when mushrooms
are not available, I resort to the hojas de la Pastora. . . .
Of course, the Pastora doesn't have as much strength. . . .[1]

MARIA SABINA

Salvia divinorum is the botanical name of a visionary plant,* which,
despite the words of Maria Sabina, is the source of what is now widely
regarded as the world's most powerful natural hallucinogen.

---

*Albert Hofmann, who collected the first Salvia cuttings with Gordon Wasson,
objected to the botanical name, however, on the grounds that the literal translation of
Salvia divinorum is "Salvia of the ghosts" whereas "the correct name" according to him
should have been *Salvia divinatorum,* "Salvia of the priests." "I was not very happy," he
said in his typically understated way. Nonetheless, the botanical name is now in common usage and will also be used in this book.

More commonly known simply as "Salvia," its other names include "diviner's sage" and "magic mint" (the genus is part of the Lamiaceae or Mint family). The genus name, *Salvia,* comes from the Latin *salvare,* to heal or to save, while its complete botanical name, also translated from Latin, is generally understood as "sage of the seers."

The Mazatec shamans of Oaxaca, Mexico, where Salvia grows, use the plant for divination, visionary, and healing purposes and know it by many other names, all of which are associated with the Virgin Mary who is apparently regarded by them as the representation of its spirit (see my footnote on page 112). Among them are *Ska Maria pastora* (the leaf or herb of Mary The Shepherdess), *hojas de Maria* (leaves of Mary), *hojas de la pastora* (leaves of The Shepherdess), *hierba Maria* (Mary's herb), and simply, *la Maria.*

In its traditional shamanic usage the fresh leaves are rolled and chewed as a quid or made into a tea and drunk. When taken in this way the effects are usually (but not always) mild. When the active ingredient, salvinorin A, is extracted and smoked, however (the more frequent way of working with Salvia these days), it becomes highly—sometimes shockingly—potent.

SALVINORIN A

Salvinorin A was first isolated from Salvia by Alfredo Ortega in 1982 although he did not investigate its psychoactive properties. Another group led by Leander Valdes III did—but only on mice. Valdes tested it by administering injections of the compound, the results confirming that salvinorin A was the visionary component although its effects on humans were not tested.

That came in 1993 with the work of Daniel Siebert who was the first to produce concentrated extracts and, in the spirit of many psychedelic pioneers, to explore their effects on himself. As he reports, his first encounter was as strange and dramatic as others have subsequently found their own experiences to be.

I placed 2.6 mg of the material to be tested on a small piece of aluminum foil. I held a small torch under it and as soon as the substance vaporized I inhaled the fumes through a piece of glass tubing. I waited for a while and decided that nothing was going to happen. The last words to pass through my head went something like, "Just as I thought. This stuff is inactive. I'll go toss it in the trash." Then quite suddenly I found myself in a confused, fast-moving state of consciousness with absolutely no idea where my body or for that matter my universe had gone. I have little memory of this initial period of the experience, but I do know that a lot was happening and that it seemed quite literally like an eternity when in fact it must only have lasted a few minutes.

I knew something had gone wrong and I wanted desperately to get back to the "real" world. I searched my memory trying to remember the living room I was sitting in just moments before. I tried to remember what my body felt like. Anything, just something to reconnect me with the "normal" world. But the more I looked for some little thread of "normality" to get a hold of, the more it showed me something else. At some point I realized that what I was trying to get back to did not exist. It was just an ephemeral dream. I suddenly realized that I had no actual memory of ever having lived in any other state of consciousness but the disembodied condition I was now in. So I decided to stop panicking and just relax. After all there was no place to get back to. I was totally convinced that this state of existence was all there ever was.

Then, I suddenly found myself standing in the living room. . . . I was glad to be back. But then I saw that something was wrong! This was not my living room. It was the living room of my deceased maternal grandparents. And it was furnished as it was when I was a child, not as it was later in their life. The most extraordinary thing was that this was the real world, not a memory or a vision. I was really there, and it was all just as solid as the room I'm sitting in now.

I had the sudden realization that although I had managed to pull myself back into my body I had somehow ended up back in the wrong spot in the timeline of my physical existence. I was convinced that I might be stuck in this situation and would have to continue my life from this point in my past. As I panicked and desperately tried to remember where it was that I was supposed to be, I lost awareness of the physical world again, and found myself without a body: lost. Then it happened again. I found myself regaining consciousness in the real world. And again as I saw everything clearly, I realized that this was not my home, it was the home of a friend of mine. Then again I panicked and lost consciousness.

This cycle repeated at least seven or eight times. Always I would find myself in a familiar room. Some of these places were from my childhood, and some were from my more recent past. In this state all the points of time in my personal history coexisted. One did not precede the next. Apparently, had I so willed it, I could return to any point in my life and really be there because it was actually happening right now . . .

A little later the physical world all started to work properly again. As the effects began to subside I managed to piece together what had happened. When I remembered that I had tested the extract and that it must have been responsible for what I had just been through I felt ecstatic. I was literally jumping for joy. I wanted to say "EUREKA!" I had stumbled upon the psychedelic essence of Salvia divinorum. *I grabbed a pen and tried to write down a few notes while the experience was still fresh. The first thing I wrote down in BIG letters was, "IT IS TOTAL MADNESS," then, "TEARING APART THE FABRIC OF REALITY." . . . I had been shaken to the soul.*

Siebert wrote in *The Entheogen Review* the following year that salvinorin A is

an extremely powerful consciousness-altering compound. In fact it is the most potent naturally occurring hallucinogen thus far isolated. But before would-be experimenters get too worked-up about it, it should be made clear that the effects are often extremely unnerving and there is a very real potential for physical danger with its use.

When the herb . . . is consumed either by smoking the dried leaf or chewing the fresh leaves the effects are usually (but not always) pleasant and interesting. This is because when used this way the amount of salvinorin A absorbed into the bloodstream is usually very small, and in the case of the chewed leaves it is absorbed into the blood very gradually. The pure compound salvinorin A [however] is active at 200–500 mcg when vaporized and inhaled . . . [and] when the dose goes above 500–1000 mcg the effects can be very alarming. I have seen several people get up and lunge around the room falling over furniture, babbling incomprehensible nonsense and knocking their heads into walls. . . . When the experience is over they have no memory of any of this. In fact they usually remember very different events. To an outside observer people in this condition have a blank look in their eyes as if no one is present (and perhaps no one is).[2]

Dr. Bryan Roth of the University of North Carolina agrees with Siebert about the potency of the extract. In 2002 he discovered that salvinorin A, uniquely, stimulates a single receptor site in the brain, the kappa opioid. LSD by comparison stimulates about fifty receptors to produce its effects, which, even then, are not as potent or immediate. "Dr. Roth said salvinorin A was the strongest hallucinogen gram for gram found in nature," the *New York Times* reported.[3] He added that "its chemistry may enable the discovery of valuable derivatives [and] there's good evidence it could treat brain disorders including depression, schizophrenia, Alzheimer's, maybe even HIV."[4]

Although usually a much gentler experience, even chewing the leaves of Salvia (one of the more traditional shamanic ways of ingestion) can have profound effects as the anthropologist Bret Blosser discovered in the mid-1980s. He writes at The *Salvia divinorum* Research and Information Center about an experience he had in Oaxaca.

I never noticed the transition. I was not aware that I had eaten an entheogenic plant, was in Mexico, was with friends, or had ever had a body. I was engulfed in a complex, fluctuating environment. Much hung in the balance. I was facing awesome challenges and knew that I lacked the skills to deal effectively with them. However, I also knew that I might somehow do OK.

I remember very little of this first plunge into the world of the *hojas,* but toward the end I recall an intricate, neon-pastel, slick-lit, all encompassing, non-Euclidian topography. This sense of a distinctive topography has characterized each of my Mazatec Salvia experiences. Of course, what I can describe begs the question of what I cannot describe: being out of the three dimensions and linear time.[5]

MY INTRODUCTION AND REINTRODUCTION TO SALVIA

My own experiences with Salvia began in 2003. At that time I was working extensively with ayahuasca (*Banisteriopsis caapi*), the visionary "vine of souls," and San Pedro (*Trichocereus pachanoi*), the "cactus of vision," both of which are native to Peru. I had first visited the country in 1998 to drink both medicines and had started to take groups of people there for healing encounters with these plants a few years later. My first plant teacher was ayahuasca, which I went in search of, like many others, to find meaning in my life and gain new understanding of where I had come from and where I was going. Ayahuasca has the effect of taking you outside the body and into the spiritual universe, showing you all possibilities open to you. I also drank San Pedro at that time and realized that it had a complementary effect in the sense that it brings the spirit of the universe into the body and shows the possibilities open to us in *this* world.[6]

Over time my main plant teacher began to change from ayahuasca to San Pedro as I realized that it was more important for me to learn how to live properly and deal with "real-life issues" than seek the new options that ayahuasca reveals. The infinity contained within ayahuasca can be confusing, showing us too much. What I needed was practical, down-to-earth advice about how to *be* and how to be a better person. San Pedro provided that, and with its help it is a lesson I am still learning.

It is against this background of faith in the benefits of entheogens and many plant ceremonies of my own that I first heard about Salvia.

I believe it was one of my students who told me about it. It was the world's strongest visionary plant, she said, although its effects were short-lived and often very peculiar. I was intrigued by this because I had experienced some extremely strong (and sometimes also very peculiar) journeys with ayahuasca and wondered what a more intense experience could be like.

What also interested me was that Salvia is native to Mexico, and in that country there are four main teacher plants: sacred (psilocybin) mushrooms, the seeds of the morning glory, Salvia, and peyote. The latter is a mescaline cactus like San Pedro, my ally, and it seemed to me that Salvia might therefore be compatible with it since peyote and Salvia are both used by the shamans of Mexico, albeit independently of each other and, historically at least, in different parts of the country.

My first explorations with Salvia took place in the United Kingdom but were less than successful. When you work with any teacher plant you have to learn how to, and then learn the language of the plant and the way that *it* works with you. I didn't know how to use Salvia then and was really just experimenting. I drank the leaves as a tea and on other occasions chewed them, in the way the Mazatec shamans did. Apart from a slight sensation of numbness and a little light-headedness not much happened, certainly not the strong visionary experience I had been told to expect. No deep insights resulted, and since my interest was San Pedro I didn't have the intent to explore much further.

Salvia came up for me again in 2009. The book *Peopled Darkness*, written by J. D. Arthur about his experiments with the plant, was about to be reissued by Inner Traditions under the name *Salvia Divinorum*, and as an author of books on plant medicines myself I was asked to write an endorsement for it. I read Arthur's book and was surprised by it. He had worked with extracts of the plant, most often 5X concentrates,* and

---

*The "X" (nominally) denotes a multiplication of strength or effect, so that a 5X concentrate, for example, should be five times stronger than a single Salvia dose, although it doesn't always work out that way since nobody quite knows what a "typical" dose might be.

his experiences were nothing like mine; he had gotten a lot from it in terms of new understanding, enhanced creativity, and a unique sense of the world. My interest was rekindled, and I made a mental note to do further work of my own. It would have to wait for a while though as I was making preparations to go to Peru for several months to begin long-term work with San Pedro as well as running the ayahuasca healing center where I was then the co-owner.

Salvia was not going to let go of me this time though, and within a few weeks of getting to Peru the subject came up again. I had just appointed a new shaman, Jungle Svonni, to be the center's resident *ayahuascero,* and he had some limited experience of Salvia and wanted to explore it further. My co-owner and I were interested in it as well to see how it might fit into the therapeutic programs we had developed for our clients.

Following Arthur's lead we ordered Salvia extract (20X concentrate in our case) and began a series of experiments with it. I will talk about these in the next chapter but let's begin with an introduction to the plant.

WHAT IS SALVIA?

Salvia divinorum is a perennial herb in the mint family. Native to Oaxaca, Mexico, it grows in the humid forests of the Sierra Mazateca at altitudes of between 750 and 1,500 meters (2,400–4,900 feet). It can grow to over a meter (thirty-nine inches) in height and has large green leaves, hollow square stems, and white flowers with purple calyces.

The ritual use of psilocybin mushrooms by Mazatec shamans had been documented as early as the sixteenth century but information on Salvia is rarer and much more recent, dating mainly from the 1930s. During a field trip in 1938 the American anthropologist Jean Johnson learned that Mazatec shamans used a tea made from the leaves of Salvia for the purposes of divination in a manner similar to the mushrooms, primarily when the latter were out of season.

In 1952 Roberto Weitlaner also reported the use of the plant,

noting that its leaves were gathered by *curanderos* (shamans or healers)*
who harvested them after a session of prayer. In healing ceremonies an
infusion of 50 leaves was prepared (for the treatment of alcoholism the
dose was usually 100), and around midnight the curandero and patient
would go to a dark room where the patient drank the potion. After
about fifteen minutes he would enter a trance state, and from his speech
or during a subsequent discussion of his visions the healer was able to
make a diagnosis of the cause of his illness and know how to cure it.
The session ended by bathing the patient in some of the same infusion he had drunk. Weitlaner noted that Salvia was used for divination
as well as healing (for example, to trace lost objects or identify thieves
when a robbery had been committed).

Gordon Wasson was the first to describe the Salvia experience.
During a ceremony in July 1961 he drank the juice of 34 pairs of leaves
(68 in total) and noted that the effects came on faster than those of
mushrooms although they lasted a much shorter time. He reported seeing colors and three-dimensional designs.

The first Salvia specimens were collected by Wasson and Albert
Hofmann a year later while traveling with Weitlaner. The plants were
brought to them by the shamans who would not allow them to see
where the sage itself grew. They drank the brew again, and Hofmann
said that his experience was more intense this time and created a state
of heightened "mental sensitivity" although it did not result in "hal-
lucinations." His wife, who accompanied him and also drank, reported
seeing bright images.

Jose Luis Diaz studied Salvia in the Mazatec highlands during the
1970s and '80s, drinking an infusion of the plant on six occasions, noting like Hofmann that its potency increased each time. He saw visual
patterns, which he described as "complex and slowly changing," but
only in complete silence and with his eyes closed. After a while he also
noticed a lightness in his arms and legs and an "odd sensation" in his

---

*Curandero (curandera, if female) comes from the Spanish *curar:* "to heal." In the
Mazatec language they are instead called *cho-ta-ci-ne:* "one who knows."

joints. These feelings lasted for about ten minutes although more subtle effects persisted for a few hours.[7]

MAZATEC HEALERS AND SALVIA SHAMANISM

Wasson, Diaz, and Richard Evans Schultes have all commented on the difficulty of making contact with and gathering information from Mazatec shamans because of what Diaz calls their "jealous and secretive nature." "Visiting many shamans in a single area can actually lessen the amount of information gathered," he remarks, "as each curandero may fear the visitor is telling their secrets and giving their power to a rival. To them magic can hurt or kill." Despite this Diaz was able to find one informant, Don Alejandro,* from whom he was able to gather information during fieldwork in the summer of 1979 and spring of 1980. He tells us,

> The Mazatecs (the name, taken from the city of Mazatlan, was imposed on the natives by the Spanish) are nominally Catholic Christians but they have incorporated many features of their traditional beliefs into their conceptions of God and the Saints, whom they consider to have been the first healers. The most prominent among them is San Pedro, or Saint Peter, who is said to have cured a sick and crying infant Jesus through the ritual use of tobacco (*Nicotonia* spp.).
>
> For the Mazatecs, as well as for almost all Mesoamerican Indians, [tobacco] is the most important curing tool in the pharmacopoeia. The fresh tobacco leaf is ground, dried, and mixed with lime to form a powder known to the Mazatecs as San Pedro (Saint Peter); the best is prepared on the Saint's day, June 29th. . . . It is worn in charms and amulets as a protection against various diseases

---

*"Don" is a title like the Western equivalent of doctor but it also refers to a gift of healing given to the shaman by ally spirits.

and witchcraft, but its most important use is in *limpias,* or ritual cleansings. Anyone who comes to Don Alejandro to be treated usually gets a *limpia.* This ritual cleansing may be the cure in itself or it may be accompanied by other medicines. The patient is given a pinch of the San Pedro powder (wrapped in paper) to carry with them and use during the healing period.[8]

It is often given to patients during a Salvia ceremony as well.

Training to become a shaman is through an apprenticeship, which lasts for two or more years and teaches the shaman-to-be the practicalities of healing. Spiritual instruction comes through plant-induced visions and the teachings of angelic beings. Teacher plants are taken as part of this training at intervals of a week to a month. The process begins with successively increasing doses of Salvia, and through it the shaman-elect is said to become familiar with the route to Heaven.

In common with all plant work, a strict diet is followed during the training, with hot foods such as chili prohibited and abstinence from sex and alcohol, although Diaz remarks that some shamans allow the drinking of beer during the diet and other alcohol, principally tequila, may be taken in a ceremonial context. The first Salvia diet lasts for sixteen days; subsequent diets are a minimum of four days in length. Breaking it can lead to madness according to Don Alejandro.

The shaman learns that Salvia can be used as a medicine as well as for visions. For example a tea made from five pairs of leaves will cure anemia, relieve headaches and rheumatism, and regulate alimentary function (for example, to stop diarrhea or aid defecation in the case of stomach blockages). Diaz reports that there is also a magical disease that is cured by Salvia. This is known as *panzón de borrego* ("lamb belly") and takes the form of a swollen stomach, which results from a curse made by a *brujo* (sorcerer) who has placed a stone inside the sufferer. Salvia removes it, and the stomach returns to normal.

The future healer also takes Salvia to learn how to identify and use medicinal plants. Mazatec shamans believe that there is a tree in Heaven on which all healing plants grow, and under the influence of Salvia they are able to talk to God and the saints and learn the uses of these plants.

Aside from healing, Salvia is known for its divinatory powers and for this purpose it is prepared as an infusion of 20 to 80 pairs of fresh leaves, which may be taken by the curandero, the patient, or both depending on the situation. Salvia will then foretell the future and provide answers to detailed questions.

The observation that "20 to 80 pairs" of leaves are used comes from Diaz but it is very vague. There is a 60-pair (120-leaf) difference between these extremes, which is a wide margin for those who wish to explore Salvia themselves. To add to the confusion, Christian Rätsch in *The Encyclopedia of Psychoactive Plants* tells us:

> The Mazatec take thirteen pairs of fresh leaves (twenty-six leaves in all) and roll them into a kind of cigar (quid) that they place in the mouth and suck on or chew. . . . At least six fresh leaves are needed to prepare one quid (threshold dosage), while more distinct effects will occur with eight to ten leaves. . . .
>
> Dried leaves are best smoked by themselves. Here as little as half an average-sized leaf (two or three deep inhalations) can be sufficient to elicit profound psychoactive effects. Usually, however, one or two leaves are smoked. . . .
>
> Tinctures are prepared from fresh or dried leaves by using an ethanol-water mixture (60 percent alcohol). . . . Dosages appear to vary considerably. . . .[9]

Salvia can therefore be drunk as a tea/infusion, which is also the way to diet it (see chapters 2 and 4), chewed, smoked in a pipe, or held in the mouth as a tincture and not just in the way (or in the quantity) that Diaz describes. Additionally, in modern usage the extract can be smoked.

Karl Mayer remarks that "to date little that is certain is known about the Salvia ritual as corresponding ethnographic or historical evidence is lacking,"[10] and it may be this as well as the secrecy of Salvia shamans that gives rise to the confusions surrounding this plant in terms of its methods of ingestion and the number of leaves to use.

This, however, is how I have proceeded:

Tea/infusion: Thirty pairs of leaves are added to approximately half a pint of hot water and left to soak overnight. The leaves are removed, and the cold juice is drunk first thing in the morning as part of a shamanic plant diet.

Chewed: As part of the Salvia diet I have also chewed the leaves from the tea (30 pairs) and held them between the teeth and gums for about fifteen minutes so that the active ingredient passes into the bloodstream. Swallowing the leaves or their juice does little in this respect, although no harm results from ingesting them (see chapter 4).

Smoked: Four or five pairs of dried leaves can be crumbled into a pipe and smoked. Some say that two or three pipes of leaves smoked one after the other in this way will produce salvinorin-like effects. More usually, however, I have used the leaves as a substrate for a pinch of salvinorin extract (see chapters 2, 3, and 4).

Tincture: Twenty pairs of leaves in alcohol are held beneath the tongue for fifteen to twenty minutes, then the liquid is either spat out or swallowed.*

THE SALVIA CEREMONY

Salvia divinorum rituals almost always take place at night in complete darkness and silence. . . . After chewing the leaves the participants lie down and try not to make any sound. Both sounds and

---

*The reason for holding the tincture beneath the tongue is so that the active Salvia ingredient can more easily enter the bloodstream through the delicate tissues of the mouth. If simply swallowed the liquid has little effect, and salvinorin is inactive in the stomach.

sources of light will greatly disturb the visionary experience. Because the effects of the leaves are much shorter in duration than those of the [psilocybin] mushrooms Salvia rituals rarely last more than one or two hours.[11]

Diaz provides an account of two ceremonies he attended with Don Alejandro but these differ again from the description offered by Rätsch. It may simply be, as Mayer remarks, that not enough is yet known about Salvia shamanism to determine what makes a "typical" ceremony or, as I have discovered with San Pedro and ayahuasca shamans in other contexts, that not much is rigidly fixed in any ritual encounter, the shaman preferring to exercise his intuition and creativity according to what each circumstance presents, the needs of his patients, and the guidance he receives from spirit.[12]

In the ceremonies Diaz attended the curandero began making the Salvia infusion as darkness fell. The leaves were counted out in pairs and put into piles before being crushed by hand into a bowl of water. After the potion was prepared it was poured through a sieve into a glass. The spent leaves were set aside for bathing the participant's head to refresh him after the ceremony or to be discarded later in a location where they wouldn't be found.

The curandero picked up a glass of the infusion and called upon the Holy Trinity, the Virgin Mary, Saint Peter, and other saints to watch over participants. Those present then drank the brew, and following Mazatec tradition an assistant was in attendance who didn't drink in order to safeguard the others. As a last protection before their visionary travels the curandero performed *limpias* (ritual cleansings) on the participants by reciting prayers over each and anointing them with a piece of copal dipped in San Pedro (tobacco). He also gave them a pinch of San Pedro to carry.

During the first ceremony Diaz drank an infusion made from 50 pairs of leaves and after about fifteen minutes began to see visions, like columns of smoke in the darkness; then as the images increased in intensity, a mountain of ice, lights of various colors, a dark sky with bright objects in it, and a native village. The session lasted about an hour with a further hour spent in discussions about what he had seen.

In his second session he drank an infusion of 60 pairs of leaves and after fifteen minutes again felt the effects of Salvia: a sense of relaxation and colorful images of plants and flowers. A little later he reported that "I feel like I'm being twisted around inside of my body. Very strange sensations, like I'm being . . . twisted . . . like I'm spinning." He also recalled seeing "a large boat or something like that. And as if all the things inside were all very mechanical like a machine that was very, very precise and very geometric. . . . And again I began to see many flowers, but as if they were all mechanical, as if they were not . . . real." These sensations of being twisted or pulled and visions of things mechanical, of being inside a machine and of reality being not quite "real" are characteristic of the Salvia experience as we will see.

He remarks that even when the ceremony ended he still felt the influence of Salvia. "It is as though the body is intoxicated (*borracho*) and the mind isn't." While being driven home that night his visions continued. "Among them was the Virgin of Guadalupe amidst red, white, and green streaming banners."

SALVIA EFFECTS

Don Alejandro encouraged Diaz and his companions to talk about their visions throughout the ceremony and afterward in order to clarify them although this seems less common among other curanderos where ritual use involves silence so that the plant itself can be heard. (Mazatec shamans say that "La Maria speaks with a quiet voice.")

For many who have taken Salvia (especially in extract form) the immediate effects can be so extraordinary that they *do* wish to talk, but this is to risk prematurely deconstructing their journey or becoming so caught up in their descriptions that they do not hear the information that may still be being passed to them by the plant. In my experience the more useful insights and realizations from the journey tend to arise during the thirty minutes or so after the peak experience (or they may come in dreams following the ceremony), and it requires continued silence and introspection to hear them.

There are other effects, too, which are subtle but ongoing if attention is paid to them. Researchers (from the University of California and California Pacific Medical Center Research Institute) conducted a survey of five hundred Salvia users, for example, which suggests that post-ceremonial effects have a completely different character from the peak experience. About half of the users reported a pleasing "afterglow" and it is in this state of relaxation and expanded consciousness that the real work of insight or divination can best take place, and where questions can be put and answers received.

The study also showed longer-term effects that might last for days or more. These included:

- Increased insight: 47% of respondents
- Improved mood: 44.8%
- Feelings of calmness: 42.2%
- Increased connection with the universe and nature: 39.8%
- "Weird thoughts": 36.4%
- Things seeming unreal: 32.4%
- Increased self-confidence: 21.6%
- Improved concentration: 19.4%

Salvia may also have even longer-term therapeutic potential. We have already heard from Professor Bryan Roth who believes that drugs derived from the active ingredient could be useful in combating diseases such as Alzheimer's, depression, schizophrenia, chronic pain, and AIDS. Thomas Prisinzano, assistant professor of medicinal and natural products chemistry at the University of Iowa, has suggested that Salvia may also help treat cocaine addiction: "You can give a rat free access to cocaine [then] give them free access to salvinorin A, and they stop taking cocaine."

Finally, clinical pharmacologist John Mendelsohn confirms that "there may be some derivatives that . . . would actually be active against cancer and HIV . . . there are a lot of therapeutic targets that have many people excited."*

THE MYSTIQUE OF THE SHEPHERDESS

There are, however, mysteries to Salvia.

First, there are no creation myths that tell of its origin. Unlike ayahuasca, for example, where shamans have legends to explain the origins of the plant and its purpose on Earth (see my book *Plant Spirit Shamanism*[13] for a discussion of these), or San Pedro, where curanderos tell of the hummingbird bringing the secrets of God to Earth in the form of the cactus (see my book *The Hummingbird's Journey to God*[14] to read this story), with Salvia no such stories have yet been heard. From this we may conclude that Mazatec shamans are either extremely secretive about their Salvia myths or else they do not have any.

D. M. Turner, in his book *Salvinorin: The Psychedelic Essence of Salvia Divinorum,* also remarks:

> In a recent paper, Jonathan Ott has noted that the Mazatecs lack an indigenous name for *Salvia divinorum,* both the Christian theme of Mary, as well as sheep, having been introduced to the region during the Spanish conquest. The Mazatecs also list a method of consuming this plant that does not efficiently utilize its psychoactive content, and seem to be generally unaware of its tremendous potency. Based on this information . . . Ott has suggested that *Salvia divinorum* may be a post-conquest introduction to the Sierra Mazateca.[15]

---

*Other potential targets include treatments for eating disorders, motion sickness, convulsions, ischemic brain damage, hypertension, depression, arrhythmia, and for heroin, cocaine, alcohol, and amphetamine dependency. Kappa opioid agonists like Salvia are also antagonists for other receptor sites so further applications may include rheumatoid arthritis, systemic lupus erythematosis, Sjogren's syndrome, multiple sclerosis, chronic lymphocytic leukemia, type 1 diabetes, Epstein-Barr virus, coronavirus, and cytomegalovirus.

It is not uncommon for conquering nations to impose their ideologies on those they have conquered. As professor of cultural anthropology Irene Silverblatt puts it, "History making (which includes history denying) is a cultural invention. . . . History tends to be 'made' by those who dominate . . . to celebrate their heroes and silence dissent."*[16] Thus, for example, *huachuma,* the sacramental healing cactus of Peru, was renamed San Pedro by the invading Spanish to reflect their Catholic beliefs. In the case of San Pedro, however, the original name is known and ritual artifacts and depictions of the cactus have been found dating back 3,500 years BCE or more, proving the historic use of this plant well before the arrival of the Spanish. With Salvia no such evidence exists.

> *Her real name must not be told—*
> *Her real name is closer to Medusa than to Mary*
> *"They came with crosses—*
> *They came to drag us*
> *From our huts, from our beds,*
> *The soldiers that serve the priests"*
>
> DALE PENDELL

And it is not just the shamans who are mystified. Botanists have no definitive answer for the origins of Salvia either. They have been unable to determine whether it is a naturally occurring species or a cultigen, for example. The plant's partial sterility suggests a hybrid—although no likely parent species have been identified—and if the plant was created it begs the questions why and by whom?

Turner again:

Salvia divinorum . . . is not known to exist in the wild, and the few patches that are known in the Sierra Mazateca appear to be the result of deliberate planting. A Mazatec shaman informed Wasson that the Indians believe the plant is foreign to their region and do

---

*Quoted in my book *Cactus of Mystery*

not know from where it came. And if *Salvia divinorum* is a hybrid, there are no commonly held theories on what its prospective parents may be.[17]

A further puzzle is that although salvinorin A is by mass the most potent natural hallucinogen it has no actions on the 5-HT2A serotonin receptor, the principal molecular target responsible for the actions of psychedelics such as mescaline and LSD.

Shortly after discovering salvinorin A's effects, Siebert sent a sample to David Nichols who initiated a NovaScreen receptor site screening. The screening results were in contrast to those of all previously tested psychedelics. Salvinorin A did not affect any of the receptor sites tested, which included all of the likely known receptor sites for other psychedelics.[18]

Turner was writing in 1995, just prior to his death,* but in 2002 Bryan Roth partly solved this mystery when he discovered that salvinorin A stimulates a single receptor—the kappa opioid—but even that is strange and unique since other psychedelics stimulate multiple receptor sites. In other words, no one still quite knows how or why Salvia works.

As with all great entheogenic detective stories, therefore, the answers must be found by the individuals who choose to work with the plant themselves.

---

*D. M. Turner (DMT) was the pen name of Joseph Vivian (1962–1996), a psychedelic researcher who wrote books on entheogens. He died on New Year's Eve 1996 after injecting ketamine while in a bath of water, perhaps trying to emulate the scientist John Lilly's work with ketamine, LSD, and flotation tanks (the basis for the Ken Russell film *Altered States*). It is believed that Turner drowned.

2

THE QUEST IN PERU

Beginning the Shamanic Exploration of Salvia

(Salvinorin 20X Concentrate) in Iquitos • The Search

for the Spirit of the Plant and Its Applications

for Healing • A Diet of Salvia and Its Use

with San Pedro and Ayahuasca

*Most people who have ingested Salvia . . . reported very
bizarre and unusual psychoactive effects that are difficult
to compare to the known effects of euphoric or psychedelic
substances. Space is often perceived as curved and surging,
and rolling body sensations or out-of-body experiences are
frequently described. . . .*[*1]

CHRISTIAN RÄTSCH

The Encyclopedia of Psychoactive Plants. Quoting Bolle (1988) and Jansen (1996) he
does add, however, that "these effects are strongly reminiscent of those that are experienced at subanesthetic dosages (50–100mg) of ketamine." In *Ketamine: Dreams and
Realities,* Karl Jansen, M.D., summarizes the main effects of ketamine as follows, and
they do indeed seem reminiscent of Salvia (as later examples in this book will show):
"Those who have experienced ketamine . . . may become convinced that they are dead

Daniel Siebert summarizes the characteristic effects of salvinorin intoxication as:

- The resurfacing of past memories, such as revisiting places from childhood
- Sensations of motion or being pulled or twisted by unseen forces
- Visions of membranes, films, and various two-dimensional surfaces
- Merging with or becoming objects
- Overlapping realities, such as the perception of being in several locations at once*[2]

These effects are typical, and all of them may occur—and occur all at once—in any journey. Dale Pendell quotes one Salvia explorer in his

---

(continued) or that they are having a telepathic communication with God. They may see visions and describe leaving their bodies, dying, and entering other realities and alternative universes. Old memories may emerge to the point of being re-experienced, sometimes leading to a life review that is occasionally perceived as having moral, spiritual, and therapeutic value. The loss of contact with the external reality and the sense of being part of other 'much more real' and 'fundamental' realities may be very strong. Some people find this interesting while others become disturbed. . . .

"One of the more dramatic types of ketamine experiences involves the sudden conviction that there is nothing real except the self as a point of awareness floating forever in eternity with no external world to return to. Life was but a dream, and this is the one reality to which the person has just awakened. . . . Many users are absolutely convinced that their ketamine experiences were real. They insist that the drug opened a door into other worlds. Sometimes participation in these 'other worlds' can cause problems in this one when the realities collide. . . .

"[The ketamine explorer Marcia Moore] described how prolonged use resulted into *fragmentation into subpersonalities [which] usually came in pairs of opposites, such as the Nun and Prostitute.* [My italics since this aspect—and indeed this very symbol—is certainly a key feature of my work with Salvia: again, see later]. . . . The boundaries of existence seemed increasingly permeable. . . . This was linked to a dramatic increase in apparent synchronicities (coincidences that are highly meaningful to the person who notices them) and what [Moore] interpreted as magical events." Such synchronicities in the forecasting of future events are also a feature of Salvia—diviner's sage or the sage of the seers—as my own experiences suggest (again, see later in this book).

*Quoted in D. M. Turner

book *Phamako/Poeia—Plant Powers, Poisons, and Herbcraft* who said of his experience:

> It's very intense. I call it a reality stutter or a reality strobing. I think that having been a test pilot and flying in that unforgiving environment with only two feet between our wingtips helped to prepare me for this kind of exploration.[3]

Our Salvia, 20X concentrate, arrived in August 2010 and we began our own explorations. Three of us were present at our first session: Tracie, my partner in the healing center, Jungle, our shaman, and me. At this time I had also begun my apprenticeship to San Pedro, and it is within this context that I had decided to work with Salvia, sensing that there might be an affinity between the plants.

Some of the reasons that San Pedro ceremonies are held, for example, are:

- To cure illnesses of a spiritual, emotional, mental, or physical nature
- To know the future through the prophetic and divinatory qualities of the plant
- To overcome sorcery or *saladera* (an inexplicable run of bad luck)
- To ensure success in one's ventures
- To rekindle love and enthusiasm for life
- To restore one's faith or find new meaning in life by experiencing the world as divine

All of these are typical reasons for a Salvia ceremony too.

The famous San Pedro curandero Eduardo Calderon said of the cactus that "participants [in ceremonies] are set free from matter and engage in flight through cosmic regions . . . transported across time and distance." Words that a Mazatec shaman might also have used about Salvia.

Finally, there is a symbolic connection between the plants via the hummingbird, which is the pollinator of Salvia and the spiritual guardian of San Pedro.

Because of these obvious connections and, more fundamentally, because San Pedro, my ally, had asked me to pay attention to Salvia, our work with the sage began immediately.

Jungle had more experience smoking the extract, although he had only taken it a few times, so he smoked first, followed by me, and then Tracie. These are my notes after our first session.

I had to smoke two pipes—with no immediate effect. It was only when I was about to give up and pass the pipe to Tracie that the Salvia kicked in. I felt myself pulled physically backward and as I fell, saw my arm dissolving and separating into hexagonal molecules of red, green, and yellow. (At that time I had no knowledge about the molecular properties of Salvia. The plant is, of course, however, drawn with a hexagonal structure when depicted by chemists, and these six-sided shapes were clearly visible as patterns in the room whenever we smoked it and during my subsequent journeys with ayahuasca and San Pedro when I had previously taken Salvia. At first we puzzled over them, unsure of what they were, where they came from, or whether they were octagons or hexagons. We finally decided on the latter but had no idea why we were seeing them. I believe now that Salvia imposes its structure, or its will,

The structure of salvinorin A

on the world and it is from these hexagons that it creates reality in its image.)

Space around me curved and seemed to flow backward, as if I was being rolled or sucked into a tunnel or vortex of some kind. When I passed through it and landed on the other side I found myself in a childhood scene. I had an idea of a bus stop being important and of being a child and my mother pulling me toward it by the hand—but it was like being pulled backward in time as well as physically. The experience lasted a lifetime, although from her perspective Tracie said I was "away" for only two or three minutes.

It can take a while to learn the language of a new plant, the way it wants to interact with us, and how it communicates its meanings. It took me two pipes, but that is a vast improvement on my previous (U.K.) Salvia experiences, and I feel that a connection was at least made between us even though the content of the journey isn't clear to me and didn't go very far in terms of immediate insights. The general theme of childhood and its significance seemed important, however, and the whole experience ties in with what Siebert describes as the characteristics of Salvia: past memories, childhood, being pulled or twisted, and a sense of overlapping realities. I felt all of these, so I think I have at least been "properly introduced" to Salvia although I don't know what the information in the journey means yet. It was brief and strange. What I remember most is the physicality of it: the feeling of being pulled through time and space and my body coming apart.*

Tracie smoked next. Within seconds she was reaching for Jungle and looking frightened. When she came round she said it felt like—

---

*I came later to describe this sensation of being pulled apart as a "dismantling." I meant it to suggest a physical quality, but it is also appropriate from a psychological perspective since the word *dismantle* literally means *to uncloak*—which is what I now understand Salvia to do: uncloak us and lay our patterns, habits, and subterfuges bare and available to scrutiny so that we can learn from them and change our behavior by way of healing where it does not serve us. The word became even more appropriate when I finally met the spirit of Salvia and took note of her appearance—see later in this book.

no, not felt like, she *had*—lost her identity and had no sense of who she was anymore. She said it was as if her whole life had been a dream but she didn't want that dream to end "by going to another dimension." "Even dream characters have a life and don't want to die," she said. The ego endures, at least for a while during the first stages of the Salvia journey, and it wants us to continue being who we *think* we are and always have been.

When Jungle smoked he also lost his identity. He was looking at us and asking, "Who are you? Who am I?" He said the thing that brought him back was not remembering *who* he was but *what* he was: "That I am a shaman, and I help others through places like this." He identified with a role not with himself.

Our next session was a few days later; Jungle, Tracie, and I again, and once more we smoked the 20X concentrate.

> *It took me one pipe this time. Easier. Faster. And the effects lasted longer: about ten minutes. I was pulled backward again, my whole body leaking away like sand through an hourglass or iron filings being pulled by a distant magnet.*
>
> *I had an idea that I could be an insignificant object from the story of my life, and an image of walking down a street again as a small child (an event that felt as if it had actually happened and may have done), being pulled by the hand by my mother, but also of being something other than human, like a brick in a wall in that street or a leaf (or even a cell in a leaf) and watching myself pass by—so that every object in my life was also me; like our realities were interchangeable. I could look at myself from the perspective of everything in that street and feel its connection to me—and me to it.*

I was not sure yet how you would use this plant for healing or how it might fit with San Pedro. During the journey I was looking for Salvia's spirit as I thought I might then understand it better but I couldn't find it, and in fact it seemed to me as if the plant didn't have one (Jungle couldn't find it either). It felt like there was no "humanity" to it, just a sense of something mechanical and dismantling. If anything the only personality I did detect felt like a *male* rather than a female energy, and it seemed almost matter-of-fact in its behavior toward me. I can see from that how it *might* work with San Pedro as the cactus is also very direct (although much gentler and more forgiving) but I have no idea of *how* the two work together. In the morning we all agreed that we slept deeply after the ceremony but none of us had dreams we could recall.

My next session was with Josephine, a volunteer at our center. While she had some experience with psychedelics and had attended one or two ayahuasca ceremonies with us she had never smoked Salvia so I went first.

Felt the pulling/dismantling again (a bit like being in a wind tunnel and having the flesh ripped from my back, piece by piece, or as Josephine felt it, of moving quickly forward through space) and once again I ended up lying down—there was no way to resist this pull or to get up again—like there was a weight on me. The "pulling apart" started in my lungs as the smoke was inhaled and then followed the Salvia through the blood. As it reached each part of me, that part dissolved or was dismantled. I had no visions or realizations, just this feeling of being dismembered, but maybe that is significant in itself. Whenever I have worked with a new teacher plant before—whether ayahuasca, San Pedro, or mushrooms—the first journeys were always more physical, as if the plant was checking me out and preparing my body for deeper work to come.

Josephine said her experience was like sitting in a pool of water that rose up her body from the feet until she went under. She felt a rolling sensation and saw a huge wheel in the room—like a waterwheel. She had a sense of something from her childhood but didn't connect with its meaning.

• • •

Our next session, still with 20X concentrate, took place the next day. All of my previous sessions had been in the moloka, the ceremonial temple where ayahuasca rituals are held. Molokas are thatched, open-sided roundhouses and although ours was screened against mosquitoes and insects it still allowed a fair bit of light in, and Salvia ceremonies are traditionally held in darkness. Thinking that the ambient light of the rain forest might have affected our previous experiences, Josephine and I decided to begin the ceremony later this time so this was our first session held in full darkness.

This time my experience was more subtle and less physical—no pulling backward. My mind felt relaxed—an almost "can't be bothered" feeling. When it came to "thinking" I felt unable and unwilling to rationalize; I was more in touch with the intuitive and "knowing" part of myself. My rational mind seemed dull and blunted in fact, like my brain wasn't making the same connections or going first to that place where it habitually goes to "understand." I felt as if "I" was more in the back of my brain. It was not a visionary experience although I had a sense of being out-of-body and seeing myself and the world from space.

Josephine's experience sounded similar: subtle, gentle, and no great insights; maybe a sort of "settling in" and getting familiar with Salvia. In the morning we also agreed that we had both slept deeply that night.

DIETING SALVIA

A few ceremonies ago I decided that the way to get to know the spirit of Salvia—a first step for all shamans in developing a connection with a plant—was to diet it.

The diet is a ritual process that involves the restriction of certain foodstuffs that might interfere with or overwhelm the subtleties of the plant you have chosen to work with, so there must be no chili, for example, or other strong herbs, no lemons, limes, or salt as these cut through magic and can kill the spirit of a plant, which, when you first begin to work with it, is very fragile within you. There can be no meat on the diet either (pork especially, as the pig can become possessed by a forest spirit, which shares an affinity for human beings and can be passed on to us if we eat this meat; it will then interfere with the dietary process and harm us spiritually or physically) and no alcohol or sex.

The restriction on sex is because during orgasm men give away their power—the energy of the plant that has built up in them through the process of dieting it—while women can take in the energies of a man while he is inside her, and especially if he is not in a state of dietary purity she can become disempowered by this or infected by unclean energies.

Essentially a diet is a meditative fast that allows for deep connection with the plant that we hope to become our ally. It is like making a new friend so we choose to spend time with them, focusing as much as possible on the development of our relationship until we feel that it is established.

> The ally is the one who helps you. That is what an ally
>   should do . . .
> Allies may also have agendas of their own, however. That
> is, an ally is not like a fairy god-mother, but is a powerful
> force in its own right . . .[4]
>
>   DALE PENDELL

The typical shamanic diet is followed for seven days, during which the shaman hopes and expects that a subtle alchemy will take place in his body and spirit, whereby the plant is transformed through intent and gentle coaxing, by the romancing of it, so it changes its form from material to essence or soul and finally into an ally when that essence becomes part of his own. Then there is an after-diet for a further seven days so that the new friendship can be cemented.

During the initial period it is important to develop as close a connection as possible to the plant, and I had decided, as is customary in Amazonian diets, to drink a cup of the plant tea each morning, made the evening before by adding the leaves to hot water and then leaving them to cool. In addition I would bathe in the tea each day and, finally, make a tincture of the leaves in *aguardiente* (cane alcohol, also known as "fire water" in Peru), which I would sip in the after-noon and hold in my mouth for fifteen minutes to allow the essence of the plant to be absorbed.

During the after-diet it is no longer necessary to follow these prac-tices, because the spirit of the plant is now in you, but the fast and other restrictions continue as its spirit is still young and can be over-whelmed by alcohol, for example, or lost through sex. It is not unusual for people to lose seven pounds in weight during a typical two-week diet.

The following notes are taken from the journal I kept at the time and reflect my day-to-day experiences (see chapter 4 for a more detailed account of shamanic dieting).

Day 1: Sorrow and Connection

Through my work with Salvia so far I feel as if I am more in touch with my emotions. This may be one of the subtle effects of the plant. The visions and the experience of smoking it can both be dramatic, but it is the after-effects that bring the emotional insights, not the dismantling and drama of the immediate session.

I feel sad today and a little lost. It seems like through the diet my body is coming back into balance and my "self" is therefore moving its energy away from physical needs to deal with deeper emotional issues. From what is arising these have something to do with my experiences of childhood, power, disempowerment, and the feelings that come from this. It may also be the "S"* thing. Perhaps this is enhanced by Salvia too: a

---

*"S" was a volunteer at our center who was causing problems of a particular and rather persistent nature. It is not useful to discuss the details here.

sense of empathy and connection between people and the sadness of seeing something beautiful that is also so damaged.

I found a quotation from Man in the Landscape *that is like the experience of dieting.*

> *To the desert go prophets and hermits*
> *Through deserts go pilgrims and exiles.*
> *Here the leaders of the great religions have sought the*
> *therapeutic and spiritual values of retreat,*
> *not to escape but to find reality.*
>
> PAUL SHEPARD

On the diet we withdraw from the world and embrace solitude. Through this we hope to find something real. (Although, as I later discovered, with Salvia we are just as likely to find out what is not real.)

Day 2: Emotional X-rays

Bathed. Drank. Sipped the tincture. My emotions are pronounced again, experienced today as frustration. I've been thinking about "S" again. There seems such sadness and tragedy in her but hidden beneath a tough, almost emotionless exterior. It feels somehow like she has a business arrangement with life: to use and be used in equal measure, calculating the cost and reward in each relationship before she commits to it; and then making her commitment contingent anyway, just in case things change.

It is interesting how Salvia seems to be amplifying my sense of her, as if it provides a sort of "emotional x-ray" of the people around me. San Pedro operates in the same way, another plant affinity. Mexican curanderos use the term placitas *to describe the heart-to-heart, soul-to-soul connection they try to develop with their clients to make their counseling and healings more effective, and I can see how Salvia could be useful for this. For the same reason it might be valuable in Western therapeutic work.**

---

*See chapters 5 and 6.

This sense of empathy and seeing into the soul of things is what Dale Pendell meant, I am sure, when he wrote that after his work with Salvia "everything around me gradually became more intelligent."

It is usually best to follow a diet in isolation, away from daily concerns, so we tune in to the plant and learn from it without these connections to other people getting in the way and confusing things. I can see how this might be especially important with Salvia even though our concerns will follow us anyway because they are in our minds and not "out there" somewhere.

Day 3: A Change in the World

My senses feel changed today, as if my perceptions have altered: the world looks brighter and sharper, and my hearing is more acute, especially after the tincture. My spirits have lifted as well, and I have the sense of an initiation or journey through Salvia into the dark places then an ascent back to light.

Day 4: Ayahuasca Ceremony

Same dietary procedure but there was also an ayahuasca ceremony in the evening. Not all shamans agree but I believe it is important to drink ayahuasca as part of a diet so you can get closer to the plant you are dieting and see its spiritual nature. Then you can learn from it. I'm reminded of something that Jungle's teacher, the ayahuascero Don Luis, said about San Pedro, that "I can see San Pedro from ayahuasca but I can't see ayahuasca from San Pedro." He means that ayahuasca is "of the universe" so it has a more expansive perspective whereas San Pedro is "of the Earth." I suspect it is the same with Salvia: that it is possible to see and meet its spirit with the aid of the vine but not the other way around.

Things didn't go entirely to plan, however, since Jungle was unable to run the ceremony, and I had to do it. Some beautiful new icaros *sang themselves through me but I can't remember them all; they arise in the moment when they are needed.* Running the ceremony didn't give me*

---

*See chapter 4 for an explanation of *icaros*.

much time to focus on Salvia but I was told by ayahuasca that in order to meet its spirit we have to "change our shapes" because Salvia has a different form to human beings, more like pyramids: triangles and angular lines.

I had the sense that I was a part of the Salvia mind—that I am being dreamed by it—and that for me to try to locate its spirit is somehow the wrong way around: like I'm trying to hold on to God whereas God, of course, holds me and is too big for me to comprehend or contain. I feel that I am a thought, that Salvia is thinking me—even though I think I can think about it! Its spirit felt just too big for me to stand back from and observe, like trying to look at a house with towering walls: no matter how hard you try you only see the bricks. I did have a fleeting idea of Salvia as a lady in white but I may be imagining that.

Day 5: Knowing the Mind of God

Out of the blue Ranolfo, a shaman I have worked with occasionally and whose knowledge I respect, arrives at the center and although he has no idea I'm dieting Salvia that is exactly what he starts talking about. He says that he has been dieting it for thirty years and offers to teach me its icaros. Salvia he says "brings us closer to God so we can see Heaven and know the mind of God," which is interesting, in view of my visions last night. For him the spirit of Salvia looks like a small (3–4 feet tall) black man! Very different to my image or even my expectations of what Salvia might look like. He says that when he diets the plant he uses 60 leaves in a tincture of agua de rosas [rose perfume] and drinks it for three days.

Thirty pairs of leaves sounds about right according to Mazatec tradition, and it is what I am using now. (It is amazing how shamanic lore tends to correspond on such practices even when two cultures have never exchanged views. When asked how they know to use 60 leaves rather than 80, for example, or how to undertake a diet of any kind the standard response of all the shamans is, "the plants told us.") I am not sure about agua de rosas though; Mazatec shamans make a tea of the leaves in water, as I am doing, and this seems more appropriate to me as *there is less room for confusion over where the effects are coming from: the rose essence, the alcohol, which contains it and is the base for the perfume, or the sage itself.*

Day 6: Transformation

Same dietary procedure, then in the evening there is another ayahuasca ceremony. Again I wasn't able to focus on Salvia due to the "battle of the moloka": a rival shaman had sent bad energy to disrupt the ritual for our participants, and Jungle and I had to fight to keep it out. Rivalry like this—brujeria, or sorcery—is common among Amazonian shamans. I didn't think it was a serious attack, more a test of strength, but it still got in the way of my personal work.

Because of the disruptions I decided immediately after the ceremony to do some further work with Salvia and, still somewhat in ayahuasca, smoked two pipes of 20X concentrate. I wanted to see how the plants worked together, bearing in mind what Don Luis had said. I sat on the floor in Tracie's room while she sat on her bed to watch me.

Sometimes the ally rolls over and crushes a person without warning.

DALE PENDELL

Suddenly I felt myself physically pulled up by my shoulders and knew that I was not human at all but a bedspread being laid on a bed. My body slithered upward by itself (or was pulled by unseen hands), and there was nothing I could do to prevent it. The last remnant of "me" knew that I didn't want to be a bedspread—I didn't like my pattern!* I panicked and grabbed Tracie as I was pulled up and over the bed. She held onto me to prevent further movement as I lay flat on my back.

As the consciousness of the bedspread I was fully aware of my surroundings and was no longer in a jungle hut but owned by an elderly woman in Idaho who had decorated her bedroom in chintz. I could see

---

*This seemingly stupid observation would turn out to be much more prophetic and important than I thought at the time.

farmland through her window and dust in the air as the sun shone through it; all of it in intricate detail. It was my reality.

All of my humanity was slipping away. I was a bedspread and always had been. I abandoned the attempt to be anything else and became just an item in the room with no thoughts or judgments. Even the chintz didn't bother me anymore. It had nothing to do with me but had its own existence to contemplate, as did the wooden wardrobe at my side and the white lace curtains moving gently in the breeze above me.

A little later, from somewhere off in the distance, perhaps from one of the fields outside, among the calls of crows and the stillness of the day, I thought I heard a human voice. It was saying nothing remarkable however, just repeating a simple question over and over in a combination of amusement, fear, and confusion: "What the fuck? What the fuck?" At some point I realized it was my voice, coming from some place in me that vaguely remembered a human existence and had no idea what was going on now.* But at least that meant there was an "I" and that it/I was finally returning from somewhere.

It took me some minutes to fully shake off the bedspread consciousness, with Tracie holding me down until I returned to human awareness. Then I literally ran (stumbled) out onto the balcony overlooking the jungle and whooped for joy at being human again. Having a head, two arms, and two legs, even if they weren't working so well, had never felt this good before.

> *A kind of wild orgasmic paroxysm of self-affirmation . . .*
> *He had said the words before. But he had never said and*
> *understood them in this way before. Ta vodos! Ta vodos! I am!*
> *I am!*
>
> TERENCE MCKENNA

I had read the accounts of other Salvia users who had turned into objects when they smoked the extract—it always seemed silly: one had

---

*As our research progressed I would come to hear this question repeated by a number of participants for the same reason, as you will see in later chapters.

reported being a wardrobe, another said he was a suitcase under a stairway at an airport—but it didn't seem so silly now. In those accounts I'd always assumed that the writers meant that they "thought" or "felt" or "had a vision of being" whatever they turned into. But it isn't like that. I was a bedspread just as they were wardrobes or suitcases, and the sense of losing all human consciousness was alarming. It is what Tracie meant, I am sure, when after her first experience she said that she lost her identity totally, as if being human had just been a dream.

When I recovered I smoked again, and this experience was even deeper. I am not sure where I was but certainly not in a jungle: an urban street somewhere. It felt similar to my first time with Salvia where I could have been a brick in a wall I passed by in childhood. At one point the entire room became a wall, and I was a part of it.

When I thought about these experiences later I realized that the afterglow (those moments immediately after the blastoff experience) is where the real work with Salvia is done. The moment for reflection, divination, or the asking of questions is not during the experience itself because then we are way beyond thought or even humanity, but in the integration period, which follows, when we are not fully back in the "real" world but not so distant from ourselves that we are incapable of processing anything.

I looked in J. D. Arthur's book again, the one I had endorsed some months previously but couldn't really connect with at the time because I hadn't yet had the experiences he was talking about, and found a passage that I now understood completely.

> *It was as if I might actually "awaken" in one of these realms with no memory to serve as a way of returning . . . as if I would awaken over there, and this world would be a dream that would fade [or] I might "come to" in someone else's body—in someone else's life—and have no memory of my other life.*[5]

Day 7: Stuck and Learning to Stand

Last day of drinking the tea, tincture, and bathing. I spent the evening with Josephine, and this time we decided on three sessions—three pipes of Salvia each—one of us after the other, taking it in turns.

It was a breakthrough for both of us. Having given me the experience of full transformation into a different consciousness it seemed that Salvia had found its route into me and that this was a means for us to connect. The first time I smoked I became another object—or aspect of myself. I was chewing gum stuck to the wheel of a pram that was being pushed along a street. I even knew when and where it was: Birmingham, United Kingdom, in the 1960s. The pram was a Silvercross. I was the baby in it (and also the gum and the wheel) and my mother was pushing it. Again it was like viewing myself from another perspective and feeling that I had made some sort of agreement with everything that was a part of my life before I was even born (no matter how seemingly insignificant: a bus stop, a brick, or a piece of gum), that this was a spiritual journey we would take together and a consciousness we would share. It was as if these things were my soul companions and there was a contract of some kind between us.

Every time the pram wheel turned I turned as well and felt myself rolling around the floor of the moloka. I was ground into the earth repeatedly so that my body (or my consciousness of even having a body) disappeared into it, and only when the wheel rotated upward did I have any remotely residual sense of "me." I surfaced one time and had an awareness of Josephine sitting close to me and, just as I had with Tracie the night before, I grabbed her to stop myself being pushed into the earth again. She held me as I returned gradually to a sense of myself. It was one of the strangest experiences I've ever had.

Josephine smoked next, and hers was a positive experience. She found herself in a variety of landscapes with people around her and was told by them that she "belonged" in their world and could stay if she wanted but that "he [me] can't come with you."*

I was annoyed that I was being excluded from the world that Josephine was allowed into (SalviaWorld as I came to call it) and that while she saw

---

*In terms of the future relationship that developed between us these two different messages —me feeling safe with Josephine in the ordinary world and her feeling safe in a different world, which also represented an escape from everyday reality—would prove to be portentous and significant: a pull in different directions. But I didn't understand the language of Salvia well enough to read the signs then.

people and fabulous landscapes I was immediately thrown out and ended up as bricks or gum. I'd read in Arthur's book his theory that Salvia takes you to the Land of the Dead, and if that was true, my sense was that I was being prevented from entering that landscape now because as a shaman I have often rescued souls from it so I was not welcome because, from the perspective of those who lived there, I had been stealing souls and citizens from them. In their view of things I was a death bringer, a virus, a disease.

I was determined to get into that land though, and I smoked again with that intention in mind. I was dropped into a busy street with many people present. I felt small, child height, and became aware of a hand reaching down to me, like an adult picking up a child who had tripped. There is kindness even in that colder, more clinical world. I took it and in my journey (and in physical reality) stood up and looked around. One of the people walking toward me in the street was a young girl with brown hair wearing a pink duffel coat, patent leather shoes, and white socks. I had the idea that it might be Josephine as a child.

Standing up, I realized, is what had at last got me into this landscape; Salvia was teaching me how to be in its world. The man who had helped me up said, as if to a child or someone who knew no better, "Is that what you wanted [to be here and to see us]? Is that what all the fuss was about?"

The next time I smoked something had changed. I made a point of standing up straight away (it was a struggle because my body felt heavy) and noticed that while in previous "transformations" I had always been small, nonhuman things—a brick, a bedspread, chewing gum—now I was human-sized and a human being of a sort: more phantom than flesh but at least not an object. Furthermore, I could interact with what I was seeing and had some control over it instead of being subject to forces that acted on me.

A "wave" of the same street scene as before appeared in the moloka, like a wall of different reality that moved through the room toward me. As it reached me I felt its particles pass through me like pins and needles, and I realized that I could move around and through it as it swept across the floor. When I stepped into it I was in the street, when I stepped back I was in the moloka watching the reality wave approaching.

I asked Josephine if she could see what I was seeing. It seemed so real to me that I couldn't imagine why she wouldn't, and in fact, with a residue of Salvia still in her from her last pipe, she said she could. She saw blurred outlines of people—ghosts in the room—and me with my arm around someone as I surfed the reality wave and walked with the people in the street. I took Josephine's hand, and she felt solid, cold, meatlike, architectural even, while the others felt ethereal and tingly, like energy or vibrations (and so did I when I was in their reality). I had a sense that even in everyday life, if I am reflective and pay attention, I can also feel these pins and needles, and I wondered if other dimensions are always passing through us.

Josephine smoked again and found herself in the body of a machine in an alien factory. The machine is like a giant multileveled mangle, each layer a different scene—a beach, stars, country fields, a wall, standing stones—each of which is a vast, self-contained world, which she is a part of: like rolls of living wallpaper. A blue creature turned a handle, and each of these worlds rolled forward until it folded in on itself. The people in these worlds panicked and ran as their reality slipped into the mangle and ended. The creature controlling it was stoically amused at their reactions, their fear of annihilation, as if they/we really should have evolved beyond that.

Josephine had previously seen herself in individual landscapes interacting with people there but now she saw the entire and intricate picture: that "reality" is actually multiple realities, and it is all just a play, maybe literally rolls of wallpaper each with a pattern, which contains its own consciousness and is controlled by something bigger than us (the blue creature), which we in our dreaming might, I suppose, call "God" and project all sorts of illusions onto but is actually ambivalent, uninterested, and just a functionary in a factory. The world—or these multiple worlds around us—means very little in the whole scheme of things, as does God or the factory-world he occupies because "He" and we are all just cogs in a wheel.

Day 8: Tearing Through the Fabric of Reality

Josephine is with me but only I smoke—another three pipes.

I am back in the same street again but something is not quite right. The people here are all dressed as if from the 1950s. The men wear hats, tan suits, and brown brogues; the women wear flared knee-length dresses, again in beige or tan; it is a limited palette but all of the colors are bright and pastel-like. Its just-so perfection reminds me of The Truman Show *or* Pleasantville, *as if the clue to its manufactured nature is that it is too nicely engineered. There is something else too: the flesh of the people. They are just too pink, as if they are drawings, cartoons colored in by a child or by a computer badly programmed to replicate skin tones but doing it just well enough to fool most of us most of the time. "They're too pink," I find myself saying to Josephine. "That's how you know they're not real." It is like I have discovered a secret: how to tell from Salvia the things that matter in life and those that have been put there to deliberately mislead us by some agency or intelligence, which is bigger than us and controlling our lives from a distance. I could see how conspiracy theorists like David Icke might conclude that the world is manipulated by powers we cannot comprehend but to name these powers as "Illuminati" and pretend to know who (or what) they are is woefully simplistic. The truth that Salvia was hinting at was even more disturbing: that we are nothing more than characters in a computer game perhaps played by an insignificant kid who really doesn't care about us at all. At least in Icke's cozier view of things those who seek to control us can be located in time and space and care enough about us to bother with their manipulations of our reality. What we learn from Salvia, however, is that we have no idea who is "playing" us but we can be sure that, like any kid with a toy, we are no more important or significant to them than the next distraction.*

My next journey continues the theme, and I find myself back in a street, but this time with no people, just an empty road with houses on each side, something like the street I grew up on. I know, however, that this is just a film, a projection onto fabric, and it feels like this is what all reality is: a projection we make onto fabric.

We live as film, on a film, the skin of a bubble. What is real
lives behind, waiting to push through, swallow us up, reclaim us.
   It may not be nice.

THEODORE ROSZAK, *FLICKER*

Kneeling in the moloka I begin to physically tear the screen apart; I want to know what is on the other side. The fabric rips as I claw at it, and once shredded there is only blackness behind it.

I smoke again, and the next journey begins where I left off. I enter the blackness I discovered last time and begin to drift through the emptiness of space. Looking back I see that Earth/the reality I've left is a cube, and there are other cubes/planets/realities all around me. Within each of them is a multiverse, and I realize just how vast and intricate and wholly mysterious what we call "reality" is. The cubes also look like the geometric patterns that Salvia produces when it is smoked and perhaps, I think, Salvia itself contains these realities; that it is a plant that enables us not just to explore multiple worlds (like ayahuasca) or to more fully experience this world (like San Pedro) but that gives us access to completely other dimensions.

Day 9: The Meeting of San Pedro and Salvia

It is my birthday, and my San Pedro mentor and friend La Gringa has sent me a bottle of San Pedro to celebrate. It is the best I've ever had—intense and beautiful—like an all-day, all-over massage. It has arrived at the perfect time in the diet since my explorations with Salvia stem from a desire to better understand and connect with the cactus.

I drink a glass of San Pedro and find that the two plants work well together and seem to like each other. I still have a lot of Salvia in me from all the journeys I've taken and from the diet, and I can feel the sage and the cactus meeting in me. They remind me that reality is pliable and there are whole other worlds or dimensions within us, and we can therefore choose our reality—and ultimately it's all a game anyway—one which exists within and not outside of us because nothing is really real. This, then, is one of the applications of Salvia—and San Pedro—for healing:

to remind us that we have free will so we can also choose to abandon our sad stories if we wish and believe something better of ourselves. Josephine's "blue Salvia God" has no agenda either way and finds us amusing no matter what we do, so we do not have to be accountable to him, only to ourselves for what we want from and make of our lives.

Day 10: A War of Realities

There was another ayahuasca ceremony tonight, and we had another fight on our hands, this time in the form of an entity—like a huge scorpion—that had taken possession of Veronica, one of our clients. Its agenda was to change her thoughts, and ours, so that its will and not hers would be served and it could gather power in the world by stealing her energy. In that way it could live through and off her while she would become weaker and sicker.

In the end it couldn't win though because I knew from yesterday's experience of Salvia and San Pedro that there is no reality it could control. Or, to put it another way, my reality—anyone's—was as valid as its reality, and if I believed more strongly in mine than it did in its own then Veronica would be well. As soon as it understood that I knew that, the scorpion-spirit left.

Ridding her of this entity took time and concentration though so I wasn't able to focus fully on Salvia again but I did feel its presence, and my visions took on the familiar hexagonal designs that now characterize the sage experience for me.

Day 11: Love and Melancholy

Spent the day with Josephine sharing the remainder of my San Pedro with her in the moloka from noon until around 6:00 a.m. the next morning. We both felt the presence of Salvia in us as it mingled with the San Pedro, especially in the geometric patterns that became part of the experience and were particularly pronounced when I was playing the drum. Synesthesia can be a characteristic of Salvia and San Pedro—the translation of sound into images—and this may be another way the plants connect.

There was a lot of love in the medicine and in us for each other. We got close and spent hours holding each other. I felt that melancholy that as human beings we all sometimes feel when we are with those we most love: that we are always separate and apart, that we can be inside each other's bodies, sometimes each other's minds, but we can never share a soul or truly know one another. The best we can hope is that our spirits and destinies merge but we can never be our lovers. Reality may be whatever we choose but we have to live it alone.

Days 12 to 14: Many Masks

Completed the Salvia diet, and looking back on it I can see that I made progress with the plant. However, I am still not sure I have met its spirit. Mazatec shamans say that she is "elusive" and during her journeys Josephine was told that Salvia "wears many masks," a point echoed by Pendell in his book Pharmako/Poeia.

> *She has many epiphanies. Not all of them are shy and not all of them are "she." One person encountered the ally as a giant . . . wearing a belt of human skulls. . . . The giant wanted to know why he had been summoned. The giant did not want a trivial answer. . . . She can be shy [however]. Sometimes she has to get to know you for a while before she will come out and say hello. But once she appears, are there any who are more direct?*

> *I feel that I have learned a lot about how to work with her, how Salvia may be used for healing and about the nature of reality itself. I am also clear that Salvia is compatible with San Pedro. It may also be with ayahuasca, although whenever I tried to meet it during ceremonies, some distraction always prevented me from doing so fully. With San Pedro, however, the two plants merged beautifully.*

EMERGING THEMES

During this early work with Salvia I had smoked it twelve times in all, Tracie and Jungle had both smoked twice and Josephine had smoked five times: a total of twenty-one journeys. I had also followed a shamanic diet with the plant, which I had shared in part with Josephine, had drunk a tea and a tincture of leaves, and had looked at Salvia three times from the perspective of ayahuasca and twice from the perspective of San Pedro. From this body of experience what messages or themes begin to emerge? What is Salvia trying to tell us?

Looking back over my journeys the first thing I noticed was how Salvia had taught me to work with it. In my first session it had taken me two pipes of the extract to feel any effect but as I continued the plant showed me how to gain more control over myself and the experience, first taking me deeper into its world and enabling me to explore reality from the consciousness of different objects, then (literally) lifting me up into the "human" world and teaching me to stand and move so I could interact with the beings who occupy SalviaWorld.

This is not the Mazatec approach. In their shamanic rituals, darkness, silence, and stillness are more common, with the participant lying down with eyes closed and allowing the visions to unfold. But retaining a degree of control through movement seemed to work better for me and, indeed, despite the traditional shamanic approach there is still a degree of flexibility in the structure of ceremonies, as we saw with Don Alejandro, for example, who encouraged his participants to talk about their visions in order to understand them. So forming one's own relationship and way of working with the plant should not be considered disrespectful or "wrong" as long as it is positive and helpful.

At first I had felt excluded from SalviaWorld when I had been transformed into various objects while Josephine was able to meet and talk with the beings there, but now I saw it more as an initiation and almost a tour of the vast consciousness of Salvia, which, it seemed to me, contained all things and the aware perception of everything. What I had turned into was significant too: a bedspread whose pattern I didn't like, chewing gum stuck on a wheel, a brick in a wall. Salvia was teaching me through these symbols I now realize, and this also contained its divinatory potential.

The most important thing in the bedspread journey, for example, was that I didn't like my pattern. Reflecting on this now, years later, from the viewpoint of my life and the turns it has taken since that experience I believe that what Salvia was telling me was that there were patterns in *me* (thoughts, beliefs, behavior) that were not healthy and that I didn't like at a soul level but of which I was not consciously aware. Especially in my relationships, I would come to learn, I had particular responses that were not useful but that had become habitual. I had become "stuck on a wheel" and kept turning—repeating the same mistakes and finding myself in the same place again.

Had I better understood Salvia's language and teaching methods at the time I would have looked more closely at myself and been able to prevent some of the mistakes I would make and the outcomes, which would arise—for example—between Josephine and me as our relationship developed.

By the same token there must be information for those who become wardrobes or suitcases when looked at from a symbolic perspective and measured against their lives. After all, from all of the billions of points of consciousness in the universe, why these particular objects? An abandoned suitcase at an airport might, I suppose, be a teaching about how we are allowing ourselves to be left behind or hiding away from the world. A wardrobe is a container for clothes and a metaphor for identity: how we present ourselves to others. Perhaps there is a message in this too for those who have had such visions.

I had also been a brick, part of a structure, and maybe the teaching here was that I should know that I am not separate but the same as others (bricks, people) around me and that I rely on them for my sense of self and community, that I should therefore treat them with empathy and respect, sharing my "brickness"—or humanity—with them rather than standing alone. This realization, too, would have helped my relationships with others, and again, had I understood and followed the advice of the plant Josephine and I might be in a different place today.

For Tracie, Josephine, and myself Salvia gave us a sense of our childhoods. The meaning behind this was not fully explained because our intentions during these journeys were simply to explore the plant. In general with plant work having a defined intention is important so that its spirit can offer specific advice and answer our questions precisely. In Mazatec shamanism, for example, the patient comes to the curandero with a question in mind such as where an item has been lost or who has stolen something from him or else the healer has a particular purpose such as looking for the cause of an illness.

Although I didn't follow up the childhood theme at the time, my sense of it now is that it related again in some way to the patterns of my life, which I have mentioned, that they began in childhood through interactions with others, most obviously my mother since she was the one I grew up with (my father was absent for much of the time) and who appeared in my Salvia journeys. I suspect that the same sorts of childhood issues were also important for Josephine since she had a sense of childhood too and that the relationship between us and the problems we would face were influenced by these dramas.

Because our experiments were more general and exploratory, what Salvia chose to show us instead was the nature of reality, a revelation that is the first initiation into the spirit of this plant. What we learn is that reality is fluid and can be viewed from many perspectives and orders of consciousness, that nothing is fixed, that, as Tracie put it, our whole lives are a dream. But they are dreams we choose to believe and become attached to. Hence she didn't want hers to end by "going to another dimension."

This experience is consistent with the accounts of others, many of which can be viewed at the Erowid website (www.erowid.org), and with the experience summary created by Daniel Siebert who mentions the sensation of "overlapping realities" and the sense of merging with or becoming objects and experiencing reality from their perspective.

For some people, especially those new to Salvia, this shift in reality and the realization that nothing is what we thought it was can be confusing or even terrifying. Turner writes that

I can confirm from my own experience that [Salvia] can instantly obliterate any reference to sanity, logic, or even the idea of existing, and make one feel that either one's self or the entire universe has gone entirely and permanently crazy. Occasionally people who have been given salvinorin A, even highly experienced psychedelic users, feel that a bad joke has been played on them by whoever gave them the substance. One person who tried salvinorin A, who is quite experienced with DMT and most other psychedelics, remarked, "It made DMT look like a water pistol, at a dose 50–100 times less."[6]

The intensity of a salvinorin A journey is often experienced as being an order of magnitude more potent than smoked DMT, in much the same way that DMT seems an order of magnitude more potent than a typical LSD journey. A large percentage of salvinorin A users also report that the fear factor is much greater than with DMT, which is saying a lot. I feel that no person, no matter how experienced with other psychedelics or altered states of mind, can be prepared for the intensity of a full-strength salvinorin A journey. It is common for users to be shocked, amazed, and frightened at finding themselves in a state they could not possibly conceive of being induced by any psychedelic substance.

In an Erowid account titled "Mind Shattering" Andreas writes that

[I] felt as though "I" was no longer "me." All I can say with any certainty is that I had completely lost any sense of myself in ordinary reality. I was completely disconnected from any physical body and had traveled to God knows where.[7]

A 10X concentrate user, Roadhouse, writes that

at the peak of the trip I was completely merged with the surface of reality. I felt like I was one with everything, yet unable to discriminate between individual objects or occurrences. . . . I looked up and saw the surface of reality extending into the space above me. Simultaneously I looked down and saw myself fused with reality, looking up in awe. I turned to my friend and asked him what was happening, to which he replied "Oh, it's the end of the world." I felt content in knowing this, as if this was the nature of reality. I felt that the end of existence was just supposed to happen right now, at that very moment. I was faced with total non-existence. . . . It was as if the surface of reality was a sticker, and someone was peeling it from the paper backing. My friend and I were at one corner of reality, the last part left stuck to the backing of existence. Finally I felt myself being torn away.[8]

Somatzu writes about the terror that such an experience can bring.

I was shot through different memories from the distant past. Each memory was its own consummate reality, and I felt completely out of place in each one, not understanding that it was all part of the trip. The terrifying part of this was that I was launched through dozens, if not hundreds, of these different memories. It was as if a gun shot me through a book where each page represented a memory-reality, and I busted through the pages violently, as if being born into each one. Soon after, I felt a complete break with all these realities, and my whole existence was torn apart. . . . I felt a deep terror that still haunts me when I think about it. I started screaming for help. . . .[9]

> *You monkeys think you control the show. Not only do you*
> *not control the show you don't even know what show it is.*[10]
> DENNIS MCKENNA, *VINE OF THE SOUL*

Trendal's account (also at Erowid) is worth reporting at length as it illustrates not only the strangeness of the Salvia experience but, again, the terror that can arise from it when we realize that nothing is as it seems.

Suddenly I became aware of a series of strange zipper-like patterns across the room, running parallel with the floor. . . . Then I noticed the presence of a few beings around me, whom I thought to be my friends . . . Each of these beings was attached to one of the zipper lines in some way I can't describe. . . . The idea was passed to me from somewhere that these people were the heads of the zippers that held reality together. This was, I assure you, one of the most intricate horrors I have ever come across.

The idea that these people were all that stood between reality and nothingness scared the living shit out of me. To my complete horror I watched as one of my former friends began to walk along his zipper-line with an insane grin on his face. Reality began to "unzip." I don't know how else to describe it. It looked *exactly* like a zipper being undone. The two sections of reality that were previously joined by the zipper began to spread apart. An infinite blackness was the only thing left between the sheets of reality. My friends, I realized, were only some benevolent consciousness wearing their skin. Each one moved and acted precisely the same way. Each with the same sick grin on his face, they would unzip their zipper while goading me into letting it happen.

This led me to the conclusion that I, somehow, was in control of the fate of reality. I fixed the idea firmly in my head that everything would stop, and reality would zip itself back up. This did not work.

Now I realized that I had no control over the situation and never had. The beings wearing my friends' faces changed from goading and sneaky to angry and forceful. I was chased out of my room, into the kitchen. I became aware of the fact that I could not move as I thought I should be able to. There was some form of resistance whenever I moved, accompanied by a strange zipping sound. I was now a zipper head, and as I ran I was unzipping reality behind me. Panic hit me very, very fast. I tried to flee the kitchen as the other zippers had followed me and were trying to "catch up" to me for what I thought was some purely evil reason. It was imperative that I stay ahead of them if I were to survive. I made my way through the living room, down the back hallway of my house, out the back door.

Reality was now completely coming apart around me. Everything had gone quiet except for the noise of the other zippers following me, and the noise my own zipper made as I moved. All other noise seemed to disappear as reality was unzipped. I was now in a very real state of panic as I watched in horror as my house unzipped from reality. I was not safe outside either, I realized.[11]

Such feelings are very real when we realize that we are nothing and never have been, that all we are is a dream. Pendell calls it "the terror of absolute emptiness." And yet there is a possibility that with the proper shamanic or therapeutic support the experience of nothingness could also be liberating and healing. Its underlying message after all is that if nothing is real then nothing really matters because things only exist when we lend them meaning and sense. This would include our most painful and debilitating life stories and therefore reveals another healing application of Salvia: to show us that ultimately we are free to choose any story we wish, including one that describes us as "unwell" or "healthy," "blessed" or "cursed" because if nothing is real in itself then all things are possible if we have sufficient faith to create them. This was my experience in the moloka on the night of the ayahuasca ceremony for Veronica, when she needed to be freed from a possessing entity, and I realized that the battle between myself and this spirit was really one of faith, and if I believed more strongly than it did that my client would be well then that is what would inevitably follow.

> *Everything is energy and that's all there is to it. Match the frequency of the reality you want, and you cannot help but get that reality. It can be no other way. This is not philosophy. This is physics.*
>
> ALBERT EINSTEIN

The complete physicality of the Salvia experience is another of its unusual aspects compared to other entheogens. Siebert refers to it as "sensations of motion or being pulled or twisted by unseen forces." Josephine mentioned it as the feeling of moving very fast through space or being in a wind tunnel. Others describe it in their own words.*

"The pulling feeling that others have mentioned is definitely what I felt at this point, it ripped me into many pieces."

"Some part of me is aware that my torso is falling back so that I will lay prone on the bed, only it seems like an incredibly long fall. A very long fall indeed."

"I had the sense of being catapulted head over heels through some kind of warp in space or time."

"The tingling sensation became more intense, and I felt that my entire being was being torn apart at a molecular level."

The last account is similar to my sense of this effect, which I have described as a dismantling or dismemberment.

Such dismemberments are often referred to in the shamanic literature, particularly during the initiatory crisis, which signifies a spiritual death and rebirth and heralds the calling to shamanize. According to Mircea Eliade in his classic work on this, *Shamanism: Archaic Techniques of Ecstasy*, the shaman-to-be is typically presented with a healing crisis of some kind, an illness, for example, that defies medical explanation and treatment. The only way the sick person can survive is through the intervention of spirits who will save him if he agrees to do their work on Earth and become a healer himself.[12]

When he makes this agreement he is taken (in his dreams, visions, or feverish imagination) to a place where his body is torn apart, ripped limb from limb, and all parts of him are boiled in a cauldron or cleansed in some other way before he is "remembered" and reassembled, often with some other gift of healing or foresight. He then begins his work as a healer, spreading the message of the spirits and the greater truth of the universe: that it is bigger, more expansive, more mysterious, and more healing than we have been taught to believe.

---

*These accounts can also be found and read more fully at Erowid.

This is similar to the Salvia experience. We are torn apart and washed clean in the flow of the universe where we come to realize—sometimes to our horror, sometimes in awe—that infinity is all around and within us, that nothing and everything is real and that we can be and do whatever we wish.

When we emerge from Salvia and are put back together again—that is, when we come back to *this* reality—the gift we are given is the new understanding that nothing and everything matters and that life, while insignificant, is also the most precious thing we have, and we should live it honorably, respectfully, and wholly, as best we can.

3

THE QUEST
IN SPAIN

Working in a Ceremonial Context

(5X–100X Concentrate)

• Using the Mesa • Ritual Experiences

and the Beginning of a Dialogue

with Salvia

If there is bad or good, save him
Help him out of sincerity and love
In nomine Spiritu Santo
Most Holy Lord Saint Peter
You too, Maria, show him
Set him free that he may see it.
　　　THE SALVIA PRAYER OF DON ALEJANDRO,
　　　　　　　　THE HISTORY OF SALVIA

As I said in the last chapter, Josephine and I were beginning a relationship somewhere in the middle of our Salvia experiments. Ours was

a "whirlwind romance," which began "officially" in September 2010, and by the end of October we were married, a San Pedro wedding at the Temple of the Condor Heart, a mountain shrine in the hills above Cusco.

Our honeymoon was a semiplanned tour of Peru. I'd been taking groups there for years to drink ayahuasca and San Pedro so I knew the jungles and mountains but had never done the tourist route. Josephine had never visited the country before. So it sounded like a great idea to us, and we traveled to Colca Canyon (deeper than the Grand and more beautiful); Nazca, to see the famous lines; Chavin (the birthplace of the so-called San Pedro cult); Titicaca and the floating islands, each handcrafted from reeds, where individual families now lived. The rest of our half-formed plans involved traveling north from Chavin, taking in more sites, and ending at a beach town where we would celebrate my wife's birthday. We were married on October 30, however, and by now it was late December. Christmas and other necessities interrupted our plans, and my wife flew back to England to spend time with her family while I returned to my home in the mountains of Spain. She joined me in January and our work with Salvia started again.

Until now we had worked only with 20X concentrate but felt that experimentation with different strengths would be beneficial. Most of the literature we had read on the contemporary exploration of Salvia (e.g., Arthur's *Salvia Divinorum*) used lighter concentrates of 5X strength although some reports on the Web used 10X or higher. We decided on a range—from 5X to 100X, the strongest then available—in order to test the outcomes of each. Our idea was that we would start with the extremes, first 100X, then 5X, and then explore the grades between until we arrived at the best for us. While we waited for the new extracts to arrive we continued with 20X concentrate.

In Peru our experiments had been informal but at our home in Spain we decided to introduce ritual procedures, which are more common when working with teacher plants. In particular we thought it important to work with the *mesa*.

THE MESA

The mesa (the word literally means "table") is the most important part of South American shamanism. It is an altar composed of a single piece of cloth woven with symbols and patterns, which is charged with spiritual power and becomes a gateway to beneficent energies. On it are placed ritual objects, which are also rich with healing intent. When not laid out as an altar the cloth and the objects it contains are typically carried by curanderos as a medicine bundle, and it may be used to heal in its own right. Josephine and I had both experienced healings in Peru, for example, where the curandero ran the bundle over us or rested it on our heads in order to remove negative energies and infuse us with new, more positive ones.

When used as an altar during a ritual, however, it becomes the center of the ceremony and controls the flow of energies within the room, acting as a *punka* (a Quechuan word that means "doorway") to spirit. The Peruvian curandero Eduardo Calderon described the mesa as "the important part of a curing session for the simple reason that it is the panel where all the elemental forces are computed."[1]

Placed directly on the earth, the mesa contains objects (or *artes:* "arts") that hold spiritual energy in the form of artifacts from archaeological or ritual sites to represent the power of the ancestors: herbs and perfumes in ornate or antique bottles that bring good luck and healing, swords and statues or stones from cemeteries and sacred sites, which stand as emblems for the powers conferred on the shaman by his guides and allies in the Land of the Dead. Other objects might include hardwood staffs, bones, quartz crystals, knives, toy soldiers (for the powers of opposition or victory), deer antlers and boar tusks (for strength in the face of challenges), shells, and photographs or paintings of saints. I have also seen torches used on mesas (to represent spiritual illumination), mirrors (for self-reflection or the return of evil forces), and carvings of various animals that are symbolic of particular qualities.*

---

*For more information on the mesa and how to work with it see my book *Cactus of Mystery*.

Josephine had begun to create her mesa while we traveled Peru on our honeymoon. I had given her an antique cloth from Cusco, hand-woven by one of my brothers in the Q'ero community. The Q'ero are the first people of Peru who live at high altitudes and in such rugged conditions that they were never conquered by the Spanish who never even knew of their existence. Indeed, most people in Peru were unaware of them until a few decades ago when these wisdom-keepers arrived in Cusco from the mountains to deliver the prophecies for mankind, which they had safeguarded for thousands of years. In 2008 I had become friends with Juan, a member of this community, and was also godfather to his daughter. It was a mesa cloth he had made, which I had given to Josephine.

On our travels around Peru she had collected various artes for it such as stones from Machu Picchu, the "crystal city" of the Incas, and gifts I had given her including an antique key (to "open the doors to Heaven"), a *seguro* (a talisman in the form of a bottle containing magical plants for luck and protection), crystals, and other items.

Her layout was based on the one I use for my San Pedro mesa, which is, in effect, a medicine wheel. The east represents fire; it is the place where all life begins and represents potential, passion, creativity, and courage. I keep a lit candle in this quadrant. The south represents water and is the place of the emotions, of power, identity, and self-awareness. I keep bottles of perfume and holy water here. The west is for air and the mind and signifies clarity, vision, and clear direction. A crystal and a condor feather sit in this place. The north is for the earth and for spirit, the ability to bring spirit into matter, and the desire to give birth to God's will in daily acts of healing and beauty. In this quadrant I place a live San Pedro cactus in a pot of earth.

In this way the four aspects of the soul—body (fire), emotions (water), mind (air), and spirit (earth)—are all included, and the mesa becomes a living thing: the soul of the universe itself. In the center, to represent stillness and balance, as well as the power that makes us whole, is a lithograph of Saint Peter—San Pedro—the gatekeeper to Paradise and the palaces of Heaven.

San Pedro is my ally but Josephine had begun to feel a growing affinity with Salvia so she had adapted her mesa accordingly to call in the spirit of this plant and at my suggestion became the officiating shaman for our early ceremonies in Spain.

THE MESA CEREMONIES

Our first ceremony had four participants: our friends George and Gina who were staying with us for a few weeks and Josephine and me. Josephine began them in darkness, as is traditional when working with Salvia, by laying out her mesa and offering a prayer to God, the saints, the elements, and the artes on her altar, and to the spirit of Ska Maria. She then loaded our pipe with a little tobacco and a pinch of Salvia.

A pinch is literally all that is needed. Many people (especially if they have experience with other psychedelics) are surprised at how little is required to create an effect. As Diaz remarks:

Salvinorin A is active at 200–500 mcg when vaporized and inhaled. Since very few people have the costly equipment necessary to accurately weigh anything close to this small an amount, it is inevitable that people will try to visually estimate the dose. Unfortunately there is little room for error. . . .

Because the dose is so small and insignificant looking, there is a tendency for people to think they need more. . . . I have seen more than one intelligent, careful, and experienced person accidentally do too large a dose because of this. Fortunately they had sitters and managed to get through the experience safely.[2]

Because of our research in Peru, however, Josephine had become quite practiced at measuring by eye. Some Salvia researchers recommend the purchase of delicate weighing equipment to be sure of an exact dose but the more this technology is used the less spirit is involved in the process, and if we trust our spirits and engage with our intuition we open the ceremony to the experience of what we *need* rather than what we *want,* which is often the point and the purpose of shamanic healing.

Josephine smoked first while I watched over her journey. It is important always to have a sane and sober person present during Salvia rituals so they can take care of those on their journeys and intervene if needed to offer help and support. Diaz mentions this, too, as part of Mazatec ceremonies: in his experience there was always one person present who had not taken Salvia.

I took the pipe from her after she had taken a few draws on it, and she lay down quietly on her back with her eyes closed. She was "away" for about five minutes and when she returned, still somewhat under the influence of Salvia but able to express herself, she spoke of her experience.

I had noticed that Salvia seemed to be taking me on a progressive journey through its world, familiarizing me with the territory, a sort of initiation where my experiences got deeper but always included a linking theme of some kind. The theme for me, had I been aware of it then, was related to issues from childhood that were affecting my relationships now: "patterns that I didn't like."

Something similar was happening for Josephine. In a previous journey she had found herself in a landscape—a country field—that seemed to be moving. Being present in the landscape itself, she hadn't noticed the movement at first but became aware of it when she saw that the scene had an end to it, that as she looked forward the field disappeared and was replaced by blackness. As she explored this she realized that she was, in fact, on a conveyor belt on which this landscape rested like a product on a factory line that would eventually roll off the end to be processed further. It was as if reality folded as it reached the end of the line and that stage of the process concluded.

From a wider perspective—standing back from the scene—she was able to see that there were actually several conveyor lines, one on top of the other, each one containing a different slice of reality, on this world or another, each stacked horizontally, and each being propelled forward from existence to annihilation. Her "blue God" turned a handle in order to move these layers on. The "reality-machine" itself was mechanically very simple: the handle connected to cogs, which caught on zippers beneath each layer of reality and pulled them toward their destiny.

A few of these themes are consistent with other Salvia users.

> **Zippers:** We have seen from Trendal's account that zippers (in Josephine's case, parts of her machine) appear in Salvia journeys. "Suddenly I became aware of a series of strange zipper-like patterns across the room, running parallel with the floor." DoOr (also at Erowid) mentions something similar: "I saw/felt . . . my Self being completely and quite literally *unzipped*. I saw the fucking teeth of the zipper separating."

> **Flat Planes:** For Josephine, when seen from a distance, each of the conveyor belts within the reality-machine represented a different horizontal plane of existence, which was absolute and self-contained, like a memory, a fragment in time, an experience within the context of the entire reality-picture of a life and a world. Seen from a perspective outside the machine each plane looked flat and two-dimensional, again like an item on a conveyor belt, which, face on, seems two-dimensional, even though we know it has depth and is a separate thing in its own right.

Trendal again:

I became aware of the fact that everything I was seeing was losing its depth and becoming flat, like a piece of paper. Except there were "layers" of these papers . . . I could move around between the layers in my bedroom. It was kind of like walking through a room filled with freestanding cardboard cut-outs with pictures of my room on them. One cut-out would be my computer and desk, another my bed, and so on.[3]

Alien Intelligences: Some entity—a blue being not of our world or perhaps our dimension—stood outside the reality-machine and controlled it. The machine was hardly complex and, with "his" wide-mouthed, inane grin, the "alien" in charge of it hardly fulfilled our expectations of a sophisticated extraterrestrial race— more like a functionary in a factory. The point, perhaps, is that human beings believe themselves advanced and intelligent, and this arrogance distances us from the truth: that in the wider scheme of things we are nothing and our entire life experiences may be controlled by an intelligence outside of ourselves. We call this "God" and presume in our projections that since we are so great "our" God must be extraordinary and magnificent too, but he may just be a factory worker, creating and destroying worlds because that is his job and he is after a paycheck. In fact, our God may be the base of the chain, himself controlled by a supervisor who is controlled by a department head and so on. Even the factory owner, like any "boss," is just part of a system and insignificant in the whole scheme of things. Who—what one person—is in charge of planet Earth for example? Why then should we believe in a single creator-God who controls all things? Pondering this question brings us back to our insignificance as human beings.

Something of this may also be present in the accounts of other writers. Glassalchemist, a 20X-concentrate user, in a report titled "How the Machine Works," writes for example:

Where am I? How did I get here? What is the meaning of this? Immediately, a voice jumps into my thoughts, explaining that this is where you go when you fall asleep. All of the races go there. Together, in their slumber, their thoughts intertwine, intermingle, to form the web I would best understand as the multiverses. The voice explained that our collective consciousness is what keeps the multiverse in existence. It was horrible. We are enslaved in our sleep, harvested to allow this gargantuan machine . . . to pump all of our energy around at high speeds.[4]

When back to normalcy his realization was that

this place [planet Earth] is so strange. So pointless. We all need to set aside our differences, our greed, our anger. We need to live in a state of love, rhythm, joy. I hope one day we will all wake up, and smash that fucking dream machine. It is a trap. It is there to enslave our energy. We should be in control of our own souls, our own destiny. Collectively as a race and separately. No more war. I am not afraid of death, but I truly appreciate the beauty of life quite a bit more.[5]

Somatzu smoked a 40X concentrate and agreed that his friend Joe could video his journey. He writes,

Everything around me was very alien. I looked at Joe; he was standing behind the camera and let out a couple of laughs. This had a terrible effect on me and constituted the hardest part of the trip; I now thought Joe was some alien being who videotaped all of human existence for his own pleasure, and he was laughing at how ridiculous this silly little human was. I totally freaked out and curled up wondering if he would kill me or keep me alive in his dimension.[6]

Karl Jansen in *Ketamine: Dreams and Realities* relates a comment made by a ketamine user, which is also pertinent given the similarities between "K" and Salvia: "I'm on a guided tour through the subatomic factory, which continuously generates the universe . . . countless other universes are rolling off the assembly line." The key difference between this account and Josephine's vision is that here the machine *creates* realities, whereas in Josephine's "world" it is a reality-annihilation machine, the purpose of which is to *destroy* all that we know and love or are attached to.

In her journey now Josephine found herself back in one of these reality-machine landscapes. She was enjoying a picnic by a river in the English countryside. Other people were there too, children and adults—a tranquil scene. She, like everyone else, was unaware of the fragility of her existence against the apparent solidity of the reality they had created for themselves through their relationships, jobs, families, salaries, expectations, belongings: all of which gave them the sense that their lives were real and permanent. Then the blue God began to turn the handle, and the conveyor belt started to move. Way off in the distance, this scene, this reality, began to fold in on itself. People became aware of it and started to panic and run from their impending annihilation, including Josephine. But death—the end of "reality"—is inexorable and inevitable for us all; we can't run forever. And so her last image was of herself standing alone as the world collapsed and darkness rushed over her.

Josephine was not scared by the imagery, but as she told her story she was reflective. Annihilation is the truth of human existence, which makes it important for us to engage with the life we have in an authentic and genuine way, not be driven by fear, patterns, or things, which do not matter, so that we get the most from our lives and share them with those we love. What exactly is "authentic and genuine"—what is real and what is true love for us—is not a trivial question but possibly the most important we can ask, so we do not waste our energy or our time here.*[7]

---

*Plants like Salvia, whatever else they may show us, reveal areas of ourselves that require attention or where healing may be needed. Another way of interpreting a vision like this, therefore, of an annihilation machine that ends all life around us—from a psychological or metaphorical perspective rather than a metaphysical one—might be to say that each of these different landscapes represented one aspect of that person's personality, one of the "selves" that she could further explore to understand its particular view of her life or the healing needs of that part of her personality, its drives and "issues" and so on.

From this analytical point of view it is significant (and disturbing) that reality was ending in each of these landscapes (i.e., for each of the separate personalities that these scenes represented) and that the predominant character (the blue entity) was in

Glassalchemist again:

It was as if I had been pretending all along that reality was the
way it is, and that somehow I had forgotten the nature of my true
existence. . . . Do what thou wilt. That is the power of man.[8]

The mood of Josephine's journey reminds me of something Einstein
said when he was asked by a journalist what the most important question of all time was for the human race. "Is the universe a friendly
place?" he answered.

Our individual perspectives on this—whether we feel comforted or
confronted by life—could determine our whole existence. Furthermore,
no matter how we answer and what we believe, how we *act* in the face
of our conclusions changes the nature of reality itself. Even if we believe
the universe dead and destructive if we hold onto love we can change
it. "Think with the heart and feel with the head," is how my San Pedro
teacher described this.

PATTERNS AGAIN

Josephine handed me the pipe next. Our ceremony this night was in our
workroom, the space where we held workshops and rituals for participants. There was a bookcase in the room where the books I had written

---

(continued) control of the annihilation process. Freud, Nietzsche, and others have written about *thanatos,* the unconscious "will to death" or desire for final endings, which
may, in the personal context of this vision, be revealed as a drive that is part of a "master program" or controlling personality. A person who has a vision like this might,
therefore, want to give urgent attention to it since the image *could* be read as a warning
(or in Salviac terms, a divinatory forecast) of their own (self-directed) death, telling
them in a symbolic way why and how it will happen unless they choose to change their
programing. And if the Fool spoke he would say, "Did you know that transformation of
consciousness is possible at any moment, that you can suddenly change the perception
you have of yourself? . . . If you wish to act in the world you must explode that perception of the ego that has been imposed and imbedded since childhood and which refuses
to change."

were displayed, as well as crafts and art for sale. I couldn't remain still during my journey—since I had learned to stand and walk on Salvia, movement had become part of my experience—and I sensed myself slithering over the floor, away from the ritual circle and toward this bookcase. It wasn't a willful or intended movement; rather, it was as if I were being pulled, exactly as I felt when I had become a bedspread or a wheel, a motion that was out of my control. I ended up hugging the bookcase with my head beneath it.

In my journey I was back in darkness, in that space again where during one of our final ceremonies in the jungle I had torn through the fabric of reality, which had the appearance of a street from my childhood, and ended up in a void, drifting away from the Earth. I feel now that the void experience, while in some ways unnerving, also offers us the possibility of new beginnings: the knowledge at an inner instead of a rational level that everything is available to us if we dream hard enough because it is through our dreams and creative acts that we make life whatever we want it to be, fashioning it from the nothingness that surrounds us.

Others have written about this void experience too.

MacExistence: All around . . . was a giant empty void, not really black, just sort of no-thing. I totally felt as if my body was this giant void. . . . Then after what seemed like near eternity . . . the perception of my body went from being that huge void to being trapped in a small container about the size of my head, which was very confusing and confining, as if I was forced in it.

Vulpine: I thought about the notion I heard from the Tibetan Book of the Dead, which suggests that when you die entities come whose job it is to dismantle your ego—what makes you the person you are. If you are ready for them, they appear as angels, but if you struggle they seem to be demons.

For me there was nothing—no thing—no angels or demons, and I think that whatever part of me continued (the ego perhaps) had grasped for what was familiar: my old ideas and my "me-ness" represented by the books I had written, which is why I had ended up hugging the bookcase.

With hindsight there was a message from Salvia even in this simple involuntary action. I had recently married, and my wife had just joined me in Spain to begin our new life together. *Now* was exactly the time for me to enter the void and lose my identity so we could create a new shared reality. It may have been different if I had reached for her when faced with the void—that would have been future-looking—but instead I reached for myself, my old self.

Again, learning the language of a plant is essential to working with it. Salvia is a plant of divination—of seeing a possible future so we can act on it or change its nature if we feel that we need to. Hindsight is easier—learning the lessons when that future has already taken place—but not such a useful gift. All it can really do is prepare us, through awareness, for different possibilities now that the "future" has happened, but it doesn't serve us in the way that foresight can, to preserve our relationships, for example, by acting on the information we are given at the time.

George was the next to smoke. He had limited experience with mind-altering substances of any kind. Seconds after smoking he fell backward and then sideways into Gina's lap, holding on to her, saying, "Help me. What's happening to me?" Gina held him and talked him around, and because of this he seemed to come back to normalcy a lot faster than Josephine and I. When he spoke of his journey he also described the void and "falling backward through darkness." In contrast to me, however, he had reached for the woman he loved.

Finally Gina smoked. Gina smokes marijuana as a daily practice and says it helps her sleep; otherwise she is a restless dreamer. She takes at least one joint a day and has also worked with entheogens. She had been a student of mine on plant shamanism courses and in ayahuasca ceremonies. Perhaps because of this and because her mind was making associations between the two plants to understand her Salvia experience she described a jungle scene, walking among trees—"very bright and real"—and becoming the roots of a tree. The sense of merging with and becoming something other than human is common with Salvia although the context of her experience seemed more ayahuasca-like. It is also true, however, that Salvia grows in the cloud forests of Mexico so that could also have been the context. Josephine thought that there was an affinity between Gina and the plant, especially given her calm demeanor throughout, and as the shaman in charge of the ceremony she suggested to Gina that she might do further work with it.

Looking back on this ceremony what arises for me now is the sense that Salvia understands our relationships and passes information to us against the background of our lives and where we find ourselves in them. By so doing, it hints at our futures and the directions we are likely to travel if we continue our present courses. This is what shamans mean when they talk of its divinatory powers. But Salvia cannot do it alone. It is down to the shaman or the participant to understand the language of the plant and interpret the information given. Awareness is therefore required.

In our case, during this first ceremony in Spain there were two couples, each of them in a loving relationship. George and I both underwent a "void experience"; he reached for his lover to help him through it, whereas I broke from the circle and reached for myself. Josephine saw a machine, which taught her that reality is an illusion and necessitated endings, whereas Gina saw a natural organic environment—"very bright and real"—where things grew and new life emerged. The theme of Gina and George's journeys was to do with nurturing, mutual support, growth, and togetherness, whereas Josephine's and my own were characterized by separation, aloneness, and endings and, as it turns out now, Gina and George are still together and part of a mature and loving relationship while Josephine and I are not. It is the job of the shaman to interpret these signs during ceremony by "keying in" to the divinatory quality of the plant and acting as its ambassador, suggesting remedial actions and routes forward that might help his participants. But none of us were Salvia shamans, and as I say, hindsight is a wonderful gift but it does little to help us at the time.

• • •

Gina and George returned to the United Kingdom shortly after this, and Josephine and I were alone in our mountain home. We loved it and had nothing but love for each other. Every day was a miracle. Our Salvia selection—from 5X to 100X strength—arrived shortly afterward.

100X AND 5X CONCENTRATES

Our first explorations with these concentrates were in February 2011, and we decided to begin with 100X strength; the idea being to then work with 5X and from these extremes to find our preferred level.

I had read very few accounts from people who had smoked 100X concentrate but those I did were not reassuring. In general the headlines for their reports were along the lines of "Nightmare," "Madness," or "To Hell and—*I think*—back."

Josephine was again the officiating shaman and smoked first while I sat for her. From the outside it looked a very different journey to those I had seen her take before. She sank backward and lay down on her back (normal for her) but was then immediately on her knees, staring into the darkness of the room and evidently in conversation with someone in front of her that I couldn't see. She put her arms out before her, beseechingly, and asked, "Really? What do you mean? How does it work then?" There was a pause as she waited for answers. I sensed that she was asking questions about her reality-ending machine or the nature of reality itself from the spirits of SalviaWorld or perhaps her blue God. She seemed to understand the answers given. Then she went into a child pose with her head on the floor, then turned and fell against the wall, clawing at it as if she wanted to merge with it or break through it. It was the most agitated I'd seen her on any Salvia journey. Finally she lay down on her back with her eyes closed and was "away" for what seemed like a further five minutes.

We recorded this session, and when we played it back, although not much more can be added in terms of words spoken or clues to the journey, we noted the time signatures and, in fact, her whole journey lasted around twenty-five minutes before she came back to normalcy. She could remember nothing of it and had no recollection of talking to anyone or, disappointingly, the answers given but at least the journey was not as horrific for her as I feared it might be after reading other 100X accounts.

I smoked next and, as usual for me, I moved. As I felt the onset of the journey I stumbled to the door. I didn't get very far though before I was on my knees on the flagstones outside the room. That is not entirely accurate, however, as from my perspective I was not "on" anything; I *was* the flagstones, I sank into them, and my body was composed of them. The residual part of me that could still remember "me" was amazed once again at how easy it is to forget SalviaWorld—its potency and how real is it—compared to the world we think we know. Josephine followed me out, and I looked up at her and said, "I remember this, I've been here before." Exactly what I remembered I can't say; maybe a feeling or the sense that nothing is real, or rather that SalviaWorld is as real—or more real—than the one I am used to.

There are gaps in my memory then, but when I came back to a sense of myself I had moved again and was lying next to our swimming pool. I also remember standing and looking over our fence, but instead of seeing the familiar olive groves and mountains I saw a car park in London and a housing estate in the 1970s and had a feeling that some sort of criminal activity was taking place. Then I was lying on my back again, staring into the night sky. The stars were pinpricks in velvet, beyond which there might be anything. I had a sense of someone near me, a woman looking down at me. "Josephine," I said. It was a statement but also a question: "Are you Josephine?" which meant, "Am I coming back?" She took my hand and helped me up, and I hugged her. *She* is what is real. I had been away for about twenty minutes. It felt like another life.

Daniel Siebert created a scale for Salvia experiences—the SALVIA Experiential Rating Scale—which uses the mnemonic S.A.L.V.I.A to describe the intensity of the journey.[9]

Level 1. *S* is for Subtle effects: "A feeling that 'something' is happening although it is difficult to say what. Relaxation and increased sensual appreciation may follow. This mild level is useful for meditation and may facilitate sexual pleasure."

Level 2. *A* is for Altered perception: "Colors and textures are paid attention to. Appreciation of music may be enhanced. Space may appear of greater or lesser depth than is usual. But visions do not occur at this level."

Level 3. *L* is for Light visionary state: Closed-eye visuals occur ("fractal patterns, vine-like and geometric patterns, visions of objects and designs"). "The imagery is often two dimensional. . . . Visions are experienced as 'eye candy' but are not confused with reality."

Level 4. *V* is for Vivid visionary state: "Complex three-dimensional realistic scenes occur. Sometimes voices may be heard. With eyes open contact with consensual reality will not be entirely lost but when you close your eyes you may forget about consensus reality and enter completely into a dreamlike scene. Shamanistic journeying to other lands, foreign or imaginary; encounters with beings, entities, spirits, or travels to other ages may occur. You may even live the life of another person. At this level you have entered the shaman's world. Or if you prefer you are in "dream time." With eyes closed you experience fantasies (dreamlike happenings with a story line to them). So long as your eyes are closed you may believe they are really occurring."

Level 5. *I* is for Immaterial existence: "Consciousness remains, and some thought processes are still lucid but one becomes completely involved in inner experience and loses all contact with consensual reality. Individuality may be lost; one experiences merging with God/dess, mind, universal consciousness, or bizarre fusions with other objects—real or imagined—e.g., merging with a wall may be experienced. . . . To the person experiencing this, the phenomenon may be terrifying or exceedingly pleasant but to an outside observer the individual may appear confused or disoriented."

Level 6. *A* is for Amnesic effects: "Either consciousness is lost or at least one is unable to later recall what one is experiencing. The individual may fall or remain immobile or thrash around; somnambulistic behavior may occur . . . on awakening the individual will have no recollection of what he/she did, experienced, or said. . . . This is not a sought-after level as later nothing can be recalled of the experience."

Journeys are unique and personal of course and depend on many factors including preparation (Josephine and I always dieted ahead of a Salvia ceremony and fasted on the day itself), body weight, age, previous entheogenic and shamanic experience, intention, and other circumstances, but I would guess that most of our sessions to date registered on Siebert's scale at around the 4 or 5 level. Tonight, however, I would say that Josephine entered level 6 while I was at 5–6. We never used 100X again, not because of the terror supposedly inherent with it but because it offered no useful information, or if it did we were unable to recall it, so this strength of concentrate seemed rather pointless.

Our next ceremony was with 5X concentrate, and for me there felt little difference between this and 100X except for the duration of the experience and the ability to remember more. The intensity was the same, the themes were similar but the journey lasted around five minutes rather than twenty-five.

I was back in the housing estate by the car park that I had seen on the 100X journey. It was more specific than that in fact. I was a brick (again) in a wall on one side of an alleyway on that estate. Josephine was standing in front of me, and my consciousness was equally between brick and human. From this perspective I looked at her and thought, "I love you so much."

Then my human consciousness began to fade, and I withdrew more and more into brickness. My vision and awareness of Josephine narrowed as I receded into the brick. My last thought was that I had always been a brick but I had loved this woman so much and dreamed so hard about being human that I had convinced myself that I was and could love and be loved by her. But I had deluded myself and "got above my station." I was a brick and nothing more. I could never be human and didn't deserve Josephine or this love for how could she—so beautiful and perfect—be expected to love a brick?

> *Approach the God of dreams with sword drawn*
> DALE PENDELL, *PHARMAKO/POIEA*

WHAT WAS SALVIA TELLING US?

THE LANGUAGE OF SAGE

I need to interject at this point to tell you a little about the relationship between Josephine and me because, as I suggested before, it is relevant to the messages of Salvia.

We fell in love quickly and deeply, soulmates, we were sure, who had known each other for lifetimes. Within a few months of meeting we were married.

We had disagreements, of course, and because our relationship was intense they hurt disproportionately. But we always fell back in love. It was a sort of dysfunctional game we played, a pattern we had fallen into: love intensely/break away and take a breath/return once again to love. As unhealthy as it now seems it became a rhythm for us, and amazingly we never talked about it or tried to make things better. We were speechless in love, too absorbed in each other to notice—until it became devastatingly obvious.

She left our marriage on the day of her sister's wedding. She never fully explained why but no one in Spain was especially surprised. They had seen her storm out before and spend hours or days away from home. It was a problem she herself knew she had, and one she had wanted to address. This time was different though; this time she never returned.

Reality fell apart, it is such a fragile thing, and I felt myself go into shock. Whatever game we had been playing it always had rules, the most fundamental of which was that *we loved each other and belonged together not apart.* That she had abandoned our relationship so easily without even a chance to talk or the familiar return to love felt completely unreal: a Salvia moment without the smoke.*

> *Joint in one hand, cigarette in the other*
> *Glass of wine held by the teeth—*
> *Now say something cute . . .*
>
> DALE PENDELL

It was against this background that I could reflect on what Salvia had been telling me. Three of my journeys had always felt more significant, and all of them had come when I was in a relationship with Josephine and usually when I was smoking the extract with her. The first was when I became a bedspread whose pattern I didn't like. The second was when I was chewing gum stuck on a wheel, going round and round, repeating the same pattern. The third—and the last we shared—was when I became a brick that had dreamed my relationship with Josephine and felt that it (I) never truly deserved her.

It is easy now to see the meaning of these messages. The fact that they were delivered in this way also teaches us something about the language of Salvia and how it offers its predictions and healings. It is not obviously direct in the way that San Pedro is, for example. It speaks in symbols and shows us the world from other perspectives—in my case those of objects

---

*Over the next few weeks, in fact, it felt exactly like that. Just as I had been pulled by Salvia into the consciousness of a brick or a bedspread and "knew" that I had never been human, I observed myself being pulled by this new reality of a life without Josephine into a sense of myself before I had even met her. She began to fade as if she—and we—had just been a dream. I was left with a residual yearning for a life with her that I could almost have simply imagined now that only memories and a sort of "idea" of her remained without her physical presence to reinforce our shared reality. I began to understand just how tenuous "reality" is: how it is dependent on memories, choices, and the agreements we make with each other about what *is* real.

that had some relevance to my situation—but we need to know the plant in order to understand them. Had the message been clear it might have been something as simple as this: "You are following a *pattern* [the bedspread] that you don't like and that doesn't serve you; you are *stuck* in this and repeating it over and over [the gum on the wheel]. You feel that you are not good enough for Josephine [the brick] and because you are afraid you might lose her, you are creating that very outcome."

I am not going to interpret Josephine's journeys here but one thing is unavoidable: that her reality-machine was a consistent theme and it was characterized by endings, by worlds coming to a close and realities folding. So perhaps Salvia had something to tell her as well about her fears and tendencies in relationships.

The language of Salvia is dreamlike. In fact, as a healer, had clients brought dreams or visions like these to me I would have seen them as significant, and I hope I would have recognized the symbols and the underlying themes they contained so I could have worked with my clients to better understand their messages and help create positive change. I didn't do that with my own visions, and I think there are four reasons for this. First, because we were experimenting with Salvia and getting to know it, we weren't setting healing intentions for our journeys, just exploring SalviaWorld, so we missed the information it was presenting. Second, I didn't then understand how Salvia communicated so I couldn't translate what it was saying. Third, I was not even aware that Josephine and I had a problem so I wasn't looking for a solution. We were in love, newly married, and it felt so right for us to be together that we had no idea that anything could be wrong. Last, we were trying so hard to hear what Salvia had to say that we just didn't listen. Our expectations got in the way.

J. D. Arthur writes about the language of Salvia as well. "This language, which is so distinct and alien, is very similar to, if not identical with, the language of dreams," he observes. "Until my experimentation with Salvia I was never aware that such a dream language existed. I'm now convinced that it does since so many of these Salviac episodes mimic the aura of deep dreams."

It is an aura in which symbols may not be straightforward but become what Arthur calls "weighted." He gives this example: "How often have we found ourselves describing the content of a dream to someone in a fashion similar to the following: 'He told me he was going on vacation but somehow what this really meant was that he was going to the forest to live as a monk.' This is the type of weighted phrase that occurs in the Salviac state."

Words may also be represented by seemingly unrelated concepts or objects. "It's as if the word or phrase is merely a vehicle for an entire constellation of images and meanings that is complex yet completely understandable." He gives the example of a journey where he was presented by the people of SalviaWorld with a bowl that was pressed against his chest. He understood this symbol to be a word, but not the word *bowl,* which, rationally, we might expect it to be. "When I surfaced and began to reintegrate I understood the word to be 'name,' I felt the import of the experience was that I, in effect, had a name there and that this somehow insured my connection with that world."

In a world where *bowl* means "name," *gum* means "stuck," and *brick* means "identity" or "self-worth," it is perhaps not surprising that Josephine and I missed what Salvia was telling us.

After she left, my research continued alone but now with a healing intention: I wanted to understand our relationship from Salvia's perspective now that I knew its language and to draw any further lessons from it that I could. Initially I worked with the 5X concentrate, setting up my mesa in the workroom where Josephine once had hers. I said my prayers and called my allies to protect the space, as I did for every ceremony with a teacher plant. Then I blew out the candle and smoked.

> It is when you are really stuck, when you really don't
> know what to do, when you are nearing the edge of funk
> and self-destruction that the leaves are the most powerful
> and the most precise.
>
> DALE PENDELL

Childhoods Revisited

I found myself in a house, but not one I knew. From the look of the furniture I was back in the 1950s (I had no idea why this particular decade seemed to come up in so many of my journeys) with the sense again that I was not human but part of the structure of the building: a wall in a room or the wallpaper on it, watching what happened from its perspective.

A young girl came in, less than ten years of age. She was happy and smiling but her mood changed when a man entered a little later. He sat silently watching her, very intensely, and she cowered into the sofa. I had a series of flashbacks or flashforwards then and saw contorted faces and hands and voices raised. Then I was back in the room where the little girl sat. A woman watched as the man and child faced each other in silence.

Things got faster then, and all memories, pasts, futures, times, and spaces seemed to happen simultaneously, and in one rush I saw what I imagined to be the girl's life as she grew. At whatever age I saw her she was running from something, smiling but afraid, consoling herself with the illusion that she was running toward something: a new adventure perhaps, but one she could never truly have or be changed by because soon she would run from that, too. I couldn't see what she was running from but it felt like a shadow that was always over her and could never be outrun.

These images had taken seconds—an initial flash as Salvia took hold—and all of them were replaced now by the sense of a wheel spinning in the room where I sat. I had been a wheel in a previous journey but this was different. It existed in front of me, and somehow it told the story of us. Each spoke contained a different universe: a decision that might have been made, an experience that could have been chosen, an outcome that may have resulted. I didn't explore these universes but I saw them all at once: the lives that Josephine and I might have had.

Some were "ideal" and picturesque (a typical "happy family"), some hellish, some in between. In one we had a daughter, four years old, a cute blonde hippie kid, but Josephine and I were separated. After years of being apart we took our child to a football game, the first time we had been out as a family together. Josephine asked me not to tell our daughter that I was her father but then "accidentally" called me her "daddy." My relationship with my wife no longer had any emotional depth to it, but as I held my daughter's hand I was happy that we were finally being honest and enjoying each other in a real way. The love we had for our child—the life we'd created—held the promise of a more authentic future because it was based on something mature and selfless and not on our usual patterns and bullshit.

I realized that the difference between arriving in Heaven or Hell is the decision we take along the way, and that our love, while flawed because of the choices we made and the rituals and habits we'd allowed ourselves to fall into, was not the worst (or the best) of worlds that we could have created.

The image of wheels rotating may be a common one with Salvia. I am tempted to call it the "karmic wheel": that place where we create our destinies through the choices we make. I subsequently found this account.

Vulpine: I was a five-pointed wheel. Reality itself was the five-spoked wheel. . . . It had infinite depth, like each spoke of the wheel was a long shelf stretching out into the distance. It was kind of like a paddle wheel on a boat, only each of the five buckets was infinitely long and deep. I was actually a consciousness inside the tumbling object, rotating in its chambers while aware of all the chambers. They were full of light and beautifully riotous colors.

As I tumbled in my colorful bucket, through an opening in my chamber, I could sometimes see out into another world, the base or real reality. . . . I became cognizant that my entire life, or what I had perceived it to be, all twenty-seven years, was actually an illusion. It was merely a fancy I had generated while watching the interplay of light, color, and shadow in my bucket. Any minute now I would be tumbled out onto the grass, forever lost from this false, comfortable reality and loosed into the base reality outside, forever cut off from the illusion of my life I was used to.

Again, I am not going to offer a deeper analysis of my journey since it seems apparent that it concerned the life of someone else but on some nonrational level it made sense of how Josephine had behaved.

As human beings we make choices. At any point in our lives we could make *any* choice but we lend ourselves to the habits and beliefs we have grown up with to make decisions about who we are now. By so doing we may almost wilfully give away our power and happiness. As Vulpine writes, "My entire life, or what I had perceived it to be . . . was actually an illusion."

We can do anything we want but we may choose what we *don't* want because that is what we are used to. Josephine's life—like my own, like all lives—was "merely a fancy [we] had generated while watching the interplay of light, color, and shadow in [our] bucket."

> *On a few occasions I've had the feeling that there were "pockets of eternity" into which one could slip and be trapped.*[10]
>
> J. D. ARTHUR

My next journey was with 40X Salvia, to explore the same theme. I had been doing a lot of counseling and self-examination in the last few weeks, and I hoped that Salvia might offer me further insights.

From the first draw on the pipe I was in darkness—space, I thought—but there were no stars, just these cube planet-machines hanging immobile. They seemed familiar, then I remembered that I had seen something similar during the moloka journeys in Peru. I had the sense now that each one contained all the thoughts, ideas, illusions, beliefs, imaginings, histories, futures, presents, and all the possibilities of everyone and everything that has ever, could ever, or did now exist in the universe that cube contained.

I had read Michael Talbot's book The Holographic Universe *some years before, a book about quantum physics and the nature of reality. The universe "bifurcates,"[11] he said; every second of our lives is a decision point where every yes-or-no decision we make not only changes the nature of reality but creates a Y-shaped moment where yes and no and the choice itself continue to exist. So there could literally be billions of us—of every individual—existing in every moment, ghost-selves that walk beside us in some other dimension that we can't see but occasionally sense. In a way then, not even our choices matter because all of them just go on. Our tragedies and triumphs, our sorrows and joys are simply moments in time without meaning, without relevance or point. And all of this was contained in those cubes as well.*

I felt futile, hopeless, despairing in the face of this knowledge: the ultimate meaninglessness of life. I had no control over anything. Life went on, and I was of no significance. Whatever I had done or however I had behaved toward Josephine would have made no difference. It may have changed things or created a new Y-shaped moment in this world but in another dimension I would still have lost her. My comfort was the knowledge that in some other reality she and I were different, still together and happy.

Einstein maintained that God does not play dice with the universe, and this is true but, it seemed to me now, only because there *is* no God. And yet like dice we are all still spinning, waiting for our numbers to come up. I was reminded of a cartoon I once saw of a cow standing before two tunnels, one marked Left, the other marked Right, weighing the apparent choice of which to take. What the cow couldn't see but from the viewer's perspective was obvious was that both tunnels led to the same place: a destination marked Slaughterhouse. Yes, we have choice but ultimately our choices mean little because in the bigger scheme of things, from the perspective of the universe, there is only one outcome and it is a decision that has already been made by an intelligence greater than ours. Nietzsche called it the law of eternal recurrence. "What if a Demon crept after you one day or night in your loneliest solitude and said to you: 'This life, as you live it now and have lived it, you will have to live again and again, times without number, and there will be nothing new in it but every pain and every joy and every thought and sigh and all the unspeakably small and great events in your life must return to you, and everything in the same series and sequence?" You would probably want to lay down and die, but even that would do you no good since your death would also have to be lived again and, ultimately, would not bring you freedom but remain part of a choice that had already been made. There is no way out.

Then I was back in my childhood, a five-year-old in a room playing with a toy car, putting all of my attention into it. Other toys were scattered around me. I had the sense that this is how "reality" regards us: as toys to be played with and cast aside when a more interesting game comes along, that there is no love or direction to the universe, and we are all completely alone.

I heard a voice then, either in my mind or in the room (or both). It said, "The only thing that can save us is love." I understood from this that the universe is inherently unloving and ambivalent but that the human race is unique because it does have the capacity for love. That is our collateral. To make it of real value, however, we need to decide that we will use that power, commit to it, and act on it with purpose.

When I came to I was outside lying by our pool in the same position as when Josephine and I last smoked together. Then she had reached down to take my hand, and I had hugged her, knowing that at least we and our love were real. Now even that wasn't true. Everything had changed so suddenly and so unexpectedly and if something as impossible as our love ending could have actually taken place it seemed like there was nothing I could believe in or trust. Whatever Salvia meant by love, it was bigger than personal relationships.

I felt utter sadness: for my wife, for the waste of our potential, and for our human condition, all of us spinning through space, each in our own worlds, alone and at the mercy of a God who either didn't exist or didn't care. The only hope we had was love. Irrespective of the facts of our existence we had to choose love and create our reality from it. Without that we are nothing at all.

I searched the Web to see if I could find an experience similar to my own. There was one from Crystallinesheen (at Erowid) that covered the same themes.

> You know when a person gets to that point past that little crust of perception that we call "Our Lives" and "Our World"? Where they suddenly realize their ultimate position in life and the Universe? It's not fun as it totally invalidates our lives. I mean, when you realize that everybody you love and everything you take for granted about "this world" are merely props on an intergalactic stage? All of our hopes, dreams, fears, just soap bubbles on the plate of existence? I mean, we all know that we are merely shells walking around on this earth but when you actually SEE that, oh god, it SUCKS, SUCKS, SUCKS. Some things we aren't meant to see while we are still bound in meat reality. . . .
>
> At least on acid that time in New Orleans, experiencing the similar vision, I knew that when the acid faded I could return to the comfortable delusion that is (was?) my life. . . . It wasn't like that on Salvia. I was watching the credits roll on my entire life. Even if I survived what did it matter? You can't have infinity and humanity at the same time, they don't work well together.[12]

> *Ever since we dispensed with God we've got nothing but ourselves to explain this meaningless horror of life.*
> ALTERED STATES

There is a Zen legend concerning Bodhidharma's meeting with Emperor Wu who had founded a number of monasteries in China and now asked how much karmic merit he had gained from his support. Bodhidharma replied, "None at all."

The emperor asked, "Then what is the truth of the teachings?" Bodhidharma replied, "Vast emptiness, nothing holy."

So the emperor asked, "Then who are you standing in front of me?" Bodhidharma replied, "I am nothing," and walked out.

> Salvia divinorum *is what you get by crossing an entheogen*
>   *with an atheist . . .*
> *It is we who must save the gods*
> *It is we who must become the diviners*
>
>   DALE PENDELL, *PHARMAKO/POEIA*

4

CONTINUING THE QUEST IN SPAIN

Salvia Healing: A Client Study • Repeating the Diet
and the Application of Salvia for Healing Anxiety,
Depression, and Addictive Behavior
(5X Concentrate and Leaves)

Heal him, care for him
For I am going to cleanse him now
Help him at this moment that he may be cleansed
Strike out the bad illnesses that he may have
Lord (Saint Peter) attend him
That he may see the Universe
What there is in the world

THE LIMPIA [HEALING OR CLEANSING]
PRAYER OF DON ALEJANDRO

There is a curious phenomenon in healing, which all shamans know. It is that the universe often delivers a client to us who is going through almost exactly the same problems that we, through our self-healing, are just emerging from. After twenty years as a healer I am used to these little cosmic jokes.

The scholar Mircea Eliade referred to shamans as "wounded healers"[1] who know "the theory of disease"[2] because they have themselves suffered an illness (whether physical, emotional, or spiritual) and recovered from it. As a result they understand its nature and have found a way to heal it, and so the fates send them someone who is struggling with the same issue but who has not yet navigated their own course through it. It is the roll of the dice of the universe.

Within a week of Josephine's departure I was contacted by John, a young American who wanted to follow a three-week plant diet with me to deal with what he called "intimacy issues" and social anxiety. He had a growing reliance on alcohol as a way of masking his fears and a sense that he might have an addictive personality.

His parents had separated when he was a child, and his mother had remarried within a year. Now aged twenty-one, he was still fearful about the impermanence of the world, its insecurity and instability. This lack of confidence sometimes led him to become demanding in his relationships, but paradoxically his most meaningful affair had been with a woman who was avoidant and emotionally closed-off, a pattern that can lead to a difficult dynamic.

It doesn't have to. On the face of it the coming together of two people like this *could* provide healing for both of them: the possibility of lovers complementing rather than opposing each other so that the one who craves certainty can learn from his partner to let go a little by following her example of freedom, while she can learn the value of following through on love and commitment instead of running away from it. It often doesn't work out that way, however, because the issues they face—and the potential for their resolution—are rarely conscious, and each partner will therefore pull against the other because they have different agendas to fulfill. My friend and relationship counselor Emily puts it well: "Hurt people hurt people." John would drink to deaden his feelings of insecurity but this made him controlling and pushed his lover away. She would drink and smoke pot, partying to "maintain her independence," and eventually she was unfaithful.

John joined me two months later, and it seemed obvious that he would be dieting Salvia. Siebert in an interview with the German magazine *Hanfblatt* had remarked, "Salvia is especially useful as a tool for gaining insight and clarity when one feels confused about one's life path or relationships."[3] Pendell says, "It's anti-escapist, the opposite of escaping. . . . It's ideal for couples work."[4]

There are also clinical reports and case studies that show that Salvia is useful when dealing with anxiety and depression. A study led by Daniela Braida at the University of Milan provides evidence (at least in laboratory trials with rats) that salvinorin has anxiolytic and antidepressant qualities. "We found a consistent antidepressant-like activity,"[5] said the researchers.

A case study by Dr. Karl Hanes in the *Journal of Clinical Psychopharmacology* also demonstrated the effects of Salvia in healing depression and some of the other problems that John saw in himself.

Ms. G is a 26-year-old woman with a history of depression that has shown no significant periods of remission since adolescence and has been predominated by feelings of worthlessness, lack of interest in social activities, an absence of occupational satisfaction, and inability to find "purpose and meaning" in her life. After first seeking treatment for her depression five years ago Ms. G was prescribed sertraline, 50 mg daily, which she self-discontinued after three months, reporting no significant benefits. Ms. G then underwent a course of cognitive-behavioral therapy for about six months, with some improvement but no definitive resolution of her symptoms. Hamilton Depression Rating Scale (HAM-D) scores during the six-month period of cognitive-behavioral therapy were consistently in the moderately depressed range (i.e., 19–21).

During a review consultation some seven months after discontinuing cognitive-behavioral therapy Ms. G claimed to have found relief from her symptoms of depression with use of the herb *Salvia divinorum.* . . . A HAM-D score of 2 confirmed remission of her symptoms of depression at this time. Ms. G claims that she discovered its antidepressant effects accidentally after smoking the herb and had later developed a method of oral consumption, which, she claimed maintained its antidepressant effects even after she abstained from using it for up to a week.

Despite being cautioned against use of a herb whose safety profile was unknown, she has continued to use a preparation of *Salvia divinorum* leaves taken as an oral dose of 2–3 leaves (½ to ¾ of a gram of leaf material) three times per week (the leaves are chewed and held in the mouth for 15–30 minutes). During this period she has continued to show a total remission of her symptoms of depression according to HAM-D scores in the range of 0–2 and has maintained this improvement for the last six months, showing no signs of relapse and reporting only minimal side effects, such as occasional lightheadedness for up to one hour after using the herb.

Ms. G volunteered that she has also benefited from occasional intoxicating oral doses of *Salvia divinorum,* consisting of from 8–16 leaves of the herb (approximately 2 to 4 grams), claiming that this herb had engendered a kind of "psychospiritual" awakening, characterized by the discovery of the depth of her sense of self, greater self-confidence, increased feelings of intuitive wisdom, and "connectedness to nature."[6]

Finally, Salvia is now known to have an effect on the brain's kappa opioid (κ-opioid or KOR) receptor site, which binds opium-like compounds and mediates their effects, providing a natural addiction-control mechanism. Salvia may therefore have a therapeutic application in the treatment of drug and alcohol dependency so if this *was* a problem for John it might provide a solution.*[7]

---

*Childhood stress and/or abuse is a predictor of drug dependency and shows up in alterations to the KOR system.

KOR agonists have, therefore, been investigated for their therapeutic potential in the treatment of addiction[8] and been shown to alleviate stress-induced relapses into drug seeking.[9]

They also have positive effects on addictions including alcohol and opiate abuse[10] and a number of studies show a reduction in alcohol consumption with KOR agonism.[11] Heroin dependence has also been treated in this way.

Before I administered any diet, however, I needed to check my diagnosis with ayahuasca. Consulting the vine in this way helps the healer to get his own thoughts, feelings, and preferences out of the way so he acts purely in the interests of his client. It is standard Amazonian practice before any diet begins.

During the ceremony John purged a lot of negativity, and his visions—of a woman in white "radiating love and protection"—confirmed that he should follow a Salvia diet. I returned from the ceremony and made the medicine for him, adding thirty pairs of leaves to hot water and letting them soak until morning. He would drink the brew three times on consecutive days and chew the leaves, holding them in his mouth until they had completely dissolved, as part of an initial diet that would last for seven days with an after-diet to follow. I would do the same.

In the jungle I had not chewed the leaves, only drunk the infusion as Mazatec shamans do and as is traditional in Amazonian plant diets. The Mazatecs do, however, chew the leaves as a quid so ours was a fusion approach where we would do both. The other significant difference was that I had drunk Salvia for seven days during my first diet, as well as bathing in it, smoking the extract, and using a tincture, so I was fully immersed in the plant. My approach was extreme compared to standard Amazonian practice where only the tea is drunk and for just three days, although the fast continues for seven. For this diet John and I would follow the more traditional Amazonian method.

His intention was to bring the spirit of the plant into him so it became a strength and an ally for dealing with his anxieties and fears, giving him the courage he needed for better relationships and to free himself of addictive patterns. He would spend the first three days in isolation in his yurt at the camp where we were staying, slowing down and connecting with the plant. We would meet each day to discuss his insights and Salvia-inspired dreams as the plant began working with him. What follows is based on my notes from these meetings. (My comments are in **bold**.)

Day 1: Not Much to the World

After drinking Salvia I had the sensation that there wasn't much to the world apart from myself. I was able to sit still for a long period, and my mind wasn't racing. I had clarity and focus.

The sense that there is nothing to the world except ourselves— that we create our own reality—has come up many times in this book already. It is one of the consistent teachings of Salvia, although with the leaves the experience is gentler and does not give rise to the same feelings of panic, which can be part of these realizations with salvinorin. Rather, it seems hopeful.

At points during the day I was aware of a woman in the room, wearing a dress of smoke that curled around her. I didn't see her all that clearly and there was no direct message but I felt a sense of inspiration. At times I was impatient, frustrated, and doubted myself and the diet; why was I doing this when I could be anywhere else? If I'm alive why am I so still? I wanted to be occupied.

Yes, the diet can be like that. We are so used to the world of rush and deadlines and the need to keep ourselves active that the meditative state of the diet and the concentration on subtleties it requires from us as we begin to first sense the plant can lead to irritability as the mind resists the stillness and wants to fill itself with doing instead of not-doing. It is in these moments that it is important to take a breath and look more closely at what the plant may be telling us.

I was reminded of a day in the jungle when I was dieting San

Pedro, trying to relax and hear the voice of the cactus. My mind was busy, wanting to fill itself with ideas, memories, thoughts, worries, regrets; so busy in fact that I nearly missed one of San Pedro's teachings.

It was something like a puzzle or a Zen koan. I had an image of a hunter in a wood who had pursued a deer for days and now had it in his sights. At that precise moment a snake crawled from the undergrowth and wrapped itself around the hunter's leg, ready to strike. If the hunter killed it the deer would hear the disturbance and run away; if he took a shot at the deer he would kill his elusive quarry but the snake would bite him. The question was, What should the hunter do?

The answer was nothing. Now was a moment of stillness. The snake had not bitten, the deer had not moved. There was nothing to do.

The point of the story was to let go of the mind and focus on the moment because the past (all that the hunter had invested in the search for the deer) had already happened, and that time was gone, while the future (the possibility of wounding or loss) is an illusion: a dream of what might be but is not yet. Now is all that matters.

I had a few dreams in the night but they didn't seem linked in any way. In the first I was at a business show with my family and we were doing really well; it felt good to be contributing.

This was a different and more positive view of his home life than the "routines and habits" that John said he felt trapped by when he had first mentioned his family to me. In the dream-language of Salvia the message was that we can be part of something and independent. We are walkers between worlds and can create any life for ourselves. This at least offered a new perspective on one aspect of the family dynamic that John had previously spoken of as "claustrophobic."

Then I was at my friend's house, and there was some kind of purification machine there.

Reminiscent of Josephine's reality machine and the mechanical imagery that often comes up in Salvia. This one was specifically a "purification" machine but I wondered if Josephine's might not also be in some way. Hers brought endings, annihilation: the greatest purification of all.

Finally I was sitting in a church and noticing how scripted the whole sermon was. People were just sitting there listening, frozen, unchanging.

We create our realities again. Some shamans believe that all of us, every soul on Earth, came here to experience the world for God (the essence of the universe). We are God in fact or at least aspects of Him/Her/It and through our encounters, adventures, joys, sorrows, lessons, and realizations, God gets to experience more of the universe so that God can evolve, too. Part of our every experience, therefore, belongs to God, and since we are God ourselves we evolve through the process of having it.

God, of course, does not need to have the experience of our sorrows and failings ad nauseam. Once is enough for a supreme being to learn from. Then we can all move on to something better instead of repeating our saddest dreams. When we place God in a box (or a church), however, and decide to worship it we make God (and, by definition, ourselves) a static thing: an old man on a cloud, a statue, or a stained glass window. God cannot evolve then—nor can we—and the world stagnates.

It seemed to me that Salvia was already offering John some deep lessons. Pendell calls the sage "a philosopher's plant."* This concern with consciousness, thought, existence, creation, and human awareness is something else that makes the sage and the cactus compatible, and certainly teachings about reality, truth, and

---

*I have used exactly the same words about San Pedro in my book *The Hummingbird's Journey to God.*

the power of dreams to create new worlds were present in John's thoughts. And this was only day one. By contrast, I was looking for more direct answers: I wanted to know the spirit of the plant.

In my journal I noted:

There was a definite effect within seconds of drinking the tea and chewing the leaves. Physically, it felt as if I was tilting, being pulled slightly to the right; emotionally there was a sense of calm relaxation and greater focus. The landscape around me, the mountains and trees all looked brighter and clearer. The world was buzzing.

I didn't have a desire to move in the involuntary way I did with the extract and felt less agitated. I could function normally if I wanted although my body felt heavier than usual. It was, I would say, a state of light trance.

This, I felt, definitely more than the salvinorin "blastoff" experience, was the state in which to perform divinatory work. I wanted to test this so I went into the house and found a dark room (Spanish houses are always somewhat dark because of their small windows, which ensure that the rooms do not get too much of the summer sun) and lay down. Then I posed a question—something simple to test Salvia's powers of divination: "If I offer this work to a publisher will they want it as a book?"

I was asking for a clear-cut answer to a specific question. This was not the way I had worked with Salvia before. The salvinorin vocabulary was dreamlike and symbolic but the tea produced the same sort of afterglow, which follows smoking the extract, when questions can be put and answers received. So I offered a straight question, and the response was straightforward too: "Yes," said the sage, "now relax."* I had written a proposal for the book and since I wasn't following a seclusion diet in the same

---

*During the diet and after it I began increasingly to hear the "voice" of Salvia, not as a clear communication in words but more as a sense of things, an inner knowing or awareness. In this instance it just *felt* as if the answer was positive, that I could trust in the book and the interest of the publisher because Salvia wanted to be heard and would take care of the rest.

way as John, I e-mailed it to the publisher I had in mind (Inner Traditions).

The Salvia effects wore off after about thirty minutes, but I remained calm for the rest of the day. During it I looked through a couple of e-mails I had received from my wife. She had been gone for two months, and she was angry—at herself as much as me I thought, now that the implications of her decision to leave had become emotionally and practically clear. Having realized all that she'd given away she wanted someone to blame for her choices.

I reread our earlier e-mails, too, from even a few days before her departure. The contrast was heartbreaking. It is so strange and seems unnatural to be hated by someone who loved you just a few weeks before, and the change in her would have upset me prior to this Salvia diet. But now I was more bemused at what seemed like a willful intent on her part to keep hurting herself when she had other choices. (She could always return, or we could meet and talk or arrange whatever counseling we needed. I had offered her all of these things and received no reply.) But that is the nature of reality again: it's what we make of it.

It is the message of Salvia that the universe is void and formless and that we project our meanings onto it. Most people I have given Salvia to have been able to see the possibilities that it offers them to heal so that a better reality and healthier relationships follow (see chapter 5). But the universe also gives us the option of re-embracing a familiar pain and re-creating the life that goes with it. As the Buddhist philosopher Thich Nhat Hanh remarked, "Some people have a hard time letting go of their suffering. Out of a fear of the unknown they prefer suffering that is familiar."

> *It's like a mirror with no frame:*
> *Some don't see it at all;*
> *Some do, but don't like what they see . . .*
> DALE PENDELL, "ON SALVIA,"
> IN *PHARMAKO/POEIA*

Day 2: The Lessons of Commitment

Today we drank consciously. *We sipped the brew, noting how it tasted (it is not so bitter when drunk this way: it is the* expectation *of bitterness that makes it more unpleasant than it need be); how it felt in our mouths, our throats, and stomachs; how it smelled (like old churches, I thought); and how it was when its spirit entered us.*

John wrote in his journal:

I felt fatigued from the diet but after drinking Salvia I also felt heavy, like my body was twice its normal weight. There was a brightness to things and a sharpness of contrast between light and dark. I found that I was looking through things instead of at them—like a sort of gazing—and my peripheral vision was more acute. [This is exactly how I had felt the day before. —R.H.]

There was a pulsing to things too, like everything had its own vibration. It led me into a dreaming state so it felt like I was not part of anything in particular but somehow between everything. I had a sense of slowness and that I needed to embrace time as it passed, to be in the now instead of thinking ahead. I feel very different from when I arrived here: peaceful, still, slow, and I just accept things now. I began a dialogue with the spirit of Salvia and thanked her for this sense of peace. She answered me with a single word: "Commitment," like she was thanking me for sticking with the diet.

Then I began to think about that in terms of my relationships, and I realized that it's important, that if I'm going to make a commitment to someone it can't just be for the good times because all relationships are a work in progress. I have to have integrity and impeccability so I keep my promise to my partner no matter what she does.

The whole world is an act of faith—an agreement we make with ourselves and others to regard it in a certain way—where believing is seeing, not the other way round. Putting faith into a relationship and keeping our word may be the difference between happiness and a life lesson, then even if the relationship "fails" at least we leave with our integrity intact.

A lot of emotions are coming up, especially empathy. I began to feel a lot of love for my (estranged biological) father and sadness at his loneliness.

"Salvia is," says Pendell, "a plant of connection. It's ideal . . . for keeping in touch." Contact, communication, and forgiveness (of ourselves and others) are important in any relationship and for us if we want to move forward or move on. We cannot just ignore someone who has been a central part of our lives in the hope that they will go away because they have contributed to us and will always be part of our souls whether or not we acknowledge that. They live on through us and color the choices we make. Even if we decide on a course of action precisely because it is one that a parent would never make or if we do it to spite them we are still doing it *for them* because they are our reference point.

I began to think about commitment in terms of the plant as well. With the diet we aim for connection with our ally and in shamanism there must always be reciprocity: a fair exchange of energy. But if Salvia is giving us the gift of insight, what does it get from us? The answer, I realized, was mobility. Once it is ingested by a human being Salvia *becomes* human. It is then able to move and interact with others. In that way it can spread its seeds of wisdom more widely. *Human beings are its pollinators.* The plant is a social being. It is pro-evolution and through movement it can lead more people onto the path of right direction.

> *We like to walk around sometimes and to see*
> *   new places.*
> *We like some of those animal things, like*
> *   mating.*
> *Sometimes we get curious to see what it is like*
> *   to program computers.*
>   DALE PENDELL

In my dreams I was watching a TV show. It was boring and childish, about plants from outer space. Then suddenly I was in the show, and the whole thing just opened up interdimensionally. I was so terrified that it woke me up, but even awake I was scared for hours. It felt like there is something really big, something we don't understand that is controlling things in a way we can't know. A real existential terror . . .

It's called life, I think. We can sit and watch it like a show, conceptualize it and have dreams and ambitions but do nothing about them—that's safer—or we can get involved. The minute we take part in it though the concepts and ideas that gave us our security they no longer fit because we're now in the flow of life. It can be frightening then but at least we're alive and not just spectators. The way to deal with this fear is through intention: proper dreaming. We cannot control the whole of life, nobody can, but we can apply focus and commitment to our part in it and through the magic of faith and belief create the reality we want.

I always had a fear of alien abduction, of being taken against my will and being out of control and the dream felt like that. . . .

Once on a Salvia journey, I saw that aliens are interested in human beings because we are the only species in the universe who can experience love. Space aliens, at least in our myth of them, are clinical beings from a somewhat metallic world, which is why the warmth of love is fascinating to them. It is a medicine they need. They may have advanced technology, however, but they're not all that bright because looking for love with probes and scalpels will not get them very far. It is like looking for "commitment" in a tissue sample. "Human beings are gifted," Salvia said, "because we naturally have the potential for love, and it is this above all that gives our lives meaning. We have the ability, though love, to create anything."

I had another dream that I was back in high school and trying out for the football team but practice was too demanding. I asked the coach if there was an easier spot for me, and he said that was my choice. I was pissed off that I wouldn't make the team and never have the status and attention I wanted from being a player.

Let's swap the words *high school* for *life* and the word *football* for *relationship*—which is why you're here—to look at these issues. In any relationship there will be times when it gets challenging and we have problems to face. But as in football there are always options and strategies. If you find the practice tough but still want to be on the team you could try harder, you could visualize a different outcome so you become more confident and capable, you could find another place on the side. There are lots of possibilities so coach is right: it is *your* choice. But if you want the rewards of team membership and the best for the team the most useful solution is not just to quit and run because that doesn't get you very far. So we're back to the first word Salvia gave you: commitment. If you're committed—to life, to a relationship, or to the game—you can find the answer to any problem.

Salvia is telling us to be impeccable, to have integrity, to keep our promises. Impeccability does not mean rigidity, however. Once we start to develop a "code" or a set of rules and regulations for life we fix ourselves in a moment that has already passed, and then we become stuck. "Principles" are not evolutionary or real; they arise from decisions taken in the past as a result of certain experiences so they don't allow for adaptation to circumstances. What is more important is an alert awareness of who we are and how we want to live, so we develop a proper response to each situation. The first and only principle we need to embrace is *love*. If we don't we are not being real; we lose our humanity and what makes us a unique species in the universe.

In the next session I recorded:

As soon as we drank I felt calm again. It lasted beyond the thirty minutes or so of the immediate (but gentle) effects. I was back in the jungle, experiencing my emotional self as I had done when I first dieted Salvia. The emotions then (first sadness and then frustration) were nothing like those I felt now though. I'd had a hard couple of months with the departure of my wife and now her bitter distance, anger, and abuse, so if I was going to experience any emotion I would have expected it to be sorrow or disappointment in her behavior. But I felt peace.

With the extract it is difficult sometimes to feel anything but shock but by dieting the plant I was more aware of its spirit. It was not motherly but like a big sister who was wrapping her arms around me for comfort and offering advice in a practical and constructive way.

There was still something matter-of-fact about it though, as there is with the extract. Since the subject of commitment had come up I was pondering the offers I had made to my wife that she could return at any time if she would just promise to stay long enough for us to talk and see if we could work things out. I had received no response.

As I reflected on this it was as if I felt the Salvia inside me laugh, not maliciously but pragmatically. "She married you didn't she?" it said. "What bigger promise could she make, and she couldn't keep that!"

> *Sometimes an ally will tell you something that you need to know more than what you asked about. Sometimes it is not pleasant.*
>
> DALE PENDELL

What I was beginning to realize about her *wasn't* pleasant but in this case Salvia was right. I took off my wedding ring. My wife had quit the team, and we both just had to live with that. She had made her choice between fear and love.

Oddly enough, on the day I removed my ring Josephine phoned me for the first and only time although she really had nothing to say, just that she loved and missed me but had promised herself that she would never call again. She never did, so that, at least, was a promise she kept.

Day 3: The Nature of Salvia—Insights and Divination

I had suggested to John that he try to make contact with the spirit of Salvia and begin a dialogue with it by preparing some questions to ask and then listening for the replies. These are his questions and experiences.

What should I call you?

Shepherdess. [I had been calling the plant Salvia and didn't know that it was also called The Shepherdess until she told me.] You can also call me "friend."

What is your quality?

Conclusion and emptiness.

What is your purpose?

The image of a seesaw. My attention was drawn to the middle. The Shepherdess is the point of balance.

What is your shape?

A series of pulsing rings appeared. They didn't feel organic and were very solid.

What do you look like?

I saw an archetypal image of a lady with a shepherd's crook and a sword in her other hand. She is a fierce guide. I sense that she has a beautiful face but she was hooded and robed so I couldn't see it directly. I imagine her to be severe and intense, never entirely happy. She is young, blonde, and white.

What is your aid as an ally?

A crowd of robed women appeared, all identical. Then from out of the crowd came a more unique woman. She looked Middle Eastern and wore a belly dancer's costume and had dark hair. Her message was in her difference: she was powerful, confident, strong, and daring: the opposite of the first woman I'd seen when I asked what The Shepherdess looked like.

Before I went to sleep that night I asked Salvia for a dream to show that she was with me and bringing positive changes to my life. I dreamed that I was at a movie theater although it felt more like a classroom where each desk was a different film. My friend was outside watching what he called his "old movie." I nearly went out too, to the place where old movies are shown, but something told me to stay in and watch a new film. It was a hero's quest type of movie. A headless horseman rode up and handed someone a baby, which was also somehow me. But it was a mechanical baby, a false one. Another of the film characters told me to "watch the big screen" and as I did that the baby came to life and was organic, real, and no longer a machine.

As for my own experience:

I felt the presence of Salvia with me all day, its protective qualities as well as a sense of the imminent, which could be described as prophetic or divinatory. I had to drive into town to fetch supplies at one point and stopped for a while to sit in the park. All the time I was there I was uneasy, however, and instead of enjoying the view I had my eyes on my car, as if I knew that something might happen. When I returned to it I had been given a parking ticket. Despite watching the car I had not seen the officer or I might have prevented the fine but something nonetheless had made me concerned. Salvia was offering me a gift of foreboding and future-seeing.

Day 4: The Nature of Anxiety

John returned from his seclusion today. It was remarkable how similar our journeys were and the realizations we were both coming to through

Salvia. For that reason I'm not going to separate the next few days into "John" and "Ross" sections but present our discussions as a sort of dialogue. As before, my comments are in bold.

Salvia is like an aura around me now, and I don't have to concentrate on it to feel it. It is like a combination of feeling spacey and being more aware of what is happening.

For me too. Yesterday I felt the presence of Salvia all day and she had been nudging me to pay attention to certain things, like my car for example.

I felt a slight anxiety all day, but it was never focused on anything, more like a potential or energy.

Me too. Dieting with somebody else is useful because it allows you to see the common threads. Since these feelings were arising for us both at the same time it suggests that they are the teachings of Salvia and show the progression of the plant within the body. Like John, I had felt anxiety about nothing in particular but noticed that I could apply thought to it at any time and make it about something—worry about the future, concern about a move I was due to make, protectiveness toward my wife and the hope that she was okay—but it really wasn't any of those things.

In "normal" anxiety we have something to worry about, and our feelings of concern stem from that, but this was the other way round: I was having the feeling, and then thoughts would drift in and try to make themselves the reason for that feeling, but they really weren't. I suspect that Salvia has a certain homeopathic quality. In homeopathy you may be given the essence of a plant that causes the very illness or problem you are suffering from. Because the dose is small it does no harm but it prompts your immune system to develop a natural protection against the disease. John and I were both feeling anxious, and maybe Salvia was allowing us to experience that at a low level so we built up defenses against it.

In doing so it was also showing us the loops of thought that human beings can get into, believing or imagining that we are worried about something and therefore giving our attention to it, making it a concern that previously didn't exist. Creating reality again, but not one that serves us.

Day 5: In Ceremony—Reality Is Alive

On a vision quest a person will take themselves away from their tribe or community into the wild places of the world, the mind, and the soul in order to seek themselves and find answers to the questions of their lives. They return with a new vision and direction. The diet is like that, too. For the first three days John had been in seclusion with the spirit of the plant, developing a relationship with it and beginning to apply its lessons to the questions that had brought him.

The "four sacred questions" asked on any vision quest are:

1. **Where have I come from?**
   What is my history? What patterns and beliefs have I been handed or found for myself and how have they shaped me?
2. **Who am I?**
   How has my history formed me, which parts of it serve me, and which are holding me back? Taking stock of myself, am I happy with whom I've become?
3. **Where am I going?**
   What path am I on? Is it one that I *want* to be on?
4. **Who will come with me?**
   Of all the people I know, know of, or do not yet know, who (or what sort of people) best serve the ambitions of my soul? There are some that I may need to leave and others I may need to meet in order to be true to myself. How do I find these people?

Answering these questions, it is said, will tell you everything you need to know about yourself and give you the potential for a life that is spiritually and emotionally fulfilling.

Salvia had already begun to deal with the first two questions. Through his plant dreams John knew something about his past, how its insecurities and uncertainties had affected him, and how his need to be loved had led to unhealthy outcomes in his relationships. He had insight now and an ally to help him deal with these issues. He was ready to work on the third question, *Where am I going?* To explore this there would be a ceremony with 5X concentrate.

He took three draws on the pipe then emitted an involuntary sigh that sounded something like disbelief. I took the pipe from him as he fell backward onto the mat. He was "away" for about five minutes then spent a further fifteen or so in quiet contemplation, asking questions of the spirits in the Salvia afterglow. Then we discussed his journey.

Everything changed, and the catalyst for it was the noise that came from me. When it left my mouth it was spinning, like a stream of reality that filled the room, so the whole room was swirling, and the reality I was in became a pulsing fragment of something larger—real, unreal, surreal. I found myself—if I was a self—asking, Where am I? Who am I? What should I do?

Reality is alive, in a physical yet mechanical way! I realized that I am just part of it, and I can't separate myself from anything else. I found myself asking, Am I with my friends? Is this all a joke? Was I supposed to do this? At one point I opened my eyes and looked at you but I had no idea who you were—or who I was.

I could feel the floor beneath me spinning and carrying me around the outer edge of a wheel that now filled the room, and it felt like chaos. It was only when I remembered what I was doing here that I found myself at the center of the spinning, then it felt like the entire universe was moving around me. Somebody said, "You've been here before."

That is the first lesson of Salvia: that reality is not what you thought it was, that actually you're at the center of things; you create it from chaos and emptiness. You created this one with your voice: very God-like! "In the beginning was the Word. . . ."

And those questions you asked—Where am I? Who am I? What should I do?— are good ones. If we are the creators maybe we should be asking ourselves those questions each day because . . . My wife and I used to have this mantra, this ritual, when we first woke up each morning. I'd ask her, "What shall we do today?" And she'd say, "Anything we want!" And it's true. We can be or do anything. So what *do* we want? Would we rather spend this day in love or in fear and acting from that perspective? Because both of those choices are possible and have consequences for what we create around us.

I didn't feel any personality to Salvia except something metallic not flesh. There was a paradox beneath it all: like pure mathematics with an organic feel, like everything could be angular and circular at the same time.

Paradox is right. Or maybe it's that the truth is wholly inclusive, that there are no boundaries or polarities and Salvian geometry is non-Euclidean so it can be angular and circular all at once. When I saw Salvia during an ayahuasca ceremony I was told that human beings had to change their shapes to meet it. I saw pyramids. But when you asked the ally for its shape a few days ago you saw circles. Both are correct because Salvia doesn't accept the sort of limitations that human beings apply to it or themselves. It can't be understood in our terms.

When I started to come round a little I saw this huge machine and all of these people were walking out of it. They were all identical, clean and dressed in white clothes.

A lot of people mention this machine. My wife saw it as a sort of reality generator, and for her there were always endings associated with it, some form of annihilation: a current reality coming to a close.

But Salvia also shows us ourselves so maybe the desire for endings is a personal thing, and you see something else. Perhaps the machine actually exists, in other words, in some other dimension, but its meaning lies in how we interpret it. If our patterns are based on fear or endings, then that is what our machine generates and what we see. Maybe Salvia is telling us, "Look, this is how it is for you—and the way it will always be unless *you* decide to change."

> *It just gives you where you are. Wherever you are, that is*
>   *what you get.*
> *If you are in darkness, you fly through darkness.*
>   DALE PENDELL, *PHARMAKO/POEIA*

Yes. Because to me it felt like a rebirthing machine, like the people coming out of it had been washed clean in it so they were new and hadn't had any ideas or beliefs forced onto them or any experiences that had shaped them. There were no patterns.

Day 6: The Nature of Freedom

I had dreams about authority and freedom. In the first we were living in a police state but it was also like a school we were put in against our will. Some of us created a plot to get out where we dressed as police officers and stole a car but even outside the compound authority was everywhere, and they found us and sent us back. It wasn't a horrible place but it was a prison and the guards thought it important for us to be there because that was their dream.

In another I was aboard a spacecraft with lots of other people—like a kind of ark—but the engine died, and we couldn't take off. Again we were boarded by police who said we couldn't leave and searched us for drugs. We could never get where we wanted.

The third dream was different. I was alone looking at a beautiful pink dawn or dusk sky. It was peaceful, and I was calm and relaxed. I saw a medicine wheel in the sky, and all parts of it were in harmony and balance.

It sounded like a caution from Salvia. In ceremony last night John had stood at the center of creation and knew that ultimate reality was *his* reality. The trick now was not to get sucked back into the worldviews of others or succumb to their authority. Fear of the void is what leads to consensus reality, with people banding together to reinforce their views of existence in the face of meaninglessness and ultimate nonexistence. And of course they want to keep us in their worldview, too, because if we escape to freedom it becomes terrifyingly possible that they could as well.

Freedom means that we don't subscribe to the consensus in any form (even *pretending* to be a cop lands you right back in prison) but also that we don't oppose it because that is still playing the game (being a robber in a game of cops and robbers is still being in the game). True freedom comes from being in the moment and quietly following our purpose, remembering that we are the creators and enjoying the sunset we made.

Day 7: Dreaming a New Future

I dreamed that someone was standing by my bed, teaching me medicine knowledge. There was a lot of information about how to heal with plants and what conditions they cure. Then I suddenly woke up and heard something move at my bedside. It ran across the floor and out of the door even though the door was locked.

Perfect. This is exactly what we hope for toward the end of a diet, that the ally will show up and begin the process of teaching. Up until now Salvia had shown John a lot about himself; now the knowledge was widening into the arena of healing. It suggested that Salvia had plans for John, that it had chosen him as *its* ally too.

Allies are ambassadors for the shaman in the otherworld and can introduce him to other healing plants so he knows their spirit and how to use them. This had happened to me when I dieted San Pedro; it was how I had come to Salvia in fact, because the cactus had shown me a number of plants I should diet, one of which was the sage.

Plants, like humans, have particular skills and talents; Salvia will show us the nature of existence, for example, while San Pedro teaches us how to be human, but that is not all they do. They belong to the plant kingdom as well, just as every person alive belongs to the human race and shares certain characteristics in common so all of us know something about everyone else through empathy and our humanity. Plants are the same, and every plant knows the healing spirits of others and can teach us about them. Finally, all plants are aware that they are part of the spiritual universe, part of the mind of God, so they can open doorways for us into a wider dreaming. There are four levels then to the healing of every plant:

- As a medicine, used in the same way that any herbalist might (in the case of Salvia, to treat stomach problems and depression, etc.).
- As a spirit ally, which can teach us about ourselves, reality, existence, and the wider patterns of our lives.
- As a *guia* (guide) to the spirits of other plants, an educational role in which the ally begins to teach the shaman how to heal. (The Mazatecs believe, for example, that Salvia will carry the apprentice to the "tree of knowledge" where all plants grow and where saints and angels will instruct him or her in their uses.)
- As a *punka* (doorway) through which we may enter the void and learn the deepest truths of all.

My dream was postapocalyptic. I was in a house by a lake but outside was devastation, and all sorts of mutant animals were trying to get in—frogs, rats, coyotes—it was a battle to keep them out. The mechanical baby I had seen before was in the house, too, and although I didn't want to, I had to protect and care for it. It was very sick, and something told me I had to nurture it. It slowly got better and became more human. Then everything improved, and the world outside became normal. My stepdad came into the room and asked me, "Why does everything have to be so bad?" I answered, "So we can learn."

Healing the world or dreaming a new life begins with us. At first John had attempted to fight off an ugly world, the one that had led to the chaos in his previous life. Having gone through his healing process he didn't want to return to that chaos but being at war with it wasn't helping. It was only when he gave attention to himself (the baby) that things could change.

"Me first" is how one of my teachers used to put this. In other words, if we attempt to change the world or help others before we have the power to do so and have healed our comparable issues and wounds we project our sickness onto that world and make things worse. The work of changing anything always begins with us, and if we all did that, of course (since collectively we *are* the world), the planet would automatically become a better place.

> *I heard a song in my dream then, and I saw the words clearly and knew the tune of it, although I couldn't remember it when I woke up.*

Perfect again. When we diet a plant as shamans (not necessarily as patients) one of the things we hope is that when the plant is ready (often toward the end of the first week) it will begin to teach us its power song. In the Amazon this is called an icaro.

Icaros are more than just tunes sung in ceremony; they are carriers of energy and intent. It is their vibrational frequency that counts. This vibration can be used to charge or to change the energy patterns within the body of a patient, remove illnesses and blockages, and restore a person to luminosity and balance. Some icaros are learned from others (usually the trainee shaman's *maestro* or teacher), some are copied and do the rounds from moloka to moloka, but the most powerful are personal gifts from the plant the shaman is dieting. Douglas Sharon, writing about the San Pedro shaman's *tarjos* (the Andean equivalent of icaros), reported that the curandero Eduardo Calderon "learns the traditional rhythms but . . . elaborates on the basic complex with his own particular talents and according to the inspiration he receives from a variety of extrapersonal and supernatural sources." Often these sources are plants.

The most difficult part of learning a new icaro is not hearing the voice of the plant but remembering the song. I have been given many but can recall only a few of them when I try. When I don't try, however—for example in a ceremony where I drink the medicine to let go of my rational mind and hear what my soul has to say—the songs come back to me easily.

Since today is the final day of the diet, there is an ayahuasca ceremony to "bookend" it and form a boundaried space in which the spirit of the plant can continue to grow. The intention of the ceremony is for John to meet the spirit of Salvia, which is now inside him, to see it, to speak with it: to make friends. I also suggested that he allow his icaro to sing itself through him. Doing so would fix it in his mind and teach him how to use it.

John's three dreams were significant. He had come with an intention to heal himself but it seemed clear that he had also been chosen by Salvia, that a plant apprenticeship had begun. In this series of dreams he had received teachings about the plants and how to heal and been given a song of power. In the middle dream he had also been reminded that to heal effectively the shaman must be in his power and present on his own healing journey. It is not enough to heal others and forget about ourselves.

The nature of the work was changing for John in a good way. He had been selected by Salvia to help others, and if he chose to he would also gain a new purpose that would help him overcome his own problems. We are not so focused on the self—on anxiety, depression, or issues of addiction—when we are in service to others. Addiction, for example, arises from a feeling of emptiness and loss of soul. (Alcoholics Anonymous says that inside each addict there is a "God-shaped hole.") Filling that hole with service enables us to find new power and heal ourselves as well.

Salvia had fulfilled its contract: it had offered John a way to heal and gone further, in fact, suggesting a new vocation for him as a healer.

AYAHUASCA VISIONS

THE ARRIVAL OF THE SHEPHERDESS

A slut-nun with a mescal flask
in a Mexican brothel-church
birthed you Ska Maria
before an altar of snakes and flame.
Open-robed, around her waist (legs and lips apart.
  No hair)
a belt of chain, and hanging there
a skull of brass and human bone.
You were dropped into an underworld
—Scarred Maria—
a dark angel baptized in a vat of ice
(Something to cool the tequila with).
A skull-baby boiled in permafrost,
a daemon/demon owl-child,
dark-haired, pale and naked,
spitting smoke and holy water.

That was my vision of The Shepherdess during the ayahuasca ceremony, which closed the week of the diet, or at least of her birth. It was holy-unholy, Catholic-heathen, madness and wisdom. She was born of a skull and came from grief, carrying life and hope inside her. A paradox. A girl-child becoming an owl-child, the guardian of curanderos.

When you were born the stars hung sickly,
your three wise men were uninspired
Your mother's voice sang too thickly
lullabies of smoke and wine

OPENING LINES OF AN ICARO
GIVEN TO ME BY SALVIA

My meeting with her was different. In my vine-dream I was at a tourist village in Spain (the sort of place I normally avoid), sitting on a terrace by a pool. A man passed by carrying a young blonde woman in his arms. (I guessed they were both drunk; they were laughing and fooling around anyway.) He lifted her over my wall and handed her to me. She was giggly, flirtatious, and it seemed obvious that we would have sex.

As soon as I thought that another woman—a brunette with long hair—was in my face. She interlaced her fingers with mine and said, "Ross," gently but insistently. What she meant was, "Wake up." And I did. I snapped out of my vision and found myself in a dark wood. The brunette was standing on a rock looking down at me while leaves and shooting stars skittered across a midnight sky. She was earthy, primal, elemental.

> *She cums on the wind like a cool witch*
> *She rises from the earth with mulch-hair*
> *She surfs the waves like a Venus*
> *(Calva, Cloacina, Erycina)*
> *She fuels the flames with tequila*

She was holding the skull and chain, inherited from her mother in my vision of her birth, which had been her placenta, swinging it above me like the pendulum of a clock or a hypnotist's crystal. The message was, "Focus on what's important; there is no time . . ."* I had the sense that she herself was between time, the Mistress of Time, and beyond life and death but embodying both in the symbol of the skull-baby chain-placenta.

The rock she stood on was in front of a great tree, now losing its leaves in the wind. I suppose it must have been autumn, a between-time as well, change and impermanence heralding a winter-death and the potential for new growth. To her right the night sky opened, its scattered stars reflected in a still lake beneath them—as above so below—the whole picture

---

*Salvia often speaks wordlessly and in double meanings and paradox. In this case the message that "there is no time" could be taken in two ways: that "you are running out of time" and more literally that "time does not exist." Though they seem to oppose each other, within the vision both statements felt true at once and not at all contradictory.

illuminated by a faded yellow moon. An owl sat on a branch above her, a familiar silently watching.

There was an air of sadness about her, resignation and pity, as if she, too, had wounds, as if the Bringer-of-Nothing, the Priestess of Illusion, the God/Mother of Choice was herself trapped by the roles she had taken on. It made me want to hold her, protect her, and kiss away her sorrows. As I thought that the wind blew her long white dress against her, revealing the tight body of a young woman naked beneath silk. It was a sexless sexuality though— although it felt like temptation or a promise: that man can have sex with the gods again as we once did in forests like these—but I had no doubt that she would be wild, that making love with her would be a dissolution of the soul.*

> *I told her that it was a seductress not a Goddess*
> HOWARD ALLTOUNIAN, IN A WARNING TO HIS WIFE,
> MARCIA MOORE, ABOUT KETAMINE (SIMILAR IN EFFECT
> TO SALVIA), JUST BEFORE HER KETAMINE-RELATED DEATH

She looked like a tarot card, one that hasn't been drawn yet.† She was a shape-shifter too, and in my vision took many forms, all of them fleeting, just enough to give a sense of her as an infant, a crone, a grinning corpse, Liberty surrounded by waist-high flames with a torch that points to the dog star, a flower-child hippie lover dancing in an English field. All of her many faces were in some way impure or perverse.‡ There was something holy but nothing religious or reverent about her. She wants us to speak in poetry

---

*Many shamans have lovers in the otherworld, spirit wives they visit in dreams and journeys. Some even have children with their noncorporeal lovers, an extended family of the dead. Salvia as a lover though would not be Maria but the Magdalene, not Eve but Lilith, and it would not be making love but the most tender fucking, primal and feral and filled with fear and blessings. It would be the caress of a mantis where in the final communion you would know and be part of all things and then torn to pieces so you became those things: with pleasure.

†Another double meaning: like a card that has not yet been drawn from a deck or like a drawing that an artist has not yet produced.

‡References to Mary and the Virgin in the names given to her by the Mazatecs might suggest a certain purity to The Shepherdess but this may be a misunderstanding about exactly which virgin we are talking about. Albert Hofmann in *LSD: My Problem Child* mentions a ceremony he attended, for example, where "under the direction of Maria

because she loves the voice of the damned; it is a language of death and seduction, which she and all poets know. She is playful (as far as it goes) but it's a dark sense of humor, and we must prepare for the possibility that we may not get the joke. Or that we are the joke.

> *Thus it is said:*
> *the path into light seems dark,*
> *the path forward seems to go back,*
> *the direct path seems long,*
> *true power seems weak,*
> *true purity seems tarnished,*
> *true steadfastness seems changeable,*
> *true clarity seems obscure,*
> *the greatest art seems unsophisticated,*
> *the greatest love seems indifferent,*
> *the greatest wisdom seems childish.*
>
> *The Tao is nowhere to be found.*
> *Yet it nourishes and completes all things*
>   TAO TE CHING 41

And that was Ska Maria: the living Tao—protective, direct, and very matter-of-fact. It had taken me almost two years, two Salvia diets, two continents, a wife, an ex-wife, and many pipes of salvinorin but I had finally met The Shepherdess. That is the initiation, what she expects from us, and what we must be prepared to give. She can be elusive and shy as the shamans say but she is also fascinating, demanding, beautiful, unflinchingly honest, sad-eyed, crazy, and very, very dangerous.

(continued) Sabina, one of the children, a girl of about ten years of age, prepared the pressed juice of five pairs of fresh leaves. The drink is said to be especially powerful when it is prepared by an innocent child." In other words, *it may be the person preparing the brew that is virginal, not the spirit of the plant.* The focus on ritual purity enables the spirit of Salvia to be experienced in an untarnished way but that is not to say that the spirit itself is untarnished. Indeed, if The Shepherdess knows all of human nature and is the essence of reality and existence we might expect her to be a little "worldly-wise."[12]

The Shepherdess, the virgin, the ineffable:
She who cannot be effed.

That ceremony totally opened me up to the spirit world. I couldn't separate it from this world. After I purged I became nothing, then the point of conception, then I was brought into being, then childhood; I was growing up from the jungle floor like a plant, with angels and aliens watching me, and I felt like I wanted to cry. I had blocked out my natural father because I thought that I should, but there is a child in me that is still wounded from that, and I want to make peace with him. It feels okay now to remember the good times we had and forgive the distance between us.

At one point I was in darkness and woke up in another world. Complete loneliness. No one else was there, no one can save me, we're all on this journey alone, and I have to do this for myself. Time was irrelevant; I was in that sadness forever. You brought me back when you started playing the drum. Then finally I had a thought, not just a wordless vision: "I'm here!"

Some sort of brain surgery was performed on me then. I was aware of the karmic circle of thoughts and how they get trapped in my head. There was something chaotic in my head that needed to be worked on. It was painful, being awake on the operating table, but that passed too. I realized that billions of thoughts are floating around us all the time, and we can cherry-pick them. When we choose one to latch on to we take ownership of it and then it becomes us. With Salvia objectiveness it is easier, if that thought doesn't serve us, to just pick another.

A Zen interlude . . .
In my vision a teacher approached and asked me
"Have you learned NOTHING?"
I said:

Yes

I asked to see Salvia and a woman popped into my head and smiled at me. She wore a robe. We touched fingertips.* Then I was in her womb. She let me know that I'd come from her and that I was still in fact there. We are all eternally in this womb. She told me not to forget that, and I said I wouldn't. She replied, "Yes, you will. But then you'll remember."

Her love is lukewarm. It feels like cold fingers in a glove, cold bedsheets; half is worth half and no more. There was no resolution to the journey. It completed itself by not completing itself because this is a new beginning. The ally will always be with me and continue to grow. I feel different today, changed, and I didn't dream at all last night. I didn't need to because Salvia had already spoken, so in a way that is a sense of completion.

I really see how important it is now not to fall back into old patterns. Once you know a new truth you have to act on it or you just stay nothing.

It's always a choice between love and fear—or, rather, love and nothing. Every second we're alive we are offered that choice. The plants show us the consequences of our actions but what's really important is to get the message, to remember it, and to act on it, because if we do forget or don't understand it clearly the plants have a way of reminding us. They raise their voices from a whisper to a yell.

During a San Pedro journey five years ago, for example, I was told by its spirit that I must behave with Dignity (capital D). It means to be in my power, to know my boundaries, to be in control of myself but not controlling of others, and to act with humanity, love, empathy, and compassion. I only understood it philosophically, however—which means I *misunderstood* it because San Pedro meant it literally—so I sometimes forgot and didn't act on it either. San Pedro's response was

---

*This first contact with the spirit of Salvia may be interesting. She interlaced fingers with me; with John she touched fingertips. Others (see the next chapter) also talk about her fingers being significant. I wonder if this might be a symbol that we have been in some way accepted by The Shepherdess?

a sharp reminder to really grab my attention—a relationship disaster with hearts broken and bits of them still lodged in various people's souls. *Then* I got the message and now I'll never forget it. Ah, but if only . . .

So yes, we always have choice, whether to fall back into our old myths of ourselves or rise above them, but sometimes it's just easier to accept what the plants are telling us because the lessons get harder each time, and that becomes our karma.

THE AFTER-DIET

DAYS 8–14

Prophecies and Teachings

The initial diet is ended by eating onion in lemon juice with salt and sugar—a little of all the things we have denied ourselves—covering all the main taste groups: spicy, acidic, salty, sweet. The breaking of the diet tells the ally that the intensive work of connection is over, and it can now continue to grow in its own way.

The after-diet lasts a further seven days, and food is more liberal. It is still important to avoid strong spices, pork, alcohol, and sex and to eat salt and citrus fruits in moderation but apart from that food can be richer and more varied. It is like toughening up the plant to make it hardy. During the initial diet it was incubated in the greenhouses of our souls; now we plant it out by gradually introducing it to our world. The Salvia dreams may still continue as the bond with the plant develops but the after-diet is really a time of waiting for the spirit to take root.

During this week John had a few significant dreams but in contrast to his previous ones they were less symbolic and more in the nature of straightforward guidance, as if Salvia was preparing him for a return to the outside world and the choices he would make there.

One of the issues he had come with, for example, was the suspicion that he might be an alcoholic, although I had seen no evidence of this. One dream, however, began with his family trying to send him to rehab for this problem. He was angry with them and resisted their intervention. Then he woke up from an alcoholic blackout and reached for a bottle of wine as he stumbled outside his house. A Mexican approached him and asked if he was okay. He could barely stand or walk. He woke up again from another blackout, and this time he was in a beautiful apartment sometime in the future with a great life and a gorgeous woman, but she was about to leave him. He begged her not to because he loved her and her departure would leave him in what he called "an alone Hell." She left anyway, and he had the sense that this was connected to his drinking. He blacked out again and couldn't figure out which was the real world anymore because every time he woke up he was in a new place and time. Finally he awoke in a hotel lobby where a "get well" or "birthday" party was being held for him. His whole family was there, including his estranged father who had a gift for him.

John had now accepted that he was not an alcoholic but Salvia had shown him a possible future where he could be if he made that choice. As is the nature of divination, however, now that he had seen the outcome of this course of action he could avoid it if he wished, so his life would never come to that. In view of his earlier decision to make contact again with the father he had become distanced from, it was also significant that he ended the dream on a positive note with him.

Another of his issues had to do with relationships and how he handled them. In a further Salvia dream the ally presented him with two options. In one scenario he was on a beach in Mexico having fun at a barbecue. There was a beautiful woman there whom he felt an instant attraction to, and the feeling was mutual: one of love at first sight, enchantment, a magical, seductive, addictive quality. In the second part of the dream, by contrast, he was at home, pottering around his house—a much more mundane and practical scene—with a girl he had known from high school. They were just getting on with things and working together, and there was a more controlled, mature, less excitable friendship between them. He preferred this: "I didn't have to uphold some magic or keep that exoticness about it. It felt more real."

In addictive relationships magic is central to the drama the lovers create, whether "doomed love affair" or "soul mates reunited." The lovers ascribe supernatural qualities to each other and act as if they are true. As Thomas Timmreck, a relationship therapist writes, they "idealize the other person to the point of divinity. The individual is then blindly attached to the other. . . . They begin to project all kinds of illusions onto the other person." A pedestal is a dangerous place, however. If you're a God you cannot fall but one slip as a human and the whole illusion is shattered.

The message from Salvia was obvious: a more mature love, based on friendship rather than blind adoration, allowed to unfold in its own time in a controlled and conscious way was the better option for John instead of another "soul mate drama."

His final dream that week was about travel, and he saw himself on planes, on trains, and at airports, looking at beautiful scenery, meeting new people, and enjoying every moment. It was an appropriate dream, about partings and moving forward at the end of the diet. More than that though, it was a confident and optimistic dream for a man who had started the diet with social anxiety.

There was a final ceremony with the vine of souls to mark the end of the fourteen-day diet and for John to draw conclusions from his work with Salvia and receive parting advice. We fasted for the day to prepare for it and in the morning drank Salvia again to strengthen the plant in us and bring it into the ceremony. John would be searching for an icaro and wanted the support of The Shepherdess. The event was filmed by a television crew who had come to Spain to interview me, and they captured John performing his icaro for the first time. For a man with anxiety to sing in front of a camera, this was a brilliant end to his journey.

• • •

The following images, from various artists, were inspired by that artist's explorations with teacher plants, in the most part *Salvia divinorum,* and depict scenes from SalviaWorld.

Plate 1. *The Birth of Salvia—*detail (Ross Heaven). "A slut-nun with a mescal flask in a Mexican brothel-church birthed you Ska Maria." The painting depicts my vision of Salvia's birth, seen during an ayahuasca ceremony as part of my second Salvia diet.

Plate 2. *INRI—*detail (Ross Heaven). Another view of the birth of Salvia. The dark cloak and skeletal figure of the Salvia spirit are also reported by others who have smoked salvinorin and are reminiscent of Santa Muerte, the Kali-esque Mexican saint of life and death. (The name Kali comes from kāla, which means "black, time, death," all of them Salvia themes)

Plate 3. *Mama Loves Me*—detail (Ross Heaven). The face of Salvia, representing power and frailty, sadness or resignation and control all at once. (The full title of this piece is *Mama Loves Me—But She Don't Take No Shit*: the paradox, the contradiction, and the unity again.)

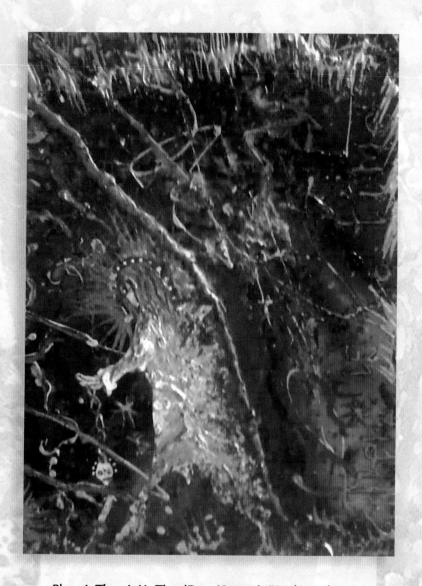

Plate 4. *There Is No Time* (**Ross Heaven**). "As the ayahuasca vision continued I was taken by the spirit of Salvia to a forest where she taught me more about herself and the nature of time. An *icaro* (a song for the plant) began to form: When you were born the stars hung sickly, your three wise men were uninspired; your mother's voice sang too thickly lullabies of smoke and wine. . . ."

Plate 5. **Salvia ceremony (photograph by Ross Heaven).** The *mesa* (cloth altar) is the central part of ceremonies in South and Central American *curanderismo* and contains *artes* (objects of power) for holding balance, protecting the space, and calling good energies. The Salvia pipe sits in the foreground. Ceremonies always take place at night and in darkness.

Plate 6. *The Origin of Salvia Divinorum* (Bruce Rimell). Few people who have smoked salvinorin, the extract of Salvia, believe that the plant originated on our planet. The consensus among them (which is shared by some Mazatec shamans) is that it is not of the Earth but an alien intelligence sent to us for an as-yet-unknown reason. Bruce's poem, written to accompany this artwork, suggests the same feeling (see page 184).

Plate 7. *Wheel of Time* (Bruce Rimell). As I saw her, Salvia was "the Mistress of Time, between time and beyond life and death." Here Rimell depicts his own experience, and time again is a motif. When independent explorers begin to agree on the message of the plant, we can conclude that the nature of time (and time travel) is a consistent theme.

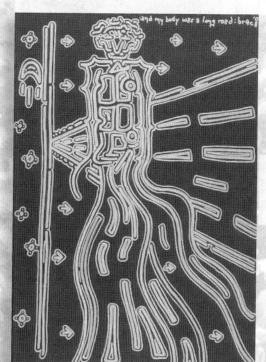

Plate 8. *And My Body Was a Long Road* (Bruce Rimell).

Plate 9. **Untitled (Yvonne McGillivray)**. Most plants have a human (female: *embra* and male: *macho*) form when seen as their spiritual essence. This is the purpose of the *dieta*: to reveal the spirit of the plant so its teachings can begin.

Plate 10. *Who Is Painting My Dream?* (Bruce Rimell). Are we the dreamer or the dreamed? This piece depicts the dismantling sensation that Salvia brings, very physical and always beginning in my back, as if my skin or my atoms are being pulled apart.

Plate 11. **Untitled (Yvonne McGillivray).** The male and female aspects of the plants, which together share a common essence. In this case chacruna (left) and ayahuasca (right) are shown coming together to make the ayahuasca potion and spirit. Ayahuasca brew is drunk by Amazonian shamans in order to meet the spirit of any plant, which is dieted to form a connection with it.

I am pleased to have met John. He was dedicated to the work, intent on healing, ridding himself of old patterns, and bringing positive change to his life. He was insightful and intelligent too. He looked at himself fearlessly and honestly, and by embracing the medicine and learning from Salvia he saw what needed to be changed and he changed it.

I learned a lot from him too. It was curious—a familiar cosmic joke as I said at the outset—how our issues and concerns were similar and how our experiences with the plant began almost to merge: our realizations about ourselves, about The Shepherdess, and how she was working with us coming more or less at the same time and sharing much in common. This gives us clues to the nature of the plant as well.

5

PLANT SPIRIT WISDOM

Bringing Questers Together • The Experiences of
Participants in Salvia Ceremonies
(5X and 20X Concentrates)

*To place oneself anywhere in space or time. To summon
the dead. To exalt senses and perceive inaccessible images
of events on other worlds, in one's deepest inner mind or
in the mind of others.*

JIM MORRISON, *THE LORDS*

Before she left, Josephine and I had planned a ten-day workshop called
"Plant Spirit Wisdom," and even though she would not now be present I decided to go ahead with it. Participants would have the opportunity to experience three teacher plants: ayahuasca, San Pedro, and
Salvia. Fourteen people gathered for the event from various locations
in Europe: a capacity crowd for our small retreat center. Most had not
worked with Salvia before. They would have two Salvia journeys each,
twenty-eight experiences in all. In fact, their first encounter with the

plant was so intense for some that they decided not to join the second ceremony so in total twenty-three accounts are included in this chapter.

PARTICIPANT INTRODUCTIONS*

Stuart (United Kingdom) came to the course because of changes in his life. He would be retiring from work in a month and also had relationship issues and a physical problem he wanted to look at. He had previously drunk ayahuasca in five ceremonies with Josephine and me.

Anton (Lithuania) had struggled with fear and depression for many years. He had tried to kill himself once. He felt he was not worthy, he said, and because of his beliefs and way of life people regarded him as crazy. He had no experience with teacher plants.

Lela (Lithuania) had spent twelve years working in advertising but saw it as meaningless and was retraining as an herbalist. Her childhood had been difficult, she said, and she carried "residual anger" from this. Her only experience of medicine plants was fifteen years ago when she smoked cannabis once.

Ronnie (from the United Kingdom but raised in the Caribbean) wanted to be a healer and had come to explore the plants and learn from them. He had only experienced cannabis but found it "very cleansing."

Sue (Germany) had drunk ayahuasca with Josephine and me and also worked with us to find a plant ally of her own. She had some food allergies and emotional problems that she felt were blocking her "connection to the world."

Ken (United Kingdom) had been to Mexico to study with the Maya and to the Amazon where he had drunk ayahuasca seven times, then a

*Participant names have been changed but everything else is as they reported it.

further five times in the United Kingdom He had worked as a journalist but wanted to become a healer.

Jane (United Kingdom) had drunk ayahuasca nine times with me in the United Kingdom and France. Her baby son died twenty-one years ago, and ayahuasca had helped her address the pain. She now had a relationship issue she needed to look at and a new direction in life that she wanted to find.

Marla (Norway) was born in Bosnia during the conflict and had been sent out of the country to live with grandparents when she was young while her parents stayed behind. She developed deep depression in 2006. Western medicine had not helped her but she got some relief from spiritual healing. She had little experience with teacher plants.

Michael, Hannah, and *Leon* (United Kingdom) arrived together. Leon experienced anxiety and fear from an early age and had ended up with an addiction to cocaine, cannabis, and methamphetamine although he had been clean for eight years. All three said they had felt the pull of the plants and had come to find their spiritual paths. They had no experience with the plants we would work with.

Alex (Greece), a student of Tibetan Buddhism and Osho, had come to "work on the nature of the mind." She had tried mushrooms in Mexico and had drunk ayahuasca twice in Greece.

Rob (United Kingdom) had drunk ayahuasca twice with Josephine and me but had left that workshop before all of the ceremonies were complete. He had returned to finish the process. He is a successful businessman but feels a pull to become a healer.

Roberta (Spain) is a small business owner who also works as a therapist. She has experimented with a number of psychedelics over a period of years and had previously drunk ayahuasca and San Pedro and smoked Salvia with me.

Their experiences follow. Key to understanding them is the intention each person brought to their ceremony. In shamanism, intention is vital for a meaningful journey, especially when working with teacher plants. If we have a question to be answered, a specific healing request, or a purpose to fulfill, intention provides a framework for our experience so we can better understand the messages of the plant and what the ally is showing us. Without this framework we might easily get lost in the images or miss the message entirely so that the plant's teaching is at best diluted and at worst leaves us confused. In this situation we will be unable to apply the transformative energy behind the symbols, and no healing at all may result since we do not understand—and therefore cannot make—the life changes we need to.

Before our first ceremony we therefore did some work on the setting of clear intentions so that for every person the encounter with the plant had a definite objective against which the experience itself and its outcome could be assessed.

The accounts that follow come from feedback sessions on the morning after each ceremony. I didn't direct participant comments or observations but interjected occasionally to ask what I thought were useful questions (e.g., when I asked Lela what she needed to be forgiven for in the report on page 135). Other than that the words used and the conclusions drawn are those of the participants themselves. I have included the intentions of each participant but I have not analyzed their journeys. I will leave it to you to make your own interpretation of the messages people received and decide if their intentions were met.

FIRST CEREMONY

"PLACES NO ANGEL HAS EVER SEEN"

For this introductory ritual we used 5X concentrate on a bed of Salvia leaves. My assistant Debs and I arranged the room so that two people smoked at once while the others sat in silence and darkness. We watched them carefully during the initial "blastoff" phase, then escorted them to their mats where each person had a thirty-minute period of reflection to explore the messages of Salvia more fully.

Some found their first meeting with Salvia gentler than others but it was still often confusing and shocking to be exposed to such a strange and deconstructed world. For others the experience was a nightmare, bringing them face-to-face with their deepest issues, those that they had hidden within themselves in places where, as one participant put it, "no angel has ever seen."

Anton
Intention: To be fulfilled

Anton looked terrified as soon as he smoked. He became agitated and stood up, using his hands to scrape some invisible substance from his arms and legs. (He explained later that he was trying to remove the new Salviac reality that was engulfing his body.) He then adopted a confrontational posture and, in Lithuanian, his native tongue, began speaking to me in a demanding way. I stood up, too, and held eye contact but did not interfere with his process.

> Reality was immediately cut in half. I was too, and a new atomic universe took hold of my right side; I was afraid and began to try to tear it off me. I had no idea who Ross and Debs were or who I was. Ross was not Ross, it was just a name he called himself. I couldn't even say he was human. I began speaking, asking, "Who opened the interdimensional gateways?" Then I became the guardian of those gateways and was trying to stop Ross, saying, "No, you can't enter. This is playing with fire."
>
> It scared me to realize how small this reality is and how thin—like a crust around something that contains all we know—but I saw its internals too, and there was something more but it was fathomless. The nothingness I saw was full.
>
> When my personality finally returned I remember that I was embarrassed because I must have disrupted the ceremony for others and I said, "I'm sorry, I fucked up; I have destroyed everyone's experience."
>
> I felt better when I went outside to look at the stars, and I was in

awe of the sky. The beauty I saw was indescribable. Flowers blossomed from my heart, and I felt Salvia as an ally inside me. She gave me a new sacred name. Today I feel I love everyone. My intention was to be fulfilled and I am.

Roberta

Intention: To explore Salvia shamanically rather than the occasional recreational use I have been more familiar with

Roberta began speaking as soon as she had smoked, repeating the same words over and over—first "I'm by my self," then "I'm by myself." The meanings were slightly different in each case. At one point she moved toward me and took my hand as if she wanted to check that I was real.

I saw my body and the whole room made of energy lines like an Alex Grey painting and although we were in darkness the room was full of bright colors. I felt my energy expand and connect with everything. This was the first meaning of the sentence "I'm by my self": that I was standing next to myself because everything was me. The next meaning of the words was that I am the author of everything, that reality is a book I am writing, which is "by myself." But there was another meaning too. I have a family issue, which may result in a separation from someone, so I could end up "by myself." In fact it was really the same message in every case: that I am in charge of my reality and responsible for my choices.

Sound became waves, and the air became solid, no different in mass from my body or the chair I was sitting in. I became aware of people talking some distance away, outside round the pool, and my attention was drawn to them. Some of their words—but only some—reached me and in a subtle way began to inform my journey. I wondered whether some words were important and that's why Salvia was selecting them for me to hear or whether they became important because I heard them, and whether this is the case in "everyday life" as well. Do we hear what is said or what we want or need to hear? It is an important question because these words create reality. I did see the shamanic use for Salvia in expanding awareness and taking attention in new directions.

Alex

Intention: To know whether I should stay in Greece in these difficult
    times or move to the United Kingdom

The second she smoked, Alex staggered across the room to another mat
but she couldn't lie still when she reached it. She was extremely agitated,
screaming and clawing at Debs who held her to give her comfort. She
was begging us to "get me out of here."

> It was a living nightmare. I became wallpaper in my family home but not on
> a wall, on the floor, and I was stuck with my family. My Salvia experience
> was like a conspiracy they had organized against me. My parents are dead
> now but I have one sister I don't speak to: they always disliked me and
> thought I was mad because of my spiritual beliefs, and it felt like this
> experience was something they'd arranged so I would finally see that they
> were right, and I was mad.
>
> I tried to pull the wallpaper off me but it was stuck, and as I pulled at
> it, it began to tear my whole body apart. I saw that Debs had become the
> same wallpaper and began to claw at her, trying to get it off her too, and
> she was also ripping apart. I was shouting, "Get me out of here."
>
> I felt betrayed by my family: they thought I was mad and wanted me
> to see what madness was like. I realize now that this affects my decision
> to move from Greece, as well. Part of me wants to stay because of the
> sense of security it offers, but I know now that it is a false security, and
> I have no family there who would ever take care of me anyway. Get me
> out of here.

Perhaps a more direct answer to her question than she was able to
see. Despite this, however, she is still, at the time of writing, in Greece.
Again, we are given information and choices but whether we act on
them is another choice entirely.

Hannah

Intention: I had a bad experience that frightened me when I was young
    and left me emotionally cut off. I want to be balanced emotionally

The first sensation was my arms tingling, like pins and needles. Then my body felt stretched, and I was afraid that when I came back I would never be able to enter myself again because my human body was just too small. The room became filled with hexagons, then I blanked out. I felt very scared, and it dawned on me that this fear was exactly what I had asked for: I reconnected with my first terror and experienced myself emotionally again.

Rob

<u>Intention</u>: To get rid of my anxiety and self-consciousness

My body was covered in—and then became—little black insects. Then they disappeared and so did I; I melted into energy. I felt anxious as if I was being watched. In the reflection time afterward I realized where my anxiety had first come from. I was a clever and confident child and was always giving others advice. I meant it to be helpful because I really did have answers, but the adults around me wouldn't listen. They saw me as precocious and called me "the professor" to put me in my place. So I zipped my subconscious mouth and started using my conscious mouth instead. I vetoed myself and became worried whenever I spoke.

Michael

<u>Intention</u>: I want to know my spiritual purpose

I was an insect trapped on a huge cog, which was rotating, going round and round. It finally came to rest at a place where there was a plank in front of me, and I could step off the cog if I wanted, but it seemed easier to stay where I was.

The room was filled with vivid colors. Then I was in a temple and a group of religious men—sheikhs I think—were talking about someone who had left their order. "We miss him," they were saying. "He was part of us." Then I was on an airplane, and my attention was drawn to another sheikh, but I was told that I shouldn't look at him or be in that part of the plane because an alien experiment was taking place. I didn't believe it but then I was directed to look at a deep incision that the aliens had made in his side. As soon as I saw it, the sheikh flew into me. My last recollection was the sound of a gong, like a wake-up noise, then a friend appeared and started telling me who and where I was.

Leon

Intention: To stop feeling self-conscious and start feeling good about myself

The room turned into hexagons, and I became disorientated. Blackness. People were looking at me and laughing. I was in a jeep then with someone driving dangerously. We crashed but we survived. Then I was on a beach watching a man playing with an octopus. He tried to throw it over a cliff but he fell instead, and I was able to rescue him.

Stuart

Intention: To heal my back pain on a physical and emotional level

This dimension folded in on itself, and I was in an intersection of blackness. I felt the immense kindness and blessing of nothingness—like a Zen meditation on the "formless field of benefaction." I understood the complete plasticity of reality and that within it I could choose to heal or be anything I wanted. In the morning I felt immense peace, as if I had been on a two-week zazen retreat: emptiness and gratitude.

Lela

Intention: I asked Salvia to give me healing. I wanted to see if the plant could heal the physical body

I had no visions but as I inhaled the smoke my whole torso filled with heat that moved through me, fixing my body so I felt changes in every cell. I still feel changed now. It is healing me. The smoke was soothing, and I felt the spirit of the plant to be nursing and protective, feminine, but it has a male energy too.

Ronnie

Intention: To love, gain wisdom, and find balance

My body merged with the chair I was on, like I was a thin piece of paper stuck onto it that would have to be peeled off. Everyone in the room also became flat, 2D. I felt like I had gone through different dimensions. Everything was spinning. I kept looking at Debs and Ross and laughing, saying, "You knew didn't you, you knew?" I was sweating profusely.* When I went outside the sky was amazing, lots of shooting stars. I felt more connected to nature and more in love with life.

Sue

Intention: How can I have a fulfilling relationship?

My body was pulled backward, twisted and contorted, and then it became a pair of scissors marching through a farmhouse. Another pair, exactly the same, marched alongside me at the same speed, synchronized with me. I had the sense that we were both cutting away our pasts and that I had found someone who had the same rhythm as me and this was important. The scissors were transparent, and this represented the honesty that is crucial for me in any relationship. Then we changed into dragons flying through the night. Our two heads became four, splitting off like fireworks and then coming back together.

I found a wounded dragon full of daggers: not sure if it was me or someone else who was in pain. I pulled the daggers out of it and breathed new life and healing in, then it consumed me, and I became its pilot. We flew into a crystal cavern, and I felt so happy, like I'd overcome all my barriers from the past.

---

*Some people do sweat when they smoke Salvia even though the temperature in the room remains constant and others around them do not perspire. Since this is an individual experience sweating may act as a form of purge as vomiting does with ayahuasca. Through the purge the plant ally is able to remove physical, emotional, and mental toxins from the body: stale energies, blockages, and "bad ideas" as San Pedro shamans call them, self-limiting beliefs and negative associations.

I think I met the spirit of Salvia too: a nun dressed in a clear latex white veil. She had very long fingernails. She told me to "shed" and good changes will come.

Ken

Intention: Some people have said they find me irritating. My intention was for people to experience me joyfully.

There was an immediate impact. The white wall opposite me became blue and crashed into me so I became a part of it, and then I was split into waves of color. My body didn't exist. I wanted to reach out to someone for comfort and protection but withheld that.* The spirits said they would look after me. Then I was taken through a scenario where I was completely irritating to others because I hadn't done something I'd promised. I got an insight into how I let people down.

Jane

Intention: To find the right path and heal myself

I was scared to smoke the Salvia but I had a very gentle experience and was glad I did it. The smoke went through my skin and into my body. What I most remember is seeing a baby—a child to come (whether it is a real baby or represents my own rebirth, I don't know). I lost my baby son twenty-one years ago and have never really recovered from that but I feel now that a new life is possible. I met the people of SalviaWorld, like you said Josephine had, and they looked like normal people to me. They told me I would be happy again and was welcome there. I feel really good today.

Marla

Intention: To be balanced and achieve my potential

I was able to observe my own reaction to the whole process. I was very concerned that I hadn't smoked it right because I had no great visions or

---

*An interesting turn of phrase given his intention for this journey.

psychedelic effects but then I realized that I was speaking, except my words weren't words. And I had the sensation that I was in two places at once, and that I wanted to be. So something was happening. My body was filled with pins and needles and reality became metallic, matrixlike, as if it had been programmed on a computer.

I understood that I wanted to be in two places at once because I had lost so much of my life to depression, and I wanted to make up for it. I wanted to share my experience immediately with others as well. I realize now that was because my parents had never listened to me. They always wanted me to do things in the "right" way, and I wanted to check with others to be sure I'd had the "correct" Salvia experience. I have never been certain that I'm okay and good enough. I have always needed confirmation and security.

THE IMAGE OF MARIA

Before our second ceremony I led the group in a shamanic journey using the rhythmic beat of the drum to induce a trance state. The purpose for this was primarily so they could reflect more deeply on the information they had received during their first experience and through this develop a new intention for the ritual to come, which would give them a useful progression from the last. In so doing I suggested that they try to meet the spirit of The Shepherdess so she could answer any remaining questions they had and, based on this, guide them in their decisions regarding their new intention. What was interesting about this for me was how they would perceive the spirit of the plant. I knew what "my" Shepherdess looked like but I wanted to see if there were any correspondences.

The answer was yes and no. As the Mazatecs say, "Maria can be shy," and as my wife had commented, she "wears many masks." Some people struggled to find her at all, therefore, at least in any distinct way, but this, in itself, is a sort of validation: if they had all seen *something*, as I would expect them to during any shamanic journey, it would not be in keeping with the elusive nature of The Shepherdess. Others saw fleeting images or had a "sense" of her but there were also accounts where common themes began to emerge.

Stuart: "I found her in a thatched hut near a waterfall. She took the form of an otherworldly, somewhat demonic child who knew everything. Her eyes were silver, and she was able to transform herself into different shapes and forms."

Ronnie: "At first she appeared as spiral energy but then she changed and became genielike. She is a shape-shifter and can be all things."

Ken: "She looked like a cat-woman, sexy and provocative. Her legs were open but instead of a vagina there was an eye. It represented fertility and her ability to give birth to consciousness: 'the eternal birthing eye.'"

Marla: "She was both male and female, a mixture of opposites: strong and loving, dark, macabre, and beautiful. Around her were triangles and pyramids, some containing eyes."

Lela: "A young woman standing in a storm at the edge of reality. Beneath her were grass and water but above her there were only molecules: the potential for reality to come into being. Everything around her was very structured but also young and new: virginal, fresh, and innocent."

Hannah: "She wore a dress patterned with hexagons and there was a lot of darkness around her, as if she was also telling me to get in touch with my shadow side."

Sue: "She appeared in a graveyard at night. She wore a black cowl and had a half-human face, gruesome long fangs and fingernails, wearing lots of rings. She was made of beauty and darkness. She said she always helps those who come to her and told me to pay attention to the plants that grow in graveyards. They have unique powers, and when you diet them they give you the ability to speak with the dead. I asked her about my intention, whether I should concentrate on healing a physical problem or focus on love and relationships. She said, 'Filling yourself with love is a good thing but rid yourself of suffering first. I have very sharp teeth . . .'"

One participant didn't take part in this journey but of the thirteen who did more than half of them met The Shepherdess in one form or another. I had seen her as a shape-shifter, able to change her appearance from a child to a crone and into other forms. Stuart and Ronnie explicitly mentioned this quality, too, and other accounts hint at the same. This ability to change shape and persona, to "wear many masks," may be why she is perceived differently by those who meet her, although it is always in a way that is generally in keeping with her "theme" or style. I had seen her as a blend of opposites, for example: as light and dark, sacred and sluttish, holy-unholy, and these attributes also emerge in the accounts of others. Marla saw her as "both male and female, a mixture of opposites." Ken saw her as "sexy and provocative" with her legs open and vagina exposed, not the usual image one expects of the Virgin.

Her darkness is also mentioned. Marla saw her as "macabre and beautiful." Hannah felt "a lot of darkness around her." She appeared to Sue "in a graveyard at night. . . . She was made of beauty and darkness." Others, meanwhile, reflect on her lightness and purity, a mixture of opposites again. Lela: "Everything around her was very structured but also young and new: virginal, fresh, and innocent."

SECOND CEREMONY

"SCARED AS SHIT WITH A HAPPY ENDING"

For this ceremony I offered two grades of concentrate: 5X as before, and for those who wanted a deeper experience 20X, both on a substrate of leaves. There were also those who had a very extreme encounter in the earlier ritual and chose not to join this session at all. Those absent were

Anton, Ronnie, Leon, Roberta, and Alex. It was a completely different ceremony, even for those who smoked 5X again, far stronger and more active.

Lela (5X)

Intention: To clean my body

Lela smoked first and within seconds began moaning. She started crawling across the floor and then making slow sideways and forward rolls, head over heels. Eventually she stood and walked unsteadily to the door. I followed her into the garden then into the house where, while standing, she began spinning, arms out at her sides. She was speaking in Lithuanian but luckily Anton had not smoked and was there to translate. She said, "Mother [referring to Salvia], what did I do wrong? Ross, what mistake did I make? Please forgive me, forgive me."

Salvia treated me in a different way this time. I didn't notice the transition from this world to SalviaWorld, but then I was flying over the room seeing it like I was an aerial camera. The room became a kitchen decorated in a 1960s or '70s style with a cuckoo clock, chair, table, and so forth, and I heard voices like a family making dinner. Someone was rolling up a magazine, and then I became a magazine and was being rolled up too [This was when she had started to roll across the floor].

I saw circles, which joined together and became 8s, with the top and bottom rotating in different directions. I felt myself being circles. Who am I? I remembered I had a relationship and a life, but then the circles came back and consumed all that.

I realized that circling is no fun. In the center of the 8 I was whole again, and things were still. Then I could see that inside the circles were lots of different life scenes, and I could join any of them.* I asked Salvia how long this would last. The plant said, "It is infinite."† I asked what the

---

*Compare this with my own account and Vulpine's in chapter 3 where reality is a wheel, the spokes of which hold buckets containing many different lives that can be entered at will.

†The symbol for infinity is of course a figure 8.

point of it all was. Salvia said none. I was standing up by then and asked if I had done something wrong. Salvia said no. But I started to say sorry anyway, and it became a chant that made me spin around, and when I did this I could control the circles. Whenever I stopped saying sorry the circles began to move in the other direction. I also remember asking "Why is this so painful?" and "Why a baby?" but I don't remember the answers.

[At this point I interjected to ask the question, which I thought was central to the story that Salvia was telling her, "Why did you need to be forgiven, Lela?" She began to cry.]

Some years ago I was pregnant and lost the child. I was asking Salvia why and what I did wrong ["Why a baby?"]. Salvia said "Nothing." I asked what the point was of this loss and Salvia said there is no point. When I asked for forgiveness the plant answered, "There are no guilty people, and there is no reason for anything." I have a strong mind and am driven to find the reason for everything; there must always be a solution, but Salvia said there are no answers to find. I felt better from this. I knew it wasn't my fault that my child had died.

What I got from the circles is that we can experience the whole of life from the void before we are even born, so there really is no point to life or birth because we can stop the circles at any moment where we already are and perceive the realities they contain. We don't even need a body.

The turning of the circles is at the speed of ultimate reality, and when we slow them down we can slip into the lives they contain and become human if we want. There is no need to but I felt happier when I did. I realized that the life I have chosen has only one purpose: for me to experience joy and happiness. Life is an artificial reality where we slow down time to experience living and enjoy it.

Then Salvia worked on my body, and I was sweating and dizzy and delirious all night. In the morning I went into the garden, and I could talk to every plant. I knew its destiny. The day before I had watered these plants but I knew now that it really wouldn't make any difference. The plants had slowed their own circles and chosen their own lives so I couldn't change the thoughts or the fate of them or anything else. But still I can make a choice to do whatever I want, to water them if I wish, and in that way our stories *become one. All of life is ultimately pointless and unnecessary but it is an adventure we can have and enjoy.*

Sue (5X)
Intention: To cure menstrual problems

I saw scissors in the room again but this time smaller ones. They were cutting around my view of reality. Then they cut me in two, as well. I lost my bottom half totally while the top was flipped upside down. Then I vanished completely and wondered where I had gone: "I" was looking for "I"! That made me laugh at the absurdity of it. I realized that "I" am not nothing or how could I witness this? But I am not just a body either; I am consciousness. A type of dismemberment had taken place where my body had been cut in two, and now my reproductive organs were ripped out, and I felt them being healed and rebalanced. There was a tingling in that area too, like the plant consciousness was zooming in on it and radiating sparkling light.

I completely became the light then and was jetted into space and looked down on myself dressed in sexy clothes with high heels, then pregnant, then raising a baby until she grew into a young woman. It was a message about my sexuality.

Then I was at my parents' house. A mouse came in; I don't like mice but this one was cute so I let it stay. Then a cat came in, and although I like cats I didn't want it there so I picked it up and put it out but it kept coming back. I realized that it loved me unconditionally and just wanted to be with me but I kept putting it out. I loved it but I didn't want it. It occurred to me the next day that I had kept something I didn't like (the mouse) but sent away something I loved and that loved me (the cat) because I was afraid it might hurt me with its claws and teeth whereas the mouse was harmless. That was the way I had been with my life and relationships too: giving away the people I loved and who loved me because losing that love would hurt me; it was safer to be with someone "harmless" whom I didn't like or want.

The experience gave me a new insight into me, my sexuality, and the way I approached relationships, all of which have a bearing on the thing I needed to heal.

Rob (20X)

Intention: To gain clarity

Within seconds of smoking, Rob began to make loud noises: slurred, unrecognizable words, screams, groans, roars, and deep vocal sounds that at times had the feel of an alien language. Those close to him who had also smoked said they could understand it and among what he said was, "Stop laughing at me." To those of us who had not taken Salvia it sounded like glossolalia: speaking in tongues. He began thrashing, flailing his arms and legs, and rolling backward and forward. After some minutes he got up and staggered to the door. I followed him out, and he stood in the night air, holding his head and muttering, "Oh fuck, fuck. What is this? What's happening to me?" He needed to be outside for the rest of the ceremony but calmed down and returned to normalcy after about fifty minutes.

First of all I forgot a promise I had made to Salvia and myself that I would treat this plant with respect, and I was greedy with the smoke. I took in a lot. I was immediately folded up into nothing. Then a sort of digital structure began shaping me, replicating me out of existence until I became everything and nothing. I felt extreme anxiety, and this increased the process of the replication to warp speed. The last piece of me was now vanishing into digital information, and I started fighting it and trying to put myself back together but I was panicking. Someone came over to help me but even his hand on my arm felt alien.

There was no "me" now and the "reality" around me, both inside the room and wherever I was, was chaos. I heard laughter and thought I was the butt of everyone's joke. I couldn't speak and felt stupid and alone, with no friends and unworthy of love: a very raw feeling. When I settled down I asked Salvia what I should make of all this, and she told me that all of my fears had attached themselves to me over many years until I had become small in the face of everyone else's ideas. Fear had tried to cheat me into a denial of myself but Salvia said I was rare and special and that I can choose love over fear any time I want because even a personality based on fear can be loved, and once fear leaves, love becomes unconditional.

After the ceremony finished I revisited Salvia, and she explained that I had time traveled. I had gone back in time and attached myself to certain situations where power had been taken from me through fear, and I had become spread out very thinly into bits of me. I hadn't been able to sleep at all, and now I heard a cock crow and saw the light of the dawn. Salvia said we are all capable of time travel. I looked around, and it had become dark and the cock crowed again for the first time. I had actually traveled in time, from the light of dawn back into darkness and then the dawn again. Salvia said she wanted to demonstrate how easy time travel was.

She said that all human beings are capable of time travel—literally—but we are not ready for it yet. We need to walk before we can run or we will fragment as I had and become attached to other existences, then we will be lost in a nightmare. We have started to learn the process of time travel because some of us now realize that what we believe to be true makes it true. This is step one.

Throughout the experience I was as scared as shit but I feel it had a happy ending, and I learned a lot about myself and what is really real.

Rob did not know this because participants had no access to Internet, newspapers, or TV at our retreat center but two days before his journey the CERN atomic research facility had announced its discovery of particles that can move faster than light, disproving Einstein's theorem $E = MC^2$,* which has become a cornerstone of modern scientific theory, and which relies on the "fact" that nothing can exceed light speed. One implication of this is that time travel, as Salvia had said, must (theoretically at least) be possible since it is already, in effect, taking place at a subatomic level. The particles that CERN explores are not unknown to us of course because they are the same ones we are made of, which means that if time travel is possible it may also be possible from within us, again as Salvia had said.

---

*Energy = Mass x a Constant squared, the constant being the speed of light.

Hannah (20X)

<u>Intention</u>: To balance the good and bad in me but also have fun (I didn't want Salvia to show me any scary stuff)

Hannah was sitting next to Rob but they had to be separated as she began moving too, crawling toward him, laughing hysterically as his arms and legs were thrashing around her and it became unsafe for both of them. Having resettled her she continued laughing, interspersing it with questions: "What's happening? Where am I? Who am I?"

Salvia was a lot easier to take this time and get an effect from. I think I had learned the technique. I wasn't so anxious either. I don't remember giving the pipe back, then I was sliding down a wall of red polyester. I tried to grab the fabric to stop falling but I couldn't; it was as if I was slipping over it but was also inside and a part of it.

Suddenly I was jerked out of the experience [she got kicked by Rob] and panicked because I didn't know where or who I was but my reaction was to laugh. When I came round a bit I realized that Rob needed help because he was in distress but I couldn't assist. I was frightened and so was he but I just kept laughing.

After the ceremony I thought I trod on an insect and was mortified that I might have hurt something. Then when I went to bed I thought I saw lots of insects crawling on the walls (they were nice) but I was still in Salvia. Then before I went to sleep I thought of Stuart and his bad back, and I wished I could take his pain for him.

In the morning what I got from all this is that I can feel frightened without it needing to be scary and that I can have fun even if things around me are frightening. I have a choice about how I react in every situation. I am the point of balance I have been looking for.

Same with the insects: why should I be distressed over the death of one when the world is full of them? We all die. The point is to enjoy life while we have it, not worry over every little thing. I realized that I have a tendency to take the blame for everything and to want to be the one in pain so others don't have to suffer, but there's nothing good in that. Stuart's back pain is his experience, for example; why would I want it?

I can feel sorry for him but his pain is not mine, and I have my own life to live.

Salvia made me look at myself and just as I asked for, did it in a way that made what could have been a frightening and dangerous experience fun. I couldn't stop laughing even when I got kicked.

Michael (20X)

Intention: I didn't have an intention, only to see what Salvia wanted to show me

Michael was lying close to Hannah and Rob and began laughing and moving too. He also had to be separated from the others for reasons of safety. The words he was uttering became a sort of slurred mantra: *"Whatthefuck?Whatthefuck?Whatthefuck?"* He came round after about twenty minutes and, having smoked before Hannah and Rob, was able to help keep the two apart.

I took three pulls and blacked out. When I came back I was laughing. Rob looked like a frightened child, rocking backward and forward. I thought I heard him say, "Stop laughing." I was worried for him and Hannah—I thought she would get kicked—but I was still laughing and happy.

It was like I had telepathy because I thought I could hear Marla talking to me from across the room, but in my mind. Just as I thought that she began to crawl over to me. [She later confirmed that she had heard Michael talking to her too, mind-to-mind.]

After this I started to come back and went to Rob to help him. He was freaking out but I still felt calm, not anxious at all, which is odd for me because I have had anxiety and depression for years. I think Salvia took it away and taught me to take care of myself and that even difficult situations don't have to lead to anxiety. There is another way.

I had a final image, of a wolf howling at the moon. It was a nice picture but it made me laugh at the stupidity of it. The wolf can howl all it likes but it will never make the moon go away or influence it in any way. I thought it was like me with my depression: I'd been howling at the moon too, wasting my time on things that didn't matter. Today I

*feel more relaxed, and I'm not concerned about the problems I thought
I had back at home.*

Marla (20X)

Intention: To reach my full potential and find better ways of expressing
myself

*I was back in the matrix like on my first journey. We were all lying down in a
perfect line like seeds or cocoons on a spaceship, and the room was divided into
squares by bright lights. It felt like déjà vu because I have seen this somewhere
before. The whole thing felt metallic. It was like we were being used in some
way or I was in an experiment. I thought Rob was on the same journey, like we
were all on the same mission. It was a dream within a dream.*

*The important thing for me is that I didn't want to be a seed because
I saw it as programmed, like it was made for someone else's use, so they
could plant it and get what they wanted. The seed represented potential,
and I wanted it for myself so Salvia was telling me not to live by other
people's rules or be part of their experiments but live in my own way.*

*I heard a voice say that I should not tell anyone about this, but it's okay
to tell you. I had no idea what this meant and did a lot of thinking about
it, and now I get the idea that I should keep my wisdom to myself because
if I let everyone have part of it I am wasting my energy and potential.
Potential is the ability to get something done, and if I reveal my plans
to others there will always be someone who wants to tell me they're not
possible or stand in my way so it's best to keep quiet until I have achieved
what I want. That was the bit about expressing myself better: maybe by
not expressing myself at all sometimes.*

Stuart (20X)

Intention: To find courage

Stuart had a bad back, a physical problem he wanted to heal, which he
felt was connected to emotional issues. During his journey to the spirit
of The Shepherdess, where he had seen her as a strange occult child, he
had been told to "be courageous and you will find healing."

The universe was constantly folding, unfolding, digesting, digested; a self-created thing. I was part of it. It rolled and I rolled and was rolling. It was orange in color and made up of millions of tentacles of live information, folding itself up, and I was folded, too, into the dissolving nothingness. Then I was ripped apart and became white light, then blue, then dark.

At some point I became aware of myself again and what was happening in the room: the ceiling seemed very close to my face, only inches away, and the flames of the pipes looked dangerous and hellish, and I couldn't move to escape it. But then I remembered that I had chosen to be scared to experience courage. I felt my back shift and get better as I thought that. I gave in to complete surrender and was profoundly enriched by the nothingness.

I was shown small examples of real courage in everyday life, like a child playing cricket even though he was ridiculed by others who were better players, and I realized that bravery doesn't have to be huge acts; it's all around us all the time, so maybe I had been looking in the wrong place or setting my standards too high. I also had some insight into my back pain, that I had a lot of anger in me, and the pain was a way of getting it out of my emotional system but still holding it in so it was part of my body not my heart but not out in the world either. In fact it was really nowhere.

I also had a pattern in my life of using pain to get attention, and I realize now that there are better, more giving and more positive ways of getting the attention I want, like playing music, for example. I don't have to suffer for it, despite what my Catholic upbringing has taught me.

Ken (20X)

Intention: My original intention was to answer the question, "Is love the answer?" but I had my own opinion on that so in the end I didn't really have an intention

Salvia sliced off my face. I became color and space and rushing sound like the growling of rolling ball bearings. I was shocked and anxious but it made me want to endure it. Then there was nothing. When I started to come back I was left with an image of mud men or plasticine characters, all gray, lifeless, and dead.

Jane (20X)

Intention: The same as my first ceremony: to find the right path and
heal myself

*I saw turtles and lizards, and they told me I had to change my thought
patterns. Then the healing became physical. It began as burning on the
right side of my head, then my throat and chest, and finally my arms and
legs. Even today they ache. I felt like I was becoming a part of Salvia, like
I'm wrapped up in it. It told me I was ready for ayahuasca and this will give
me my answers.*

JOURNEY PROGRESSIONS

Subsequent Salvia journeys often pick up where the last left off, either
literally or thematically. If there is an issue to be resolved the ally wants
us to experience it fully, from as many perspectives as necessary until
we see the truth of ourselves—the dream we have chosen to live—and
understand the message of healing.

In many of the journeys above, for example, even when the intention changed between ceremonies the participant's issue remained the
same, arising from a core idea, a self-limiting belief that Salvia would
not let go of until it had been explored and exploded.

The overriding concern for Rob, for example, had to do with identity and acceptance. His specific intention on the first journey was to
rid himself of self-consciousness and on the second to gain clarity, but
both intentions arose from the same underlying issue of insecurity and
low self-worth. For this reason his journeys were similar although they
progressed in intensity. In the first ceremony he felt anxious as if he
was being watched; on the second he experienced being laughed at and
ridiculed. "I couldn't speak and felt stupid and alone."

It may seem counterintuitive or even cruel for the plant to expose
him to these feelings given the anxieties he already had, but I have theo-
rized before about Salvia's "homeopathic" qualities; that by experiencing the very thing we wish to avoid we develop strength and immunity

to it as well as insights into its cause and nature. Rob got to see where his self-consciousness came from (being put down by adults for his intelligence as a child) and to experience its effects in his life now so he could better understand it: "anxiety . . . increased the process. . . . The last piece of me was now vanishing into digital information."

He asked for more information, and Salvia accommodated him with an even clearer answer, one that made sense to him beyond the symbolic language of the plant. "I asked Salvia what I should make of all this, and she told me that all of my fears had attached themselves to me over many years until I had become small in the face of everyone else's ideas. Fear had tried to cheat me into a denial of myself."

It then began the process of healing by showing him how he could change things in the present: "I can choose love over fear any time I want because even a personality based on fear can be loved, and once fear leaves, love becomes unconditional."

It comes back to the same message, as it always does with Salvia; that there is no absolute reality, that our life stories are exactly that— stories—and that the first essential for positive change is to make new choices based on love not fear.

Interestingly, in this case Salvia (the Mistress of Time) also introduces the idea of time travel. At the very least, shamanically speaking, this means that we can journey back to any life event where we feel that power was taken from us and retrieve it for ourselves, or revisit a time when a poor decision was made, which has badly affected our lives, and find a way to change it, whether that means apologizing to someone we have hurt, starting over, or challenging someone who has hurt us. Then we can let that energy go and move forward into a new life. We have to understand our issue first, however, by bringing it into consciousness before we can do anything about it at all.

In Lela's case her insights and healing also grew deeper even though she stayed with the lower salvinorin concentrate. Her intention for the first ceremony was for Salvia to heal her physical body, in the second for it to cleanse her. Salvia did as she asked. During her first journey this amounted to a gentle checking out and repair of her body on a purely physical level: "I had no visions" (which is unusual for Salvia). Instead she felt a heat that brought "changes in every cell. I still feel changed now."

In the second ceremony, however, the request to "clean" her allowed Salvia to go much deeper in order to purify her thoroughly by addressing the core issues that were giving rise to her need for healing. This meant bringing her face-to-face with a difficult life event (the loss of her child) about which she still carried guilt and felt the need to be forgiven.

In fact, in typical Salvia style, the sage told her that no forgiveness was necessary because nothing matters and nothing is real. "I was asking Salvia why and what I did wrong. Salvia said, 'Nothing.' I asked what the point was of this loss and Salvia said there is no point. When I asked for forgiveness the plant answered, 'There are no guilty people, and there is no reason for anything.'"

Again, this might seem like an unsympathetic lesson for a still-grieving mother but in fact the plant knows what it is doing because through it Lela was able to let go of her quest for meaning—her desire for an answer to an unanswerable question (Why?)—and realize that "there are no answers to find." This allowed her to come to terms with her loss and find relief from her pain. "I felt better from this. I knew it wasn't my fault that my child had died." It enabled her to move forward as well and to see that she and her happiness were also important. "The life I have chosen has only one purpose: for me to experience joy and happiness. . . . All of life is ultimately pointless and unnecessary but it is an adventure we can have and enjoy."

OBSERVATIONS

As far as I know this is the first time that a shamanic therapy-based workshop has been run using Salvia to explore the nature of reality.* I would say that every participant came through Salvia to understand

---

*I would like to thank my wife for the work she did with me to dream this course into being, in particular for the research we shared in Peru and Spain. Through it she helped a lot of people even though she chose not to be present at the workshop herself.

that there is no absolute order of things, no single way that things must be done, no rules or must-dos, no principles that matter, no singular and objective reality in fact; that we decide our own destinies instead by seizing meaning from the void.

Salvia makes us look at ourselves. By its process and the way it teaches it directs us, coldly and dispassionately sometimes, to ask the question, *Who am I?* Its approach may seem clinical but the answers we get are worth years of therapy.

As in the story of *The Emperor's New Clothes,* we present ourselves to the world in a particular way, dressing in roles, beliefs, myths, which we never question but assume to be true, so we do not challenge them in ourselves or others, and we will only wake up from this dream and see our illusions when we are approached by an honest child who tells us the truth: that in fact we are naked. Salvia is this child. Then in the future we can dress more appropriately.

This honest challenge—the dissolution of our personality—is a consistent aspect of Salvia journeys, especially the most intense, and it is what can be most difficult for people. But asking this question, Who am I, is one of the most important things we can do.

Many of my participants—for example, Anton, Lela, Sue, Marla, Alex, and Rob—referred at the outset to childhood issues or bad experiences with their parents. Typically this gives rise to two responses: either we have been so browbeaten and overpowered by those who raised us that we end up following their rules even if we do so unconsciously, or we reject them completely, sometimes even vengefully, to hurt our parents as we feel that we have been hurt.* In either case, we still have our parents as reference points so we cannot honestly say that we are living our own lives. To be true to ourselves we first need to *know* ourselves.

---

*A woman I worked with in Peru promised herself that she would never have children because of her experiences with a difficult father. Partly as a response to this she decided that she would not make him a grandfather. She was almost fifty when he died, and she then realized that she would actually love to have children but time was running out. She tried for a while to conceive and when that didn't work embarked on a quest to adopt a child from a local village. That fell through as well. She never had the child she would have loved but she never made her father a grandparent either.

Few of us really do, and this is one of the qualities of Salvia: it shows us, sometimes in the most brutally honest ways.

Even if we have a difficult time accepting what we see, most people come to value it. Returning from the terror of the void to look again with fresh eyes at the world around him, for example, Anton was able to say that "the beauty I saw was indescribable. Flowers blossomed from my heart. . . ."

PARTICIPANTS WHO *WOULD* AND *WOULD NOT* TAKE THESE TEACHER PLANTS AGAIN

Name	*Salvia divinorum*	Ayahuasca	San Pedro
Hannah	No	√	Probably
Rob	No	√	√
Michael	√	√	√
Leon*	No	No	√
Stuart	√	√	√
Anton	√	√	√
Lela	√	√	√
Sue	√	√	√
Ken	√	Probably	No
Alex	√	√	Probably
Jane	√	√	√
Marla	Probably	√	√
Roberta	√	√	√
Ronnie	√ As a tea	√	√
Would take it again	10 (71%)	12 (86%)	11 (79%)
Would not take it again	3 (21%)	1 (7%)	1 (7%)
Would probably take it again	1 (7%)	1 (7%)	2 (14%)

*Leon came to the workshop primarily to drink ayahuasca but after his first ceremony with Salvia felt that he had achieved all he needed. He did not attend any other ceremonies and did not believe he would work again with any teacher plant.

Despite the intensity of their journeys and the facts they may now need to look at, most of my group, in fact, said they would definitely work with Salvia again. Nine people said they would smoke salvinorin, one said he would take Salvia as a leaf infusion, and another was undecided but thought she would probably smoke again. Only three said they would never take Salvia in the future. Among those who definitely would were Anton, Lela, and Alex, who had some of the more difficult journeys but who, perhaps because of this, also had some of the biggest breakthroughs.

The value of Salvia is in the speed with which it can get to the heart of things—the core of ourselves—and in the fact that other methods of therapy may not get to these places at all. Anton, for example, had introduced himself by telling the group that he felt unworthy. His Salvia experience was a complete dissembling where he entered the "interdimensional gateways" and realized "how small this reality is." It is a classic Salvia outcome to see that the life we know, the myths we carry about ourselves, and the reality we subscribe to are, in fact, "small" and meaningless, that we are just a story that we (or someone else on our behalf) is writing about us. It is also typical of healing with Salvia to understand that the nothingness that remains when these old patterns are wiped out is filled with potential and can be used to create a new dream. "There was something more. . . . I kept saying the word *pointless* and yet the nothingness I saw was full."

What I also found interesting, however, was Anton's comment when he sensed the return of his "personality" (if there really is such a thing): "I'm sorry, I fucked up; I have destroyed everyone's experience." He immediately reached for a familiar perception of himself as unworthy and tried to grasp back the patterns that Salvia had just wiped him clean of.

Anton is not unique in this. Having realized that they are not limited but filled with potential people can become overwhelmed by the possibilities open to them and seek out old limitations so their choices are not so vast and they don't have to take responsibility for them. I remarked on this to Anton, pointing out the habits we are prone to in both thinking and action. I don't know of many therapeutic methods, however, that would have gotten us to this point as quickly and clearly as Salvia. He needed to have the Salvia experience before he could make his apology for having it and then see his pattern of apologizing for and disempowering himself.

Lela's experience was in some ways similar. She was clear in both intentions that she wanted Salvia to heal her body. The body, however, does not exist in isolation from the mind and emotions and, in order to comply with her wishes, Salvia needed her to revisit an emotional wound, the loss of her child. Lela is a very rational, analytical person, however ("I have a strong mind and am driven to find the reason for everything"), and to shift her from a physical to an emotional engagement with her problem would, I am sure, have taken a number of therapy sessions, and even then she may not have connected fully with her feeling of loss even though she might have understood the cause of her problems from an intellectual point of view. With Salvia the impact was immediate, and because she discovered the truth for herself it was undeniable and beyond her rationalizations. She *felt* it.

Alex came with a simple request as well: to answer the question whether she should move to the United Kingdom or stay in Greece. What she got was a revelation of the family dramas that caused her dilemma in the first place. As a result she was able to arrive, she said, "in a place of peace and acceptance." Salvia answered her question but also gave her insight and the ability to make better decisions about her life as a whole.

Because of its directness I have heard Salvia described as "not so much an experience as 'a beneficial ordeal.'" It will show us the truth immediately and incisively, which can sometimes feel harsh, but there is no denying that it is a time-saver ("Focus on what's important; there is no time. . . ." as The Shepherdess told me during my meeting with her) or that, with the correct set, setting, and therapeutic support, its process can be beneficial.

• • •

Hannah discovered this too. A bad experience in childhood had left her cut off emotionally, she said. Salvia's response was, again, to let her experience her fears within a safe ceremonial context: "I felt very scared, and it dawned on me that this fear was exactly what I had asked for: I experienced myself emotionally again." Having made this reconnection, a number of new directions are open to therapy.

And of course there are some for whom the experience itself is a blessing. Salvia does not *have* to be an ordeal. Stuart, for example, "gave in to complete surrender and was profoundly enriched by the nothingness."

Salvia might therefore have a number of uses in Western psycho- (and other) therapies, for example, with depressed, anxious, stressed, and addicted clients or with those who feel lost and need a new vision for their lives.

The clients for whom Salvia might be appropriate would need to be chosen carefully, and their agreement to try it would have to be gained after a full explanation of its effects. The other essentials are an appropriate set (intention) and setting (ceremonial or healing context) and the support of a therapist and ceremonial guide who is experienced with Salvia and who can, therefore, help others make sense of their own experiences. With these cautions in mind, Salvia may have much to offer.

6

THE QUESTING OF OTHERS

Accounts from Salvia Users in the
United Kingdom, Sweden, Greece,
and Spain (Various Concentrates)

*Salvia took me on a consciousness-expanding journey
unlike any other I have ever experienced. My body felt
disconnected from "me," and objects and people appeared
cartoonish, surreal, and marvelous. Then, as suddenly as
it began it was over.*

ACCOUNT WRITTEN BY A JOURNALIST IN
NEW SCIENTIST MAGAZINE

In this chapter I have included accounts from people who are carrying
out research of their own with Salvia. Most are healers, psychologists, or
psychotherapists, so their accounts are interesting both as personal narra-
tives and for their insights into the healer's point of view. In many cases
they have also studied shamanism with me or joined my journeys to Peru
to drink San Pedro and ayahuasca so they understand the principles of

shamanism and are experienced with teacher plants. Some accounts also consider how Salvia might be used in the healing of others—particularly by the therapist taking it—and enhancing her ability to tune into the needs of her clients.

I haven't changed anything in their reports, but make brief comments at the end of each on the Salvia motifs that arise.

Darryl
Shamanic healer, Sweden: 10X and 20X concentrates

I met Darryl in 2010 when he attended my Shamanic Practitioner training course to learn shamanic healing. He then joined me in the Amazon for six weeks of plant diets, ayahuasca, and San Pedro ceremonies. When he arrived in the jungle Josephine and I were involved in our Salvia research, and this kindled his interest in the plant although he never worked with Salvia there. He has explored it himself in Sweden and the United Kingdom.

Thinking of a substance that dissolves cognition to be a sacred healing thing may seem a long bow to draw. *Salvia divinorum* backs up that statement; she also gives great flight to the arrow.

Having over twenty years of psychedelic experiences and exploring the healing effects of different plant medicines, I find that when it comes to experiencing both the unfathomable mystery and getting straight to the point Salvia has it in droves. I hold *Salvia divinorum* in high esteem.

LSD is a synthetic substance that when ingested promotes the visionary experience that illuminates the Self in different ways though it does not seem, for me, to have any substantial healing effects on the body. Great master teacher plants from South America, the ayahuasca brew, and the San Pedro cactus have that profound healing effect on the body coupled with a visionary aspect that is highly illuminating to the Self. The experiences with these plant medicines or teacher spirits have explained many things in my life and for my life. Ayahuasca, to me, is an inner experience that shows the potentials of what is on offer so to speak, reminding me of things in my life I never suspected to be sacred or to be power. San Pedro shows me the good in my relationships, myself, my loved ones, and my environment: the power of the life I have to live. Both have a strong sense of Self as part of that experience. Salvia strips everything away in a very short time and points the Self to another entirely different existence. Far from what may be called any sense of the real world, I seem to be completely incarnated psychically into another very solid alternative world.

Smoking 20X: *Feeling a shift I began to laugh. The laughter was deep and building. I became aware of lights and music, then being accepted by a group and led by the hand deeper into what seemed to be a fairground at night. The lights of the rides that seemed to be packed tightly everywhere were vivid against the black surroundings.*

I was taken onto a ride by a woman/girl. She looked beautiful and exuded the persona of a happy child. There were other "adult kids," and we got onto the Cup & Saucer ride. The music was rock and roll as well as pipe organ carousel tunes. There was no conversation just joy and excitement, then the ride started up. We began to spin centrifuge-fashion, then the cup began to move quickly sideways. The motion of being out of total control, spinning with the sensation of being shunted was great. The sensation of wild abandoned fun was exhilarating. I was laughing like a kid.

She then led us to the roller coaster. The activity was frenetic around us as we began to glide. The pace quickened, and the uphill climb began. She held my hand, and I could only laugh as the knowing of the drop feeling came on. The anticipation built like a wonderful fear inside me, and all I could do was laugh. We stopped at the apex, and I felt cold with fear and so happy to be there. I looked at her beautiful smiling face and into her eyes and was catapulted into space. The speed was unbelievable, and all I could do was look at her and explode in laughter. When I came back it felt as though from a refreshing deep sleep.

• • •

The world is like a ride in an amusement park, and when you choose to go on it you think it's real because that's how powerful our minds are. And the ride goes up and down and round and round, and it has thrills and chills and is very brightly colored and it's very loud. And it's fun for a while. Some people have been on the ride for a long time and they've begun to question: "Is this real or is this just a ride?" and other people have remembered, and they've come back to us and they say, "Hey don't worry. Don't be afraid ever because this is just a ride. . . ." It's only a choice right now between fear and love. The eyes of fear want you to put bigger locks on your door, buy guns, close yourself off. The eyes of love instead see all of us as one.

BILL HICKS

Smoking 20X mixed with 10X: *Again I felt the shift and the laughing came from deep in my chest. I lay down. I was at the fairground again running from tent to tent with "Her" and others. The tents pulsated with the deepest glowing reds next to oscillating blues and radiant gold. There were people walking around that were not reacting to the environment. I ran past them looking at faces solemn and brooding. Their clothes were dark browns, black, and grey. They seemed to soak up all the glow of the shimmering environment.*

We kept running and laughing. I didn't know what we were looking for, I just wanted to follow them and keep running like laughing, happy children in a playground. The noise was again music: the music of pipe organs and the sound of an excited crowd. We continued running and dodging in and out of tents, past rides, all helter skelter. I felt powerful and had easy speed with a lot seemingly on tap. I could keep up with the group easily.

A noise began, and we stopped. Looking at the others I noticed the direction where everyone was looking, then they began to shriek in laughter and scattered, running like a crazy old uncle was going to catch them and tickle them till they wet their pants. Looking in the direction they had come I saw a moving wall; it was covering the entirety of space and time. It was moving toward me fast. Looking closer I noticed it was taking over everything, all the rides and tents and the night sky behind. It was like a billion sparkling dominoes taking over the world with a clitter and clatter that was mesmerizing. I could discern individual clattering that I knew was happening in a billion places. All together making a rumbling rushing that was background noise that the carousel music was playing on.

It got closer, and we began to run, this time with hysterical laughter. It had turned into a game of hide-and-seek. I stopped to wait and look closer at the onrushing green wall. It seemed like the hugest wave towering in height, getting bigger and bigger. I ran to its base and saw that what was folding in were 3-, 4-, 5- isosceles-type interlocking emerald-green shapes. She told me that this was time.

With welling laughter we ran shrieking with joy in all directions, and I saw she was running with me. It felt like we ran out of the fairground and into the widest expanse. On the horizon I could see something and made my way with great speed toward it. At this point I was on my own, and there was no sound—just a bright open desertlike expanse—and the figure looked to be a sphinx. As I flew toward it I saw it was shiny with radiant color. It seemed like kilometers were being traversed as I made my way toward it, all the time a feeling of exhilaration, intoxication, and joy.

As I flew to it I circled around it to take in its beautiful form. The sleek long body was power at rest, and the head was in a regal position held straight, relaxed in a state of repose. Standing before it I looked up and saw the face. I recognized it as the face of Sandra, the person whose place I was smoking at. It was glimmering iridescent reds, blues, oranges, yellows, gold, and purples around the features. It was like my eyes were being bathed in a beauty, and all I could do was grin and laugh.

I came back to find myself wrapped in the arms of Sandra. Feelings of reassurance and safeness blissed me out. I looked up at her face and could still see traces of the colors racing across her features. She later explained to me I had laid down laughing madly then had tried to get up and run. She had to stop me from bolting a few times.

• • •

The shamanic use of the plant kingdom to journey is a cross-cultural phenomenon that has been practiced for thousands of years. With Salvia the vision is intense, complete separation of reality, and a new world of existence. There is no control to where The Shepherdess takes me; she seems to be elusive to intent. With ayahuasca and San Pedro I can ask questions, with Salvia I do not. She seems to be there with a vision that has no reference to Self. She takes me beyond all attachments.

As an ally, I get a sense of great energetic transmission resulting in a sense of being refreshed. I feel lighter with an afterglow of happiness. I just need to remember and begin to feel where the laughter comes from, and it never fails to bring a smile to my face. She is a comfort and feels like a lover: all heart and excitement. Sometimes when I feel the walls close in with the downside of life's issues I go back to the sense of freedom and excitement when running from the emerald triangles to the sphinx on the horizon. I draw on this power, which turns the trough into a peak, and I overcome that little piece of living.

Where some plants use personal history as a reference Salvia seems to erase it. I get the sense of being a young child unencumbered by what I know. I get a fresh, unbiased, almost raw experience that seems "like new," an excitement of a first time.

As an avenue of exploration it may test intent. It may not be an entirely easy experience but it can be a very rewarding one. The Shepherdess helps me to see all that may ever be and to cross the uncomfortable sea. As a guide she is a great companion on an emotional level that shows the real joy of living.

Salvia motifs: The appearance of reality as an advancing "wall" or "wave" and the sense of it "folding in" bringing endings is similar to my perception of a "wave of reality" in the moloka during our jungle experiments and Josephine's reality landscapes. Salvia is also perceived as the Mistress of Time, which is how I had seen her during the ayahuasca ceremony when I met her spirit: "What was folding in were 3-, 4-, 5- isosceles-type interlocking emerald green shapes. She told me that this was time." There is also a consistency to the idea of Salvia as a medicine that "folds" reality. Even the expression "folding in" has been used by a number of participants, including the ones in the last chapter.

Bobby
Psychotherapist, Spain: 20X concentrate

Bobby is a retired psychotherapist who has undertaken a lot of personal development work with entheogens as well as psychedelics such as LSD. I met her when she attended an ayahuasca ceremony with me in Europe, and she subsequently joined another of my courses. Later she drank San Pedro and smoked Salvia with me. Because of her wide experience with plants as well as her clinical background I asked her to comment on the similarities and differences in Salvia and other psychedelics, as well any applications she might see for Salvia in psychotherapy.

I had tried Salvia a few times in the context of a social group—smoked leaves in a pipe—but given the mix of people and other substances I had nothing much to say about it except that it seemed to add to a sense of our togetherness and was a bit telepathic; I wasn't sure if we were speaking or sharing thoughts but it was just a bit of fun. It was my son who had had very powerful experiences on it and suggested we try some at his house to see what I made of it. We began with the leaf, which did not have a potent effect, just a pleasant sensation. It was when we used the 5X extract that I felt a powerful and memorable experience.

> *As usual with Salvia there was the initial "rocket launch" sensation—a whoosh and sense of rapid uplifting—I think this may be the part that concerns some people as it is somewhat out of one's control. My initial thought was that it reminded me a bit of ketamine in that it seems to be space/time bending—there is a sense of shifting perspective—literally,*

like looking at things from another part of the room from where you're sitting. The difference is that there is a sense of intelligence about Salvia that ketamine doesn't seem to produce. I have had this perceptual sense when drinking ayahuasca, as well.

This particular session with Salvia has been lodged in my mind as one of the best ever experiences although it was lacking in anything spectacular. It was out-of-body as I was looking down on myself and my son from somewhere else, and what I could see was as if I was the nucleus of a cell. It was a place of complete calm: between the outbreath and the inbreath of the universe. My body appeared to be very separate from "me" and yet not. I was not "in" it but I knew it was me. There was a rosy color, which enhanced the sense of a cell, as if I were the nucleus in the makeup of something much bigger than myself.

The overall sense was one of presence. The moment was all there was. It was the here and now that so many systems of spiritual and religious thought seem to yearn for. Everything was just as it should be. It felt very Zen—an experience of the Void, which was also completely full, a paradox that seemed to be the very essence of Zen. It was also a sense of bliss as if this was the peak experience. My mind felt completely open with no boundaries: myself and "God" or "spirit" were one and the same while at the same time there was the sense of being held in the center of the heart of "God." In one way the experience was complete enough for me not to desire to reexperience it but I was also curious to see if this sensation would be repeated on another occasion.

For the next experience I smoked a 20X extract. Again there was the whoosh of a takeoff when this time my head seemed to literally break open and expand beyond ordinary limits. I was not limited to my body but within a field of energy that could expand as far as I wanted it to. I was sitting outside and could hear some people talking across the valley. My attention went there, and I seemed to literally be pulled to them. It was a completely physical sensation; I could feel an elastic stretching of my (let's call it) energy field extending to where they were so it seemed as if I was standing with them. I could hear them as if they were right beside me and to all intents and purposes I seemed to be over the other side of the valley with them. I wondered if I was actually there with them when what I took to be my honeysuckle said quite clearly, "You're right here right now."

I played with this elastic sensation by pulling my head around to point my ears in another direction and then felt myself come back to where I was sitting. This time I could hear the television from the house but knew what it was and didn't particularly want to listen to it. Again that strong sense of immediate presence—I couldn't have been more "here and now"—and yet I was not located within my body. It seemed as if it (my body) was more of a casing for energy and waves rather than a solid group of particles. It was me but I was not it. I had a vision of an old-fashioned Bakelite radio, which was one I remembered from my childhood. I didn't feel as if I were that radio but the symbol of sound waves, transmission, and reception all seemed to fit with what I was experiencing. The analogy seems quite good for the experience; the radio is a casing with component parts for translating waves into sound. Sound was somewhat visible as the air was so dense that you could watch it rippling and moving as the sound waves moved through it. I remember now once hearing a cannon fired at close range, and the sensation was similar; the sound was visibly moving the air as it passed.

The air felt as solid as the table or any other object, and the plants around me were alive with a vital intelligence and recognition of me; actually it was two ways, I guess a bit like transmission and reception. Again it felt intelligent, as if my mind was expanded to include everything, and if I chose I could know anything and expand anywhere. Or perhaps it's better put that "my" mind didn't exist except as a part of the Mind; that feels more accurate. Overall I felt bliss. The sense of being a part of everything was complete. Time was paused. I was not separate.

As I write this I recall other "truths" it seemed to reveal. I have read many times that energy flows where attention goes but with Salvia this was an actual physical experience: it was all I could do to not "leap over" to the other side of the valley when I paid attention to the people talking there. I felt I had to resist or I would have physically flown to catch up with my attention. And yet I could choose where I put my attention; I chose to ignore the television knowing that if I did pay attention, it would activate the same pull, and I didn't want to be pulled into the television!

I believe my comment was "wow." All boundaries were gone, and it seemed possible to be or do anything as long as it didn't entail using my body. The sense of boundary-less participation in the mind of the universe was ecstatic.

I do feel Salvia to be a very wise teacher but one that needs a lot of respect. As a therapist I think it would be fairly extreme for many clients who have long lived within the safety of their boundaries. In the context of shamanic use and healing I think there would be more acceptance of the experience as the shamanic world does not work within the limits of ego; nor does Salvia. "I" ceased to exist in the way I usually do. For me this was ecstatic; for others perhaps frightening. Most people who seek therapy want to "mend" their egos, not lose them.

I particularly think of it as Zen, since from my knowledge of Zen practice there is recognition of the inherent paradox within a human, and that the practice of Zen is to learn to hold both sides of the paradox simultaneously. To be both within and without your body. To recognize the void as also the fullness from which all comes and returns. Zen also has an acceptance that here and now is all there is; enlightenment is the recognition that this is not something to be sought after but known as being present right now. This is certainly something that seems to be true of Salvia.

I was particularly interested in the way sound was working; it was neither invisible nor intangible but felt and looked like a wave through the density of the air, which was equal in density to the trees, table, or me. It was one way of knowing and literally seeing that the world is an energetic process rather than a conglomeration of matter.

I will continue to work with Salvia as I feel that perhaps it is better than anything I have so far tried to bring theory into practice. The theories of shamanic thought, the theories behind meditative practice, the ecstatic visions of God as perceived by mystics and saints throughout time, as well as the theories within quantum physics—the wave/particle phenomenon. The perception that the world is of our own making and is much more fluid than initial appearances suggest. That from nothing we come and from nothing we return, and yet as in all good paradoxes, nothing is not nothing.

Salvia motifs: An enhanced sense of empathy or "telepathy" with others. The bending of time and space. Being pulled (physically, attention). The sense of the void/nothingness and the paradox behind it ("nothing is not nothing"). The Zen sensation this evokes.

Sandy
Self-employed, Greece: 5X concentrate and leaves
Sandy is forty years old and self-employed/semiretired. Before moving to Greece she was a therapist and shamanic healer in the United Kingdom. She has experience with a range of entheogens and has administered Salvia to clients as part of a therapeutic program.

I have smoked Salvia for a number of years. It always shakes up reality and is shocking. I need that sometimes to get me out of what has become comfortable and complacent for me and remind me what is real: nothing! With psychotherapy we can get lost in concepts sometimes but knowing that they are only concepts and that I have a person in front of me whose reality is as valid as mine but just not working effectively for them has always made it easier for me to relate to them. [Richard] Bandler* used to say that it is much easier for a therapist to enter the client's world than it is for a client to enter his, and Salvia enabled me to do that. I would often smoke prior to a therapy session and found it really helped me to see my client's view of things and to feel what they were going through.

Because of the way it helped me I decided that Salvia might be

---

*One of the founders of NLP (Neuro-Linguistic Programming)

of use for some clients. I definitely wouldn't recommend it for everyone though. Some people who are suffering from depression or anxiety have responded well, however, when the leaves are smoked or chewed.

Apart from my counseling practice I also conduct shamanic healings, and in that ceremonial context I have given a few clients a small pinch of mild Salvia (5X concentrate) to smoke when I have performed a soul retrieval for them. Shamans say that whenever we are hurt, traumatized, or shocked in some way, parts of our soul (or energy) may leave our bodies. Sometimes these soul parts become lost, unable or unwilling to return, a condition known as "soul loss." Healing is through the return of these soul parts, known as "soul retrieval."

After the initial Salvia experience of smoking there is usually a new sense of peace and greater introspection, which allows the client and me to both see more clearly when the trauma occurred and where the lost soul might be. Clients say they feel much better after a healing like this, but again I wouldn't give Salvia to everyone and certainly never on a first consultation. People have to be prepared for it and know what to expect.

Salvia motifs: A number of people mention feelings of calm and empathy following work with Salvia and that this provides greater insight into the feelings of others (also see Alexia's account below).

Alexia

Psychotherapist, United Kingdom: 40X concentrate

Alexia is a psychotherapist and hypnotherapist in the United Kingdom. I met her in 2008 when she joined my healing retreat to the Amazon to drink ayahuasca. A year later she returned to take part in San Pedro ceremonies, leading to a dramatic healing, which she recalls in my book Cactus of Mystery. *Her work with plant medicines is now focused on Salvia, which she describes as "my favorite of all the plants. It's an odd landscape, the Salvia world, and the spirit of Salvia has quite a mischievous sense of humor."*

• • •

Over the years, I have worked with various teacher plants. Salvia is most certainly the one I have the deepest affinity with. The speed at which I enter SalviaWorld is almost instantaneous. The first time I tried it, one moment I was in this reality, and five seconds later I was in Salvia. I lost control of my body and any notion of time and space, as well as consciousness. I was completely immersed in the plant.

The intensity of the experience has been consistently enchanting. The colors are rich, vibrant, and intense: like ayahuasca. I recall seeing many geometric repetitive patterns (hexagons). The Salvia landscape looks very two-dimensional to me, and the spirits there certainly have a sense of humor but not in an offensive way; it just seems to be their style. The places I visited were very angular, with lots of corners. I was always walking on and through corners: there was no ground, just corners. Most of my journeys are the same, and it seemed like they were always waiting for me.

As far as I know, I didn't meet Ska Maria, I only met lions, always lions, who kept showing me really bizarre things that I cannot remember now. (I liked the lions.)

I have tried to use Salvia for divination and shamanic journeying but haven't been able to maintain a reasonable state of consciousness to do this. Interestingly though I have noticed that half an hour after using it I have felt in a very meditative state, which makes slipping between worlds easy and is good for healing work.

As a therapist, my experiences have been so insane it's difficult for me to see the therapeutic value for clients although I'm not ruling it out. I have always taken Salvia in the mornings though, and on many occasions when I have worked with clients afterward I have been hyperintuitive to their needs and issues, and they have commented on this.

Salvia motifs: The perception of "geometric repetitive patterns (hexagons)" is reminiscent of our early experiments in Peru when hexagons seemed to be everywhere. They are also referred to by participants in the last chapter. The flatness of the Salvia landscape ("very two-dimensional") as well as its angularity ("lots of corners") has been mentioned in a number of reports. Again, a heightened sense of empathy and intuition.

Martin

Psychotherapist and shamanic healer, United Kingdom:

50X concentrate

Martin is Alexia's business partner at the therapeutic practice they run. He has used the smoke for the healing of others as well as for self-exploration. Of all the accounts in this section his sounds most similar to my own.

To give this some structure I am going to split the experience into several topics:

> **Onset:** This is fast with sage, from inhaling the smoke to tripping in around ten seconds. I always have a tray at hand and make sure I'm sitting down before I take a toke on the pipe so I can drop it safely; the first time I was standing and fell over as if I had been poleaxed!
>
> **Bodily sensation:** Is the same with any strength of sage I've tried. It feels as if someone has grabbed you by the shoulders and pulled you hard backward—only you don't stop falling—receding away from your body at lightning speed; the higher the strength of sage, the more vicious the pull. From then on if I concentrate on a body part it feels as if it is churning inside out constantly in a rotating fashion.
>
> **Visuals:** At first this is nearly always a thin strip a bit like a zipper being undone, and I'm riding along it (being unzipped as well). The best image to describe this is like the one you sometimes get at the beginning of films at the cinema where you are going along a big dipper ride made of acetate film. The strip is made up of

simple bright-colored bars; the colors remind me of the ones you
get with licorice allsorts.*

Sage world: Eventually the scene changes, and I am in sage world.
It reminds me of middle world at Mardi Gras in some ways but
all the spirits inhabiting it seem to have an edge, a bit sarcas-
tic and manic at the same time. They do talk but nearly always
when I'm just arriving, they say, "Wuurp! Here he comes again."

At first I was happy to just look around and be there, but eventually
I tried to use the experience as a journey—setting up an initial intention
and so forth—and this is where the experience becomes more like navi-
gating dreams. The first time I tried to call up my lower world guides I
just couldn't think straight, I couldn't even form the notion of a "guide";
there I was trying to think (it felt like when you have someone's name
on the tip of your tongue but can't quite recall it) and all the while the
sage spirits are standing around taking the piss with me going shush at
them: it was hilarious.

Eventually I worked out that sage world is a distinct world separate
from the three we shamans usually use when journeying. Once I worked
that out I found a sage world guide and operated as normal within it.
For example, once I went there to get assistance with healing for a
friend [who was] in the hospital to recover from an operation: it was
beautiful, the sage spirit and I traveled to the hospital, and the spirit
blew a greenish smoke over her body while she slept. Later she asked me
if I had visited her while she was asleep as she had a strong feeling of my
presence; her recovery was swift and without complication.

Back in the "real" world the sage experience lasts around ten minutes for me during which time my body is completely immobile. Once
I come around, there is a period of about an hour where I'm still under

---

*Licorice allsorts are sweets or candies made from brightly colored licorice. There is
an artificiality to these colors: as if they are too bright. Martin's comment therefore
reminds me of my own observation in the moloka in Peru: that the people I was seeing
in my visions were just "too pink."

a subtle influence of the sage, and other activities such as divining or shamanic healing are greatly enhanced. The overall "spirit of sage" is seductive, and I often hear a woman's voice calling me back. "Just one more, just a little bit further," she coos. If I give in and go again the experience is usually a little harsher the second time around. The most rounds I've done in one go is four, and the fourth wasn't any worse (or better) than the third. Usually though I just do one round, as this is enough to achieve my purpose for the journey. My preferred dose is 50X.

Salvia motifs: Being grabbed and pulled. Physical rotation. Zippers and being "unzipped." The notion that the period after and not during the Salvia experience is the time to really work with the plant. The Shepherdess is far from innocent, no virgin at all: "The overall 'spirit of sage' is seductive, and I often hear a woman's voice calling me back. 'Just one more, just a little bit further.'"

James
Psychology of consciousness Ph.D. student, United Kingdom:
5X concentrate

James (not his real name) is about to graduate with a Ph.D. and begin work as a psychology professor at a university in the United Kingdom. He asked to remain anonymous.

I was working at a shop that sold (among other legal highs, herbs, and books) *Salvia divinorum,* so I thought I should give it a try so I could pass my experiences on to any customers that showed interest. I didn't really believe that a "legal high" would have any significant effect so I was surprised by the strength of the experience.

> *I was sitting in my living room at home and smoked a bowl of 5X Salvia extract in my pipe and held it in as long as I could. This was difficult because Salvia is quite a harsh smoke. Almost as soon as I exhaled, a wave of psychedelic colors washed across my vision from the top right-hand side*

of my visual field. I describe it as a "wave" because this is exactly what it looked like: a swirling wave of color that built up and then crashed across the rest of my vision and immersed me in the experience. I was genuinely shocked by the effectiveness of this herb, and as I noticed my girlfriend walk past into the next room I tried to express to her that the drug had worked. All I could manage was to nod my head (with my eyes wide and my mouth hanging open) in answer to the question that she seemed to be asking with her eyes ("Does it work then?") hoping that she would understand that this meant, "IT WORKS!"

I spent the next few minutes trying to enjoy the experience as much as possible (as I said I was not expecting to be tripping out on this mid-week afternoon from inhaling a legal high), but soon recovered enough to talk fairly normally. I went to lie down on the bed (having become exhausted from the experience) about half an hour after smoking the pipe and continued to see colors and feel exhilarated/confused for about another half an hour after this. By around an hour after smoking I was sober and felt straight enough to drive a car or work with heavy machinery if necessary (it was not).

I think some background is necessary before I describe the next experience. I was in a difficult mental space at the time: we had just moved into a new home but had soon discovered that there was no hot water, no TV, and no telephone line, so we ended up moving back into the flat we had been renting off my father for an extra week while these things got resolved, but all of our possessions were in the new flat. We did not have a good relationship with our new landlady who seemed disinterested in our concerns. In addition to this, my girlfriend's mother, who had been diagnosed with terminal cancer a few years earlier, was approaching the end of her life, and although we never really believed that she would die (she was a fighter to the end) there was a palpable tension in the air. I also had a pain in my back from all the heavy lifting and pressures of moving house, worrying about my girlfriend, her mother, and having recently started a new high-pressure job with a lot of responsibility.

I guess it would be fair to say that I wanted to take some drugs to forget my worries for a while, so I looked through my possessions and found some Salvia leaf and a couple of canisters of nitrous oxide or "laughing gas" (this is taken by filling a cream dispenser with the gas, discharging the gas into a balloon, and then inhaling the gas from the balloon). It seemed like a good idea to do it all and see what happened!

I was sitting on the sofa in my dad's living room (he was not living there while we were "between homes") with the paraphernalia laid out before me. I smoked three bowls of Salvia (I kept smoking until I was good-and-tripping, another way to describe this would be to say that the plant was communicating with me, and the burning herb in the bowl of the pipe looked decidedly "interesting") and then filled a balloon with laughing gas. I inhaled the gas, blew it back into the balloon, inhaled again, kept it in as long as I could and then exhaled. As I exhaled I leaned back into the sofa and let the experience wash over me. As I relaxed into the sofa I felt my back "click" into place and actually felt a lot better because of this. I then started to think about the healing powers of the mind and how amazing it was that a simple drug experience could be strong enough to sort out my back problems. I guess this got me thinking about how this could be, and I started to flick between about eight to ten different "parallel universes" in the space of a couple of seconds as I started to come round. These "universes" included one where my back was all better, one where I had died and my girlfriend had to deal with this as well as dealing with her mother's illness, one where I never recovered from the drug experience and went clinically insane resulting in my girlfriend checking me into a mental institution. There were others but these were the major ones that really hit home and that I still remember.

By the time I had finished flitting between these worlds I opened my eyes and was very confused about where I was, but more importantly whether I had actually woken up at all. (Of course, there was still a possibility that in the "real world" I was dying/being committed, but I was happily experiencing this world where everything seemed a bit colorful and dream-like but pretty much normal and my back was okay.) The only way I could think of to confirm to me that I was actually awake and back in "consensus reality" would be to ask my girlfriend if I was awake, but of course if I wasn't "really" awake and was still in the throes of a drug experience of course the only answer she would give is, "Yes, you are awake," so the only logical path available to me was to ask her to "wake me up." I asked, and although she looked confused at my request, she went along with it and started to say my name and say things like "wake up" and pat my hand. I told her this wasn't good enough, and although I felt like a glass of water splashed across my face might convince me, I quickly thought better of this idea and asked her to slap me across the face . . . which she did, but too gently so I asked to do it harder . . . which she did.

Eventually I was suitably convinced that I was awake and back in "consensus reality" and my back felt really good! I jumped up from the sofa feeling totally elated and very excited that not only was I back in the "real world" but I had "proved" that the mind really can heal the body. I spent a bit of time jumping around the living room waving my hands in the air feeling a mixture of happiness that I was not mad/dead and exhilaration that I had finally found some proof of the healing power of the mind. Eventually I calmed down enough to explain my experience to my girlfriend who was looking a little bit concerned, a little bit confused, but still smiling to try to keep me calm. It took a while to explain it all because I was still so excited and quite far gone. Eventually I completely sobered up, and my back trouble returned, much to my disappointment. I guess the drug experience (particularly the anesthetic effects of nitrous oxide) had relaxed me enough to temporarily realign my back, but had not actually resolved the underlying problems.

I now believe that no "real" interdimensional travel had occurred, but the drug experience showed me a selection of concerns that were troubling me at the time: having pain in my back was a pretty much constant irritation, living between homes made me feel altogether disconnected from the world, and I didn't really know where my reality started or finished, having the worry of being there to support my girlfriend through a difficult time was also a constant concern and seeing her mother's health deteriorate made me think about death quite a lot.

I was going to write how this experience made me really distrust the Salvia experience (my back was never "healed," and I was never going mad or dying) but writing this report has given me a different perspective. I think

Salvia is a very strange drug; it makes you think in a very different way and makes you totally believe the experience is "true." While I still think that Salvia experiences should be treated with a certain amount of skepticism, I think there is much to be learned from this drug. Salvia will never tell you the "truth" but it will allow you to divine some truth about your life if you are willing to spend a considerable amount of time interpreting your experience. This is certainly not a "recreational" drug and should not be treated as such. Just remember that while you are under its influence your experiences might seem to be "real" (one of the customers who came into the shop I worked in that sold Salvia said when their friend had tried it, they had become totally convinced that they had turned into a fence post), but they are the result of taking a strong mind-altering drug. When you are sober it will be clear that the experience was not really "real" but there is usually a lesson to be learned . . . and it's probably not that you are a fence post!

Salvia motifs: The reality "wave" again. The sensation that there are parallel universes/dimensions that we can move between (even if later disavowed). The notion that Salvia has its own language, which must be learned before we can fully engage with the teachings of the plant: "Salvia will never tell you the 'truth' but it will allow you to divine some truth about your life if you are willing to spend a considerable amount of time interpreting your experience."

7

THE TEACHINGS
OF THE SHEPHERDESS

Threads and Themes from the Path of Sage • Exploring

the Evidence Based on the Accounts of Nearly 50 Users

and Almost 100 Trip Reports • What Is Salvia Telling Us? •

How Does It Heal? • How Should We Interact with It? •

Its Messages for Humanity

> *It was in my first year of experimentation that my*
> *experiences with* Salvia divinorum *began to take on*
> *an increasing sense of realness that was both alarming*
> *and exhilarating. . . . What had once manifested as*
> *a meaningless cacophony was gradually becoming*
> *transformed into a coherent, approachable phenomenon.*
>
> J. D. ARTHUR, SALVIA DIVINORUM:
> *DOORWAY TO THOUGHT-FREE AWARENESS*

In this book I have included the accounts of nearly fifty Salvia users (about
a hundred accounts in all), male and female, of different ages and from
different countries, family, and cultural backgrounds, some of whom, like

John and those in my Plant Spirit Wisdom group, came with specific healing intentions. This gives us the ability to take our detective work further
by making comparisons to see what consistent themes emerge and what
you, as a shamanic explorer, can expect from meeting The Shepherdess.

I've quoted Dale Pendell a few times because I respect his work
and I trust him, so he may be a good place to start. He believes that
Salvia is about "augury . . . identity . . . borders . . . parallel universe[s]
. . . midnight . . . moon . . . birth . . . lust . . . exile . . . *Nen,* the quantum of time." [1] A number of these themes do come up in trip accounts,
although strangely enough for a diviner's plant augury (top of his list) is
less common among them.

AUGURY

The warning I received about my car on the day I got a ticket, as vague
and unimportant as it seems, is the only example I can point to of "pro-
active divination": a sense instilled in me by the plant that *something*
was about to happen in advance of the event. Interestingly it took place
during the diet when I was drinking a tea of the leaves rather than
smoking the extract. This is also the traditional Mazatec way of working with Salvia for divination, although my experience did not take
place in a ceremonial context.

There were of course more important messages for me and my wife
about our relationship patterns. Hearing (or rather, understanding) *those*
would have been worth a *lot* of parking tickets but I only saw them with
hindsight; there was no obvious indication from the plant for either of
us when it mattered that there were issues we needed to look at, which
meant that the clues could only be unraveled after the event. Not much
help then in future-seeing, or not in this instance anyway.

That may simply make us poor diviners of course (although in our
defense we didn't know we had a problem, and we weren't smoking
Salvia with the intention of looking for one or its solution) but it may
also suggest one way in which dieting the leaves differs from smoking
the concentrate: the hojas are more direct while the language of the

smoke is symbolic and harder to read, especially when you have not yet met the spirit of the plant.

Those are the only examples I can think of though where an outcome has arisen that might have been predicted or prevented as a result of a Salvia communication, and they are also subjective, but perhaps all divination is.

J. D. Arthur writes about divination too, suggesting a problem with the process that others might also encounter.

Since Salvia seemed to have so many unknown possibilities I thought it would be worth exploring this aspect as well. It was suggested in some recent writings that one should hold a question or similar thought in mind while entering the state. . . . As I began to enter the state [however] it became obvious that . . . in an ironic twist [I] would have to relinquish my ordinary thought processes, which, of course, was precisely where my question resided. Without the footing of thought there could be no question. It just didn't seem possible to bring the camel with me through the eye of the needle. [2]

I can understand the problem. It is hard to hold onto anything once the wild ride through smoke begins. A solution for those who want to try, however, is the more usual shamanic practice of having a question (or rather, an intention) in mind *prior* to the journey *and then letting it go*.

Intention alerts the spirits to our purpose so they are aware of the reason for our visit (like setting the agenda for a meeting) but we do not have to continually refer to it once they have been informed. It is *after* we return from the journey that we begin the work of decoding the symbols presented to us. If we refer back to our intention at this point and interpret the information we have been given within the framework it provides, the images make more sense, although, as I've said, salvinorin will make us work harder for enlightenment than a diet of leaves since it speaks the language of dreams and requires us to become dream analysts. Intention, however, is key—setting and then releasing it—so that the Salvia journey makes sense at all.

There is another meaning to the word *divination,* however, which might be more useful for us to consider, and which stems from its linguistic origin *divinare:* "to be inspired by a god." Perhaps this is closer to the truth of Salvia: that it makes us "diviners" more aware of our divinity as the creators of reality so we can rise above our own limitations. Perhaps the plant is not literally (or only) about foretelling the future but a means of connecting with or knowing "the mind of God," as the shaman Ranolfo said when he visited our rainforest center during my first Salvia diet.

In human terms this would mean that through the plant we are able to develop a greater understanding and new awareness of truth as well as an increase in intuition and "knowingness." These qualities *are* inherent in the Salvia experience, as many participants report, so maybe we should not equate divination too simply with augury but with the capacity to find God within us. (Although if we are truly inspired, future-seeing may be a skill we can also develop.)*

> Our entire universe is contained in the mind and the
> spirit. We may choose not to find access to it, we may even
> deny its existence, but it is indeed there inside us and
> there are chemicals that can catalyze its availability.[3]
>
> ALEXANDER SHULGIN[†]

IDENTITY

Who am I? Who are you? These have been common questions in our Salvia research from the beginning. Tracie and Jungle asked them

---

*On reflection there may be one other instance of augury that I can relate to: the incident I describe in the Overlapping Realities section on page 186. I cannot be certain that Salvia was responsible for the omens I received then as the events took place before I had met the spirit of the plant. I had, however, completed my first Salvia diet some months before. The reason I feel that these omens *may* be connected to the plant is mainly because of the sense of foreboding that accompanied them, which I also experienced in relation to my car in the example above. Whatever the source, this is another situation in which I did not listen to the advice of the spirits to my cost.
†Shulgin is being quoted by Drake Bennett.

explicitly during our first rainforest experiments but they are implied by others too, for example, in Siebert's comment about his initial journey with salvinorin: "I suddenly realized that I had no actual memory of ever having lived," and by Blosser in his 1980's experiences with the leaves: "I was not aware that I had eaten an entheogenic plant, was in Mexico, was with friends, or had ever had a body."

In fact, twenty-seven of the reports in this book, about a third of all accounts, use the word *who* in the context of a statement or question relating to identity, such as Anton: "I had no idea who Ross and Debs were or who I was"—or else make comments like Rob's, which suggest the same: "There was no 'me.'" I am sure, however, that by reading between the lines of the other accounts that figure would more than double. It is *the* archetypal Salvia question and, as I've said before, one of the most important we can ask: Who do I *think* I am? Beyond age, roles, life experiences, how others perceive me or I perceive myself; beyond principles, pride, and patterns—knowing that only love is real and my time on Earth is finite—how do I want to live? In love or fear? Choose the former and anything is possible; choose the latter and we limit ourselves.

And what, after all, is personal history if not a dream?

RAM DASS

If we clarify our identity, however, so we have a better idea of how incidents (real or imagined) like this, and our memories of them (invented or actual) have shaped us, we might also see the future more clearly and diviner's sage may better live up to its name, because if we have a greater sense of ourselves we'll have more insight into our stories and where our beliefs and patterns, our pride and principles lead. We can then predict their outcomes as well and do something to change them. Knowing the future by knowing ourselves is a different sense again of the word *divination,* but it may, in fact, be more helpful than augury because it offers us a choice not just a destination.

BORDERS AND OBJECTS

Pendell calls it a fascination with borders; Siebert talks of merging with objects. I think they mean the same thing. We have seen various accounts of people losing their boundaries and experiencing consciousness from the perspective of wallpaper, wardrobes, wheels, bricks, and suitcases . . .

In the language of Salvia there is a message for all of these people in *what* they become, which may also help them answer the "Who am I?" question. Wallpaper stuck to the floor in our parents' house is an obvious metaphor but it is also qualitatively different from a suitcase left at an airport or chewing gum on a wheel. By understanding the personal symbol we might also be able to use the plant for traveling through time: by knowing and changing ourselves so we can know and change the future.

On the other hand, there is a therapeutic value and a sense of joy and freedom for some people in simply being boundless. This might be the case in particular for people who have been "too bound up in themselves," lost in their problems and patterns, or trapped by issues and circumstances, and could, therefore, suggest another healing application for Salvia: one of simple release.

As Bobby put it, "All boundaries were gone, and it seemed possible to be or do anything . . . boundary-less participation in the mind of the universe was ecstatic."

PARALLEL UNIVERSES AND OTHER DIMENSIONS

Maybe Salvia is an interdimensional plant, one that can take us to other worlds. I have often thought so.

Anton, in his vision, talked specifically about the "interdimensional gateways" opened by it. John, during his Salvia diet, remarked that reality "opened up interdimensionally." Others, like Trendal, DoOr, and Martin, see reality "unzipped" (Martin: "like a zipper being undone, and I'm riding along it, being unzipped as well") or experience waves or walls of other realities advancing toward them in a way that is so real and inexorable that it is more than just a change in perception or consciousness. It is what it is.

In our moloka experiments I felt these other dimensions as pin-pricks when they passed through me and even without smoking, Josephine was able to see some part of my vision. (James: "I describe it as a 'wave' because this is exactly what it looked like: a swirling wave . . . that built up and . . . immersed me in the experience.")

I have speculated elsewhere on the interdimensionality of Salvia, vis-à-vis ayahuasca, and San Pedro: that the vine connects us to the mind of the universe while the cactus introduces us to the soul of the Earth. The Shepherdess, however, takes us to a place outside of time and space and links us to something greater than both. (John: "It felt like there is something really big, something we don't understand that is controlling things in a way we can't know.")

It is also interesting to observe the speed of adoption of these plants as teachers and to consider where their consciousnesses may be taking us. There has been a growing awareness of ayahuasca since the 1950s, for example, but it has taken until now, sixty years or so later, for the plant to become well-known. San Pedro first came to popular attention in the 1980s with the publication of Douglas Sharon's book on Andean curanderismo,[4] and it has taken just thirty years for it to become established as a plant of interest for contemporary shamans and seekers. Salvia meanwhile only began to come to prominence with Siebert's work in the 1990s but has now been more widely adopted than both, at least as a recreational drug, and that has taken just twenty years.

As a timeline of recent human history then, we became aware of ayahuasca, the "plant of the universe," at the time of the space race. It took us to the moon. San Pedro brought us back to Earth and was there at the beginning of the environmental movement. It taught us to care for the planet. Salvia, however, leads us away from the Earth and even the known universe. It is fascinating to speculate what its agenda may be at this point in history, especially as the old theories of science based on limitations (such as Newtonian physics and Einstein's contention that nothing can move faster than light) are replaced by new ideas based on possibilities and openness. Things are moving faster and in new directions, maybe even to new dimensions, and the plants have been guiding us from the start.

The latest quantum theory for understanding the nature of reality is membrane (or M) theory, for example, which is as strange as a Salvia journey can sometimes be. It hypothesizes eleven dimensions, each vibrating like a string, that exist all around us at all times and sometimes collide, giving birth to new universes or aspects of reality. The room you are sitting in now is filled with these other dimensions, and it may sometimes be possible to slip between them, such as the curious incident that may have taken place in Tokyo during the early 1990s.

A man arrived on a flight with a passport from a nonexistent country. . . .

Although the officials checked their records carefully, the passport had been issued by a country that did not exist. No record showed the country had ever existed. . . .

This passport was real and had customs officials' stamps on various pages including stamps by Japanese customs officials from previous visits.

The man was well-traveled, Caucasian, said the country was in Europe and had existed for almost 1,000 years. He carried legal currency from several European countries, an international driver's license and spoke several languages. . . .

After being detained for almost fourteen hours in a small security room at the airport terminal, some government officials took pity on him and transported him to a hotel. They ordered the mystery visitor to wait there until they decided what to do about the matter. From the reports, the Japanese were just as confused and flustered as the mysterious man without a country.

Although two immigration officials were posted with instructions not to permit the man to leave his room, the next morning the guards discovered he was gone. The only exit was the door they watched and the only window had no outside ledge and was fifteen stories above a busy downtown street.

The authorities launched an intensive manhunt throughout Tokyo for the mysterious traveler, but finally gave up the hunt.

The man was never seen again.*

---

*This and other curious cases can be read at http://beforeitsnews.com/story/1575/265/ Terrified_Woman_From_Another_Universe_Wakes_Up_Here.html.

"In string theory we are forced to confront the idea of other dimensions. It is the only theory that has been able to unify all the laws of physics," remarks hyperspace theorist Michio Kaku.

This historical crisis or singularity we're approaching is like a transition from a low dimensional world—say a world of two or three dimensions—to a world of four or five or six dimensions. . . . The best practice for the approaching singularity is the repeated dissolving and reconstituting of one's personality through the use of psychedelic substances. . . . *Salvia divinorum* . . . is definitely one of the plants which will shape the next few decades of the new millennium.

TERENCE MCKENNA (SPEAKING IN THE 1990s)

THE SPIRIT OF THE SHEPHERDESS

Pendell sees in Salvia the qualities of "midnight . . . moon . . . birth . . . lust . . . exile. . . ," which my vision of her confirms. After witnessing her birth I was taken by her to a forest where the moon and midnight sky were motifs. Lust—in her appearance and attitude and even the way of her birth (in a brothel-church to a slut-nun drunk with mescal)—was also apparent. A perverse virgin I have called her. My participants had a sense of this too: "She was made of beauty and darkness," said Sue, who also perceived her as "a nun dressed in a clear latex white veil." Not your average nun then.

Exile is implied in our perceptions of The Shepherdess as a union of opposites. Being both light and shade, virgin and whore, child and crone, puts her in a powerful position because it means that she is all things, but it leaves her nowhere, an outcast with no affiliations and no one like her to identify with or relate to.

Nowhere and nothingness, being outside of time and space, and the sense that nothing is real are qualities inherent in Salvia, as those who smoke it discover. Through this they come to understand that they—and everyone—are ultimately alone, exiled from all they believed to be true. (John: "No one else was there, no one can save me. . . . I have to do this for myself.")

Paradoxically, however, it is this very aloneness that unites us because it leaves us all in the same pointless position. We realize, then, that our only hopes for salvation are love, presence, and the conscious decision to make new and better choices. Then nowhere may become now, here.

Bobby: "The overall sense was one of presence. The moment was all there was. It was the here and now that so many systems of spiritual and religious thought seem to yearn for."

> *There is a field. I will meet you there.*
> *When we lie in that grass we understand that the*
> *   world cannot even be spoken of.*
> *Thoughts, words, even the idea of separate beings*
> *   makes no sense.*
>
> RUMI

TIME

Salvia is the Mistress of Time. (Darryl: "It seemed like the hugest wave . . . what was folding in were 3-, 4-, 5- isosceles-type interlocking emerald green shapes. She told me that this was time.") It is not surprising then that time travel is one of her gifts.

Siebert refers to the resurfacing of "past memories, such as revisiting places from childhood" but *memory* is not a strong enough word. In his first experiment with salvinorin, for example, he found himself in his grandparents' living room furnished as it was when he was a child. As he remarks, "This *was* the real world, *not a memory or a vision*. I was really there and it was all just as solid as the room I'm sitting in now."

> *In this state all the points of time in my personal history*
> *coexisted. One did not precede the next. Apparently, had*

I so willed it, I could return to any point in my life and
really be there because it was actually happening right
now. . . .

DANIEL SIEBERT

During my first journeys I was also taken back to my childhood. I was with my mother in streets I knew forty years ago. I can't say that these were memories though because the events that took place in my visions were not recollections of things I *know* to have happened or significant enough to have been "issues" that I have repressed. To me, as for Siebert, they were entirely real and happening now. It felt as if Salvia was giving me an opportunity to revisit the past and not exactly relive it but change my view of it (and consequently change the future and present as well) by experiencing it in a new way that might have an impact now. In other words, these were not memories in the way we understand them but a form of time travel: dimensional shifts to a place where, as Michael Talbot expressed it, "The universe had bifurcated and I had been able to take another of its paths, which I had not explored at the time, by perceiving my childhood(s) differently."[5]

Childhood and childhood-related themes were also present in the journeys of fellow explorers. Both Tracie and Josephine mentioned them during our work in Peru, and Sue, Alex, Hannah, and Marla spoke of them in Spain, most often in connection to how they had been treated by their parents. This form of time travel allowed them insight into themselves and the direction of their lives and, again, gave them the ability to make changes if they wished because, as Lela remarked, "Life is [merely] an artificial reality where we slow down time to experience living and enjoy it."

A wholly different form of time travel was made available to Rob, however. After his second Salvia journey he was shown how it might actually be possible when he experienced the dawn twice. This was not a vision or hallucination since it took place hours after he had smoked the extract; rather it was a shift in time or his perception of it. Again, the findings at CERN suggest that time travel is not only possible but already happening around and within us at a subatomic level. The warnings that Rob received from Salvia that "all human beings are capable of time travel—literally—but we are not ready for it yet," come at an appropriate moment in our evolution then. "We need to walk before we can run."

> *If, as science tells us, time itself can be altered by unrelated factors such as gravity and motion perhaps other factors of a more penetrating interior nature should not be dismissed so readily. Ironically, time, it seems, needs a perceiver of its passage to exist.*[6]
>
> J. D. ARTHUR

A Salvia-Inspired Joke

The Higgs-Boson walks into a church. The priest takes one look and is immediately rude and dismissive. "I'm sorry," he says, "but you'll have to leave. We don't allow hypothetical, elementary, so-called God particles in here."

The Higgs-Boson looks hurt, shuffles its feet for a while, and then says, "But without me you can't have mass . . ."

TIME SHIFTS

THE 1950S, '60S, AND '70S

In many of my journeys, for some reason, I found myself in scenes and situations from periods of history that I had no personal experience of. I thought this might be a quirk unique to me, but others have found themselves in the same eras and have not lived through them either—the 1950s, '60s, and '70s being most significant—such as Lela, my participant in Spain: "The room became a kitchen decorated in a 1960s or '70s style." Lela is in her early thirties so she has no firsthand knowledge of the '60s and little awareness of the '70s. This does not mean that she hasn't ever seen films, photographs, or images from that era or heard her parents talking about it, of course, but that is qualitatively different to *being* in the 1960s, which is where she found herself.

Rereading Arthur's book I found a similar reference in his experiences to "the same '50s motifs." He offers no suggestion as to why these might occur, however, and did not seem to have enjoyed them. He describes them as "meaningless, repulsive images from the '40s and '50s. Cartoon characters, crooning trios from the '40s, roller-skating carhops: all made their appearance in a maddening swirl of nonsense."[7]

Since this is not just my experience I have thought about what the message in this might be. The themes or concerns of the ages may be important. The 1950s were culturally and creatively the time of science fiction, new technology—science fact: the atom bomb—and a fascination with time travel, other dimensions, and outer space, captured in films such as Moliére's *Forbidden Planet* and *War of the Worlds*. This theme continued in the 1960s (e.g., in the classic *2001: A Space Odyssey*), prompted by our literal reaching for other worlds in the space race that got us to the moon. In the 1970s we were still absorbed by such ideas (e.g., *Close Encounters of the Third Kind, Alien*) but by the 1980s our obsession with space and other dimensions was starting to wane as we enjoyed our *Bonfire of the Vanities* on Earth. We have never returned to the moon.

Given this brief history why might Salvia want to take us back to these eras? Perhaps, in its dreamlike way, it is telling us where it came from by referencing our own cultural symbols and interests: literally from other worlds?*

As strange as this idea might sound, I am not alone in it. A number of my participants refer to alien themes and otherwordly sensations

---

*No one on Earth at least, scientist or shaman, appears to know where else it might originate; there are no creation myths to describe it, and according to Mazatec shamans it seems rather to have "just appeared" one day.

(John, for example, in one of his Salvia dreams, found himself watching a TV show "about plants from outer space") and the artist Bruce Rimell, whose work *The Origin of Salvia Divinorum* appears in this book,* seems to have arrived at a similar conclusion.

> *We were scientists and we tested xca maria,*
> *took her leaves to our labs and examined and*
> *analyzed 'til the sun was down.*
> *We found that she lacked dna, no genetic impulse*
> *at all.*
> *She is either not alive or not terrestrial*
> *And we knew then that she had come from another*
> *dimension.*
> *(I remember looking up to the sky and wondering*
> *which star she might have dropped from.)*

Or maybe Salvia is telling us where our future lies—and preparing us for the curious things we may find there as we take our next evolutionary step to become citizens of the universe? (Darryl: "The Shepherdess helps me to see all that may ever be.")

SENSATIONS OF MOTION

BEING PULLED OR TWISTED

Almost everyone who smokes Salvia experiences this. I am pulled to the floor. George, our mesa ceremony participant in Spain, fell backward through space. Hannah describes how she felt "stretched . . . I was afraid that when I came back I would never be able to enter myself again because my human body was just too small." Sue recalls how "my body was pulled backward, twisted and contorted," while Lela felt herself "flying over the room."

Arthur also writes about "the overwhelming sensation of movement.

---

*See the color insert

Initially there seemed to be a rapid forward movement as if one were plunging headlong into a pool of water," which is reminiscent of Josephine's experiences. She too described a rapid forward motion and felt the initial effects of the smoke as "like sitting in a pool of water that rose up her body until she went under."

In shamanic terms we might say that Salvia as an aid to journeying causes the soul to take flight from the body with such force and velocity that an equal and opposite reaction takes place in the physical self. Arthur does not go quite this far but he does write about his experience as containing a "seemingly very real potential for leaving the body" that felt "remarkably natural. . . . In the months to come this sensation—that I could abandon the normal physical matrix almost at will—became a regular feature of my experiences with Salvia and seems to be the mechanism of many of the transformative processes that have made their appearance over the course of time."

MEMBRANES, FILMS, AND TWO-DIMENSIONAL SURFACES

This is another consistent theme. Josephine's reality-ending machine was a multilevel conveyor containing layers of landscapes. Trendal writes at Erowid that "everything I was seeing was losing its depth and becoming flat, like a piece of paper." Ronnie, one of my Spanish participants, experienced his body as "a thin piece of paper" and "everyone in the room also became flat, 2-D." Alexia in the United Kingdom makes the same observation: "The Salvia landscape looks very two-dimensional to me."

It is as if Salvia is demonstrating the artificiality or limitations of ordinary reality by showing us a world that is itself limited and without depth or obviously not "real" ("as if it had been programmed on a computer . . . a dream within a dream," Marla). As I discovered in Peru, it is interesting to tear through the fabric of this "unreal reality" and see what lies beyond it: a different order of things for sure and one that is stranger (but may be more real) than the one we are used to.

OVERLAPPING REALITIES

"Every object in my life was also me; like our realities were interchangeable." That was my experience in Peru: that a sort of prebirth agreement had been made between me and everything I encountered, even something as seemingly random and insignificant as a brick, a leaf, or a bus stop. All of it was conscious and aware and shared a purpose and intelligence with me. Others have experienced this too, such as Alex who became wallpaper so literally that she knew what it felt like to enter its existence and *be* it.

I am reminded of Terence McKenna's statement in *Food of the Gods* that "nature is alive and talking to us. *This is not a metaphor.*" Everything has meaning and information for us because whatever shares its existence with us *is* us. John: "Reality is alive. . . . I am just part of it and I can't separate myself from anything else."

> The universe is not only stranger than we imagine, it is stranger than we can imagine.
>
> J. B. S. HALDANE

Salvia teaches us that the universe does indeed bifurcate and that—consciously or otherwise—we create new realities every second of the day through the choices we make that change the nature of our connections to the world around us.

Suppose you have a car crash, for example. Weather conditions, traffic flow, and the actions of other drivers may all be factors because they are a part of your shared reality too. But there are also other, more subtle forces at play: your decision to drive on that road instead of another, or to leave home at that precise time—thirty seconds earlier or later and the crash would never have happened—so you also have a metaphysical relationship with space and time. Even your choice of that particular car may be significant. If you had chosen another you would not have crashed; someone else may have instead.

Other more apparently random things may also be involved—like what you ate that morning, the shoes you were wearing, or how you said goodbye to your lover—because, as quantum physics tells us, everything is connected, part of a vast and changing dream, and we are its dreamers. In a sense then you and your car had a destiny to fulfil: an appointment you both had to keep at a site preordained for that crash, but make a new choice along the way and change any one of the factors above and a different outcome would have resulted.

Given the complexity of these interrelationships, however, is it really possible to change anything? Could that accident have been prevented?

Perhaps.

Because we are part of everything—and at some level we therefore know everything—we are capable of insights, glimpses of the future that hint at the consequences of our decisions before we make them, signs and omens delivered to us by the universe in feelings and symbols. What we choose to do with them, however, is up to us.

A personal example: Josephine and I separated on the night of her sister's wedding, having attended the ceremony that day. We had looked forward to the wedding for months but a few days before it I began to have feelings of foreboding. I even tried to avoid going by telling my wife that I may be late in arriving so it might be best if I didn't attend. She wanted me there, however, so against my intuition I agreed.

The morning of the event, as I dressed for it I discovered that an earring I had bought for the occasion in the shape of a heart was broken. Nothing else in my bag was damaged. Then the clearest image popped into my head from nowhere: I was dressed in my wedding suit, lying on the ground screaming while Josephine looked down on me in anger. It was so real, so unexpected, and so hideous that I had to shake my head to be clear of it.

Acting on any of those signs and avoiding the wedding would have created a new reality—a new bifurcation and outcome—but I ignored them because I didn't want to let my wife down. That decision changed everything. By the same token, if Josephine had not left on that particular night things might also be different. But once you have involved others in a personal relationship and put yourself center stage on your sister's wedding day you have few options but to end your own marriage no matter how much it hurts because that is the reality you have created, the story you have woven, and the audience you have gathered around you. Eventually you must also believe the story yourself.*

Our lives are complex, strange, and interconnected: we with everything else. But occasionally we are allowed a glimpse of the future—or of one possible future, one new dimension we might enter—and that may at least give us an opportunity to manage them better. Perhaps Salvia is a plant that can help us to grow more skillful in this by showing us the connections between ourselves and all we are a part of. Then we can make new choices, *if* we decide to.

PINS AND NEEDLES

Many people experience pins and needles when smoking Salvia. For example, Hannah: "The first sensation was my arms tingling, like pins and needles," and Marla: "My body was filled with pins and needles and reality became metallic, matrixlike."

I first had this experience when I touched the "reality wave" of the street I saw in the moloka in Peru. I had the sense then that I was feeling different dimensions pass through me and that I could sometimes feel this in everyday life, even without smoking Salvia.

Some scientists talk now about eleven-dimensional hyperspace: the notion that there *must be* (at least) eleven dimensions—most of them invisible and unknown to us—for the universe we are aware of to work. (The universe we are *not* aware of is, of course, an enduring mystery). Perhaps it is not too far-fetched to imagine that we *can* sense these other dimensions, or that plants like Salvia enhance this ability. If so then

---

*Believing our own stories is problematic, however, because it makes them part of our patterns and what I have come through Salvia to regard as the absolute reality of karma (also see the section on Love and Karma on page 192), which means that we will also have to experience them from the flipside. Not staying fluid but investing in stories told from a singular perspective links us to something fundamental and inevitable, some of which will definitely not be pleasant.

trance shamanic practices like journeying and visualization should also help us to hone this skill by taking us out of the everyday world with its own trance-based limitations and giving us access to new and more expansive realms of information and possibility.

WHEELS

Wheels and cogs appear in a number of Salvia journeys. I became a pram wheel. Lela saw "circles that joined together." Michael found himself "trapped on a huge cog, which was rotating, going round and round." Then there is Vulpine's account at Erowid: "I was a five-pointed wheel. Reality itself was the five-spoked wheel. . . . It had infinite depth, like each spoke of the wheel was a long shelf stretching out into the distance . . . like a paddle wheel on a boat."

The wheel or circle is a symbol that Salvia seems to like as much as human beings do. We have used it across ages and cultures to represent wholeness, holiness, completion, unity, love, the journey of the pilgrim soul, the circle of life, the wheel of destiny. It may mean any of these things during a Salvia journey as well and act as a reminder from the plant about what is important in life: completion of the self through our awareness of what is real and, most importantly, faith in the power of love to create beauty and growth from emptiness and potential: the void we came from and will return to. Without love there is no progress or evolution.

The precise significance of the wheel will be different for everyone who sees it, of course, but, it seems to me, often in relation to a need for love and completion. The first time she smoked, Josephine felt "a rolling sensation" and saw what she described as "a huge waterwheel" accompanied by "a sense of something from her childhood." At the time she was also working with ayahuasca and San Pedro so she could open to trust and deal with family issues and dramas that went back to her preteen years. For me it was a warning about becoming stuck in relationship patterns. For Michael it may have contained a similar caution since he was also "trapped . . . going around and around."

Once we understand the message our healing begins. Lela: "I realized that circling is no fun. In the center of the 8 I was whole again."

Then the circle can start to complete itself. John: "I saw a medicine wheel in the sky and all parts of it were in harmony and balance."

HEXAGONS

The image of hexagons is another prevalent one. The moloka became filled with them but they made their appearance in Spain and England too. Leon (Spain): "The room turned into hexagons." Hannah (Spain): "She [the spirit of Salvia] wore a dress patterned with hexagons." Alexia (U.K.): "I recall seeing many geometric repetitive patterns (hexagons)." It may simply be Salvia's "painting style" as she imposes her structure on our view of the world so we see reality through her eyes.

TELEPATHY AND EMPATHY

Feelings of connection, togetherness, empathy, and even telepathy are mentioned by many Salvia smokers. Michael: "It was like I had telepathy because I thought I could hear Marla talking to me from across the room. . . . Just as I thought that she began to crawl over to me." Bobby: "It [Salvia] seemed to add to a sense of our togetherness and was a bit telepathic; I wasn't sure if we were speaking or sharing thoughts."

The ability to instill this level of connection may be one of Salvia's gifts to healers and therapists, enabling them to empathize more deeply with clients and sense the healing they require. Sandy and Alexia, both psychotherapists, remarked on this. Sandy: "I would often smoke [Salvia] prior to a therapy session and found it really helped me to see my client's view of things and to feel what they were going through." Alexia: "On many occasions when I have worked with clients [after smoking Salvia] I have been hyperintuitive to their needs and issues, and they have commented on this."

For similar reasons couples (or those involved in relationship counseling or even tantric practices) might also benefit from Salvia. As Pendell says: "It's . . . ideal for couples work."

ZEN PARADOXES

Of all the plants I have worked with, Salvia is the one that most evokes a Zen sensation—the experience of paradox in the union of opposites—which is also at the heart of The Shepherdess: that the void may also be full, that nothing may also be something, that a virgin may be a whore.

Again more than with any other plant, *Zen* is the word I most frequently hear used by others when explaining their Salvia experiences. For example, Stuart, who felt Salvia to be "like a Zen meditation on the 'formless field of benefaction,'" or Bobby, who says, "It felt very Zen—an experience of the Void, which was also completely full, a paradox that seemed to be the very essence of Zen . . . myself and 'God' or 'spirit' were one."

Paradox is also manifested in the actions of some people who have smoked Salvia with me. During a workshop in 2012, for example, one participant was a woman who had been repeatedly sexually abused by family members and later, to escape from home, had become a prostitute. She had put that behind her now and was training with me as a healer. One issue she wanted to free herself from was a repetitive pattern of attracting the "wrong type of man"; one who typically regarded her as a sex object instead of a human being. Having dealt with her past, what was it about her, she wondered, that still invited such men?

As soon as she smoked she began to panic and I went over to help. Some residual part of her consciousness must have recognized me not as "Ross" but as "man" because she began to scream at me to get away from her and leave her alone. At the same time, however, she was clutching my arm and almost pulling me physically on top of her. That paradox or contradiction between the words spoken and the actions she used, between expressed intent and actual expression, was the crux of her issue, and in just seconds she had answered the question that had puzzled her for years and led to her relationship patterns. Saying no but meaning yes (or perhaps genuinely meaning no but not having the faith or belief in her own power to really make a refusal) was the cause of her problems, a paradox revealed by Salvia in seconds but worth years of therapy.

Another woman on the same course smoked Salvia and experienced herself being crushed by a giant boot that squashed her into the tread of its sole. Instead of panicking, however, she began laughing hysterically at how amusing she found it to be ground down into the earth. The paradox again. This was a woman who felt downtrodden in life and unable to believe in herself or express her own truth. To even attend my course she had brought with her an entire suitcase of medications. She longed for freedom, she said, but her actions—laughing at her own violation—showed the reverse.

Perhaps for these reasons of breakthrough and insight Salvia might be a useful aid to therapists and also to meditation on the core questions at the heart of our human condition and religious philosophies. Certainly it is a philosopher's plant, enabling us not just to hear and ponder a Zen koan in our search for enlightenment but to *experience* and *live* it.

LOVE AND KARMA

Salvia can feel emotionless, straightforward, and direct. Arthur calls it "almost without feeling." The passing of information seems sterile and clinical, cold even, and certainly very different from the teachings of San Pedro (fatherly and protective) or ayahuasca (motherly and supportive). John: "I didn't feel any personality to Salvia except something metallic not flesh . . . like pure mathematics with an organic feel."

Salvia just tells it like it is, like the day when, mourning the loss of my wife, the plant simply laughed and told me to take off my wedding ring because she'd already broken the biggest promise she'd ever made so it was pointless to ask her for others.

Is there any more direct?

DALE PENDELL

This absence of love—not quite lovelessness but "freedom from love" or disengagement from the illusions and projections that can accompany it—is understandable when you have met The Shepherdess and seen the circumstances of her birth. It is part of her personality. But those who meet her tend to fall in love with her anyway. Marla: "She was . . . strong and loving, dark, macabre, and beautiful." Sue: "She was made of beauty and darkness." Darryl: "She is a comfort and feels like a lover: all heart and excitement."

What is more significant for us though, when we return from our journeys having encountered the void and had our experience of no-love and no-thing-ness, is the equal-and-opposite realization that love is not just significant, *it is all we have,* all that can save us, all that is real, all that is worth fighting for, and what makes us unique as a species. It is part of the Salvia paradox: to be in the place of no-love is to know the importance of true love.

Arthur believes that Salvia takes us to the Land of the Dead. I am not sure that is true* but it certainly takes us to a place beyond ordinary life and has much in common with the near-death experience. The International Association for Near-Death Studies tells us that "almost every near-death 'experiencer' reports a changed understanding of what life is all about. . . . Becoming more loving is important. . . . Deepened belief in God or a higher power is almost certain. . . . Some people find they have an increase in intuitive or psychic abilities."

Also common to the Salviac and near-death states is the realization that karma is not just a theory. When I consulted Salvia over the end of my marriage, for example, I saw that it was inevitable not only because of how we had behaved in our relationship but how we behaved in our lives. Like the image of wheels rotating, what goes around comes around.

This has ties to another Salviac concept, that of overlapping realities, that we are connected to everything we experience and need, therefore, to act in an appropriate way toward everyone and everything we encounter *because it is us.* To remain in balance we must be as neutral

---

*I would say that it takes us to other dimensions, *one* of which is what we, from our human perspective, might call the Land of the Dead: a world of phantoms in human form.

as Salvia herself; to burn karma or accumulate merit we must behave impeccably and with dignity because if we relate to life in a way that is not in the spirit of love, we will attract those same unloving things to ourselves. Finally, in our quest for salvation we *have* to understand that love is all that matters.

Fighting Death with Love

Everything started to break down. . . . I mean literally. The room started to spin in a strange direction . . . pieces of me were being broken off. . . . I remember being disgusted at how pointless and wrong my life was [but] I wasn't ready to die. . . . I yelled out with my whole soul that I needed to go back to Earth and spend A LOT more time with the girl I loved. . . . I was driven by love, and it stopped death for me. . . . After I was completely sober all I wanted to do was go see the one I loved and just be around her. And because of salvia I'm never too far away from her now . . . because I never want to be permanently separated from her like I truly thought I was gonna be.

RELENTLESS*

---

*The account of a 5X concentrate smoker at www.erowid.org

8

DIETING THE SHEPHERDESS: A DNA FANTASY

The Purpose of the Ally and the Dietary
Encounter with Ska Maria

*At first she is elusive and fleeting as she invites one
to come deeper into the space but after a while her
manifestations become more sustained and with her
presence reason begins to break down . . . one finds
oneself asking whether the plant itself is attempting to
communicate . . .*

BRUCE RIMELL, SALVIASPACE.NET

The "success" of the human genome project and the claims of some scientists (or at least the media that report their findings) could lead us to believe that we now understand human beings, have unraveled the mysteries of DNA (the "building blocks" of life that supposedly account for all we are) and discovered through this that we're just a mechanical structure, part of a mechanical process, and there's no mystery left to our lives.

How sad would that be? And fortunately it's not true because these claims are, in fact, based on a less-than-intimate knowledge of just 3 percent of DNA. The rest of it, noncoded DNA, has traditionally been dismissed as "junk" on the basis that scientists can find no purpose or use for it. They see it as detritus instead, a useless accumulation of material from millions of years of evolution. But it may actually be where we will find the most useful answers to the questions of human existence: Where did we come from? Who made us? What are we doing here? Through junk the mystery continues . . .

Junk DNA (molecular biologists call it *introns*) got its name because the nucleotides it contains do not encode instructions for making proteins so it appears to have no use. The majority of genetic material in any organism consists of noncoding DNA, however (in humans, 97 percent of the genome), which would be an awful waste of space if none of it served a purpose: so can it all be junk? Over the last ten years scientists have begun to question their early dismissals. "The feeling," says Boston University physicist Eugene Stanley, "is that there's something going on in the noncoding region."

Physicists noticed a few years ago that there were certain patterns in junk DNA, long-range correlations called 1/f noise* that suggested that it might contain some kind of organized information, some intelligence, or message.

In an attempt to discover what it was, Stanley and his colleagues borrowed from the work of linguist George Zipf who had previously carried out a study of texts from different languages to rank the frequency with which words occur. There is a distinct relationship pattern, such that Zipf's law is able to state that for any text in any language from any era the most frequently used word will occur twice as often as the second most frequent word, which occurs twice

---

*A great name for a band incidentally, if it hasn't been thought of already.

as often as the fourth most frequent, and so on. In any text, that is—including the one you're holding—if the most frequently used word is *the* and it appears ten thousand times, the next most common (e.g., *and*) will be used five thousand times. The law was developed and successfully used for code-breaking in espionage and war scenarios.

Stanley applied it to DNA, testing it on forty sequences in species ranging from viruses to humans. In every case, junk DNA followed Zipf's law while the coding regions did not. In other words, 97 percent of us is not junk. *It is language.*

Every language also has built-in "redundancies" so that a few confused words or typos do not make a sentence incomprehensible. We can fill in the blanks and correct the mistakes ourselves so we still understand it.* Knowing this, the researchers applied a second analysis just to be sure, this one based on the work of information theorist Claude Shanon who in the 1950s† had quantified redundancies in languages. They found that junk DNA contains nearly four times the redundancies of coding segments. Again, *it is a language,* which, like all languages, follows a "hierarchical arrangement of information."[1]

The simplest way to summarize this is to say that hidden within our DNA there are libraries of books. Which begs the questions, Who put them there, and what do they say?

JUST A THOUGHT . . .

Now let's try a thought experiment, a flight of fantasy really. Just suppose that a few million years ago a more advanced alien race—from our dimension or another—for one reason or another, needed to hide or store their collective knowledge in some location other than their home world. Maybe their planet was under threat of extinction,

---

*For example, in this sentence: "You now what I man to say" (you know what I mean to say).

†That era again!

or they were at war and wanted to make sure that whatever happened they would preserve their wisdom and culture so there would be no Nazi book burnings on a planetary scale. And just suppose that on their travels they found another species (us) in which they could hide that record by storing it in their DNA, similar to what we are doing now with genetic modification. A few million years ago we were hardly likely to attract interest from their alien rivals who were searching the galaxy for this knowledge since we were still oozing around in pond slime or stumbling through forests dragging our knuckles.

Now let's skip ahead to a mere one-and-a-half million years ago because something strange and remarkable happened then. The human brain underwent what Rita Carter, in her book *Mapping the Mind*, describes as

> an explosive enlargement. So sudden was it that the bones of the skull were pushed outward, creating the high, flat forehead and domed head that distinguish us from primates. The areas that expanded most are those concerned with thinking, planning, organizing and communicating. . . . The frontal lobes of the brain duly expanded by some 40 per cent to create large areas of new gray matter: the neo-cortex. This spurt was most dramatic at the very front, in what are known as the prefrontal lobes. These jut out from the front of the brain, and their development pushed the forehead and frontal dome of the head forward, reforming it to the shape of a modern skull.[2]

Nobody knows what caused this dramatic and sudden expansion of the brain but a growth in consciousness would do it because we would need more gray matter in order to process and store the new information we now had access to.

Some, like Terence McKenna, have argued that this expansion and new capacity for thought arose directly from our ingestion of plants such as fly agaric, psilocybin mushrooms, and other psychedelic species when human beings were nomadic hunter-gatherers and would eat whatever they found.[3] Accidentally, perhaps purely in search of food, we discovered the very plants that would unlock the alien knowledge within us and allow at least some of it to leak into consciousness. And from that we built civilizations, perhaps following alien blueprints. McKenna went further, suggesting that some plants may actually be alien technologies, "space spores" sent to Earth deliberately to speed our evolution by giving us access to this knowledge. Perhaps our alien forefathers, realizing their days were numbered, wanted us to unlock their hidden wisdom to ensure that it would not be wasted, so that they could, in a sense, live on through us.*

Maybe Salvia is a plant of this kind? Until recently no one had heard of it (even the shamans, it appears), and nobody (even botanists) really knows where it came from. (Is it naturally occurring or cultivated and created?) But numerous Salvia trips do have an alien theme and point to technologies beyond our own. People are spun through time and space. They see alien beings, blue Gods with annihilation machines, dream machines, purification or regeneration machines, and landscapes that are unearthly. As often as not, they end up in outer space at the center of reality and creation. John: "I was aboard a spacecraft with lots of other people—like a kind of ark." Marla: "We were all lying down in a perfect line like seeds or cocoons on a spaceship. . . . It was like we were being used in some way or I was in an experiment." Michael: "An alien experiment was taking place."

In my fantasy this scenario might also explain alien abductions or at least tell us what our abductors are looking for when they perform their experiments on us: the secrets of the universe no less that we have locked inside us.

---

*As strange as this may sound as a theory of human evolution and consciousness it is far from unique among those who have worked extensively with psychedelics. "Like [John] Lilly [ketamine, LSD] [Timothy] Leary [most notably LSD] believed that extraterrestrial beings were more likely to contact us through inner rather than outer space on the basis that awareness can enter the inner quantum realm where the speed of light is transcended and nonlocal connections become possible." Karl Jansen, *Ketamine: Dreams and Realities*

That's all a modern myth though, a thought experiment as I said. What *is* true is that there is a language within our DNA, a library of books that plants like Salvia may help us read. And if we can do that we can at least make better sense of our lives and enhance our own evolutionary potential because greater awareness gives us more power for positive change.

> *The real secret of magic is that the world is made of words, and if you know the words that the world is made of you can make of it whatever you wish.*[4]
> TERENCE MCKENNA

We have to know how to work with these plants in order to access that information though, and in my experience (and with Salvia in particular), that begins with the diet.

DIETING SALVIA

Schultes and Winkelman define the diet as

> a tool helping to maintain the altered state of consciousness, which permits the plant teacher to instruct, provide knowledge, and enable the initiate to acquire power. The diet is viewed as a means of making the mind operate differently, providing access to wisdom and lucid dreams.[5]

From this perspective, the diet is a way of releasing the hold of the ego-mind. As it progresses the sense even of being human may diminish as the dieter becomes more "plant like," taking on the personality of Salvia, becoming calmer, more relaxed, and freeing the mind so that in contrast to the normal human condition—where we often believe or pretend that we have all the answers—we can honestly say we know Nothing. It is under these conditions that we can start to communicate with the plant in dreams and meditations and eventually in everyday life.

Alternatively you can think of the diet as like growing a plant inside you. Every plant is small and delicate at first and requires attention, care, and nurturing in order to get it established. That is what the diet does: it "brings on" the plant.

Dieting the leaves is totally different from smoking the extract. The latter is an intense experience where the lessons of the plant are dumped so suddenly and heavily on you that you are often left reeling with no time to assimilate them. The diet, however, is a gentle, step-by-step process that allows you to connect with and integrate the wisdom of the plant. This leads to a permanent change through the relationship you establish.

The connection, at first, may appear metaphorical or symbolic because the presence of the plant will be small. But as it takes root in you and your connection to it deepens and grows, that presence will start to be felt across the whole of your being: physically, spiritually, mentally, and emotionally as the plant merges with your consciousness and begins to alter your psycho-spiritual or emotional DNA. As John discovered on his Salvia diet, once the plant is in you it is "just there," like an aura around you, and it will communicate constantly, quietly, and proactively, offering advice when it is needed and not just in ceremony but with an alert watchful awareness, which, had I given it more attention, may have saved me a parking fine, maybe even a marriage.

The diet that achieves this involves certain actions and restrictions on the behavior of the dieter so he can learn from his ally and prepare his body and nervous system for the expansion in consciousness that the spirit of Salvia brings.

Dietary restrictions prohibit foods such as pork, fats, salt, sugar, spices, condiments, and alcohol, leaving the apprentice with an extremely bland menu so he is not overwhelmed with flavor and can more finely sense the attributes of the plant. This uninspiring menu also weakens his attachments to routine life, some of which revolve around meal times and typical foods. For the same reason there is a prohibition on sexual activity since sex is another distraction that will ground him in his body and inhibit spiritual progress. Detachment from the physical world and its consensus routines is, in this sense, a prerequisite to entering the Salvia mind. In the words of curandero Guillermo Arevalo, "That is why the shaman goes into the wilderness. There is no temptation there."

Whenever I diet a plant, in fact, I prefer to eat nothing and to drink water or one of the less flavorsome herbal teas. When I administer a diet to others, however, I usually allow meals made from rice, lentils, boiled potatoes, lettuce, spinach, cucumber, and chickpeas; rarely anything else. And for the three days when the plant is drunk I suggest that there is no food at all. The dieter should also avoid chemicals and chemically based products such as toothpaste, deodorant, perfume, and so on. If he wishes to wash he can shower in water, no soap.

According to Diaz, who studied with the Mazatecs, the first Salvia diet should last sixteen days. The traditional Amazonian diet for making an ally of any plant, however, lasts fourteen days and this is the method I have always followed. The Salvia is made into a tea with thirty pairs of leaves added to hot water, and the infusion is allowed to stand overnight before being drunk first thing in the morning. The leaves can then be chewed and held in the mouth between the teeth and cheek for fifteen minutes or until they dissolve, and then are swallowed. This continues for either three or seven days. Three is more usual for Amazonian diets but I have done both.

At the end of this week a little lemon, salt, sugar, and onion is eaten to break the diet and provide a safe boundary to the experience while offering a form of protection to the plant so it can continue to grow. The after-diet continues for another week, and although the same restrictions apply to sex, alcohol, pork, and strong spices, other foods can now be eaten, though it is still wise to keep salt and citrus fruits to a minimum.

The biggest challenge for a Westerner undertaking this diet is often not the requirements and prohibitions of the regime (although they can be hard as well because food is such a routine part of our lives, and we tend to crave it when dieting even if we had little interest in it before) but to accept that there is another order of nonmaterial reality that the apprentice can experience through his entrance into plant consciousness. We are born into the social paradigm that surrounds us, with all of its beliefs, myths, and institutions that support its view of the world, and it is not within ours to easily accept the immaterial and irrational.

Before we embark on such a diet then, we often need to question some of our most deeply ingrained assumptions. We need to ask ourselves, for example, if our most basic building blocks of reality—not DNA but time and space—are all there are. Is our perception of time correct: that it is linear and sequential, like a river flowing only in one direction? (Our first Salvia pipe will teach us otherwise.) Is space made up only of material things and the gaps between them? (Again, Salvia will show us a different truth, perhaps that we are not material at all. Rob: "There was no 'me,'" or that we can be any material form: a brick, a wheel, a wardrobe. . . .) Do we create our *own* times and spaces, moment-on-moment, from the data available in all of the dimensions around us? Our scientists who are now basing their theories on the existence of eleven dimensions believe so. In the new science, in fact, this is the only valid model for reality and yet most of these dimensions cannot be seen or proven to exist. Reality, in other words—even "everyday reality"—is simply an act of faith.

Ultimately it comes down to a matter of choice and belief. As John Michell comments in *Confessions of a Radical Traditionalist*:

There are an infinite number of ways in which you can see the world, and an infinite range of data to support or discredit any of them. You can believe in black holes if you like or you can believe in angels. I am not a believer but if I had to choose I would take the latter because unlike the holes, angels have often been sighted, and their influence has generally been for the good.

For shamans of all cultures, the world we perceive through our senses is just one description of a vast and mysterious unseen and not an absolute fact. The Sioux medicine man Black Elk remarked, for example (in words that seem almost Platonic), that behind our perceptions is "the world where there is nothing but the spirits of all things. [It] is behind this one and everything we see here is something like a shadow from that world."[6]

In his book *The Jivaro: People of the Sacred Waterfalls*, Michael Harner writes of a similar belief among the Jivaro of the Ecuadorian rain forests. For them, "The normal waking life is explicitly viewed as 'false' or 'a lie' and it is firmly believed that truth about causality is to be found by entering the supernatural world, or what the Jivaro view as the 'real world,' for they feel that the events, which take place within it, underlie and are the basis for many of the surface manifestations and mysteries of daily life."[7]

Mazatec shaman Maria Sabina said the same:

There is a world beyond ours, a world that is far away, nearby and invisible, and there is where God lives, where the dead live, the spirits and the saints. A world where everything has already happened and everything is known. That world talks. It has a language of its own.[8]

That language is what we learn through the diet. The way that Salvia talks is through symbols and the language of dreams, so silence, introspection, and the nurturing of the dreaming self are also important to the diet if we wish to meet the spirit of the plant.

From experience, I would suggest that you work with the extract only when Salvia is well-established as an ally within you. You need her strength to really explore SalviaWorld and avoid the confusions (and sometimes the fears) that go with it. The message, you will find, is the same—that reality is something we create for ourselves—but the leaves will make it easier for you to digest.

When you feel ready for the extract, for the same reasons, I suggest that you begin at a low concentrate such as 5X strength and build to the level that works best for you. A 5X concentrate is sufficient for a full yet controlled entheogenic experience so the traveler can enter SalviaWorld to explore it but does not get lost there and, as importantly, is able to remember its lessons.

9

THE NATURE
OF THE ALLY:
SOME QUESTIONS

On Reflection, a Summary: What Can You Expect

from Your Meeting with The Shepherdess?

*An ally is a power capable of transporting a man beyond
the boundaries of himself . . . to transcend the realm of
ordinary reality.*

CARLOS CASTANEDA, *THE TEACHINGS OF DON JUAN:
A YAQUI WAY OF KNOWLEDGE*

I hope that you will choose to work with The Shepherdess for, as
Terence Mckenna put it, the "historical crisis . . . we're approaching"*
absolutely calls for a return to love, for new faith and a new way of seeing and being: "a transition from a low dimensional world . . . to a world
of four or five or six dimensions."

---

*I would now say *facing* as the old orders of science, economics, politics, and even personal relationships spin out of control and reveal that they were always illusions.

Should you choose to, what can you expect from your meeting with Salvia? These are some questions you may have and my attempt at some answers . . .

What Is the Ally Like?
This is a fair question but there are no definitive answers. Meeting The Shepherdess is a personal quest and how you perceive the ally will be unique to you. Some see her as a beautiful woman with long dark hair, some as an occult child, others as a crone. A number of my participants saw her as a shape-shifter, a mixture of opposites, but some saw nothing at all. One of Pendell's correspondents experienced her not as a woman but as a giant with a belt of skulls. How she looks, however, may be less important than the message she brings and the feeling she leaves you with: that nothing is real and everything is possible.

This is *my* shepherdess:

> *Beautiful and dangerous*
> *Zen and Now*
> *A paradox, a contradiction: merciless and kind.*
> *Supportive but not like a mother, protective but*
>   *not like a friend.*
> *More like an older sister:*
> *there out of duty but sometimes she loves you.*
> *Hormonal too, like women are;*
> *Sometimes she's all over you,*
> *sometimes you work for attention,*
> *sometimes she won't take your calls.*
> *But it's worth it in the end—for the lessons:*
> *Reality is not real, that's the first.*
> *Nor is your life or your future.*
> *You're not even material for that matter*
> *and nor is anything else.*

It's all a potential for something and nothing:
which makes it all pointless and crucial.

What does the smoke-ally teach?
- NOTHING (Nothing matters; matter is nothing; E does not equal MC²)
- "The final truth of all things is that there is no final truth," *Altered States*
- But what is important is LOVE

How does she teach it?
- Through the dream-language of symbols

What does the leaf-ally teach?
- A more immediate and practical Something
- Relax
- Pay attention
- See your patterns
- Know the future
- Change it if you need to

How does she teach it?
- In mathematics and poetry: (John: "Like pure mathematics with an organic feel.")
- She wants us to speak in poetry because she loves "the voices of the damned"
- In feelings rather than words
- Directly ("Watch your car"), but there's a symbol in that too, about allegiance and belief: "Watch your parking meters"; remember that N/nothing is real

Something and Nothing

Something always comes from Nothing and nothing
*   always results. It's the inbreath and outbreath of the*
*   universe.*
In the beginning there was Nothing
Until Nothing got bored of its nothingness
and created Something.
Two Somethings in fact.
And because they were complementary and opposite
the Somethings were attracted to each other.
One day they made love
and created
Nothing.

What are the ally's interests?
- Time (there is no time)
- Space (there is no space)
- (No) Time + (No) Space = (No) Reality (nothing is real)
- Nothing + Belief = Creation (you can have anything you want)
- And since all acts of creation arise from desire the solution to every equation is LOVE. Darryl: "As a guide she is a great companion on an emotional level."

What are the dangers?
- Being crushed by a tsunami wave of reality, followed by the realization that there is no reality, and you've just been crushed by Nothing.
- Insanity. (In a good way. John Lilly, the LSD and ketamine explorer called it "outsanity.") The anti-psychiatrist R. D. Laing defined insanity as "a sane response to an insane world." Salvia shows us how small, insignificant, and insane our world and its concerns can be. All those who stand outside of society, space, or time or who suggest that other dimensions may be possible are by definition (by society's definition at least) insane, and they are also the only people who can move evolution forward

in the face of social stagnation and adherence to norms and principles.* Salvia frees the mind from its normal boundaries and limitations. Martin Ball in his book *Sage Spirit,* for example, discusses the value of the plant for inspiration and creativity in his work as a novelist and musician.

- Death. Fortunately not physical or permanent but a death of the ego and expansion of the self. The question, "Who am I?" is asked a lot by people who return from Salvia journeys. The danger is in the initial shock as our known identity slips away ("There was no me but there was no not-me," says Pendell. "How many people really want to see [that]?") and in the mind-fuck implied by the answers we may arrive at:

I am Nothing = I am limitless
I create reality = I am responsible for all I create

Being human is being responsible—existentially responsible, responsible for one's own existence.†

VIKTOR FRANKL

---

*The standard three-step social response to any truly novel idea is (1) *disparaging* ("That idea is crazy! Ignore or make fun of it."), (2) *defensive* ("That idea is dangerous. Burn the witch!"), or (3) *Decorative*—usually some years after the genius who thought of it is dead ("That idea is brilliant! Give its creator a posthumous award, hang her picture in a gallery, and claim her ideas as our own.").

†There has only been one actual death even remotely connected to Salvia. In January 2006, Brett Chidester, a seventeen-year-old Delaware student, suicided by carbon monoxide poisoning. His parents argued that he was suffering from Salvia-induced depression at the time, having discovered the journals he kept of his journeys, one of which included the philosophically correct and typically Salviac observation that "existence in general is pointless." As a result Brett's Law (Senate Bill 259) was passed in Delaware making Salvia a Schedule 1 substance in that state, alongside heroin, LSD, mescaline, and GHB. Since (and before) this incident there have been no other cases involving or alleging Salvia as a serious factor in suicide, overdose, accidental (or any other kind of) death, prompting the rather brilliantly named San Francisco attorney A (for Alex) Coolman to comment that "it's remarkable that Chidester's parents—and only Chidester's parents—continue to be cited over and over again by the mainstream media in their coverage of the supposed 'controversy' over the risks of *Salvia divinorum*." In the same year in Delaware there were 148 fatalities from drunk-driving, alone.

What are the benefits?

Having Nothing to believe in. Which means that everything is possible and we can make any Something we wish. Pendell: "It's not a spectator drug . . . even consciousness needs a soul."

What are the applications?

- *Educational:* Insight and clarity; knowing your beliefs, limitations, and patterns
- *Divinatory:* Seeing the future, where those patterns lead
- *Course corrective:* Avoiding the outcomes of those patterns by choosing new and better responses
- *Healing:* Learning the lessons so you never have to make the same mistakes
- *Overall:* Protective

Anything else?

Yes, take your time ("focus on what is important; there is no time"). Meet the leaves first and digest what they have to say. Hear them. This is how we learn. Then make your date with the smoke.

10

LOOSE ENDS

A Note on the People You've Met in This Book

If you want to be true to life start lying about the reality of it.

JOHN FOWLES, *THE COLLECTOR*

Before we finish I thought you might like an update on the people, places, and events you have met in this book.

Tracie (chapter 2) no longer runs the ayahuasca center in Peru where this research began, and it has gone through changes. It is now more of a tourist eco-lodge with fishing and bird-spotting trips, a sad state of affairs for a venture that began with good heart and a genuine healing intention. Jungle is no longer the shaman there, and I am no longer involved in it. They never introduced Salvia to their treatment programs.

The retreat center in Spain where Josephine and I continued our research (chapter 3) is no longer in operation either although I still run plant medicine courses and ceremonies in Spain. The center was our home, and when Josephine left the heart went out of it for me. But it was beautiful while that dream lasted.

John (chapter 4) decided to follow the advice of The Shepherdess and train as a healer.

Since you're reading this book, and it is published by Inner Traditions, we can agree that Salvia's prediction (chapter 4) unfolded as the plant foretold, which is another small but significant validation of its power as a diviner.

Many of the students on my Plant Spirit Wisdom course (chapter 5) have returned to explore these and other plants with me and some have become healers themselves. The workshop continues, along with other courses in shamanism, and is teaching us more about Salvia all the time.

Josephine never returned to her home in Spain or to her marriage. When I last heard from her she had dismissed what she once called "the love of my life" and her "ideal life" in Spain as "so much for that" and returned to England to live with her mother. She was back in her childhood home, back in the town she grew up in, and back in her old job with the same "boring" friends around her whom she had belittled because they never seemed to do anything new. Her motto at the time, somewhat ironically, was "onward and upward, never backward." I am not sure how much further backward it is possible to go without regressing to the womb but sometimes it is difficult to stand aside and take note of our own reality and we need an outsider to tell us who we really are. No doubt she will go traveling again soon because that's what she's always done. We became better people when we were together; we were learning from each other and healing, and we had the potential for so much more, but in the end she couldn't commit or forgive—herself or me—for what we had done with the love we were given. I am grateful to her for the work that we did, for the dream we shared, and for everything that I was a part of. I will always be here with smoke and water because that's what I promised her, but I would not want her back. Nor would I want her karma or the reality generated by her "machine." I hope she finds peace, that life treats her well, and that she allows it to.

I returned to England after the most amazing years of my life. I loved being in love, I loved our time in Peru and Spain, and I loved our explorations of Salvia. I came back to a new life, a new lover, new relationships, and a new way of living, having been changed by Salvia and by all that went into our research. As J. D. Arthur also found, "Salvia forced me to reexamine an entire complex of perceptions and assumptions,"[1] and I can never again be the person I was. I still lead groups to Cusco, however, to work with San Pedro in the beautiful Andean mountains, and run shamanic workshops and plant medicine courses in Spain and the United Kingdom. Our lives are as big—or as small—as we want them to be.

The way to know The Shepherdess is to go in search of her yourself. The work continues with you as I said at the beginning. Whatever happens, whatever you discover, it will be an adventure. It was for me. Some of it I would have done differently but none of it I regret.

> *Without some type of direct experience of the transformative nature of substances such as Salvia shedding light on the genuine fallacy of the validity of our normal perceptions and revealing hints about the true nature of the perceiver, any differentiation of the real from the false will remain in the realm of words alone.*[2]
>
> J. D. ARTHUR

THE THIRD
SALVIA DIET

*In Mexico it was believed that the creation of worlds
was assisted by Tocotl, the Spider God, who spins a
hammock to hold up the world. The Mayans believed
that after death the soul wanders the dark passages of the
underworld until it meets a great river, which it cannot
cross on its own. Each soul can only get to the other side
with the help of a spider person. The spider people spin
web rafts and then one spider person and one soul journey
across the underground river, linked in a spiritual bond
so that each is dependent on the other until they reach the
safety of the other side. And this, too, is the nature of love.*

SUZANNE LEE

Josephine abandoned our world of magic and returned to her old life.
The last I heard from her she was living in a box in a nowhere town
and blaming me for that: "I gave you everything; I gave you *me;* you
took everything from me" is how she put it in her last few e-mails. But
I really didn't make her choices for her. I heard from friends soon afterward that she was planning her next great escape to Canada, although

I believe it fell through. What I learned from Salvia by contrast was the importance of staying open to love so we offer even more of ourselves to new possibilities instead of old patterns and fears. As if to prove the point, a few weeks after Josephine left a new woman entered my life: Lillith (Lilly), whom I met in Spain but who relocated to London after I returned to the United Kingdom.

The coincidences were interesting. For a start she knew my ex-wife. In a certain light she even looked like her: a little younger but the same hair, same build, same interests (shamanism, massage, aroma-therapy, astrology, tarot. She was also a Spanish speaker and had plans to travel to Peru . . .). And she loved Salvia. It was as if The Shepherdess was offering me a lineage, as if (from Salvia's point of view at least) Josephine's departure had just been a blip, an interruption in a process that the plant had planned, and she was now providing a new partner with characteristics of *her* choosing so the adventure would continue. It seems possible that the plant itself has a particular "type" of woman that it calls to its sisterhood.

For eight days during Christmas and New Year 2011, Lilly and I dieted Salvia together. In my visions of The Shepherdess, tequila, perhaps unsurprisingly, had been an aspect of the plant spirit, and I was aware that Mazatec rituals sometimes included the ritual consumption of this liquor when the leaves were chewed. For my diet I decided therefore to make a tincture of Salvia in alcohol and to drink it each day while Lilly followed a more traditional diet with the leaves as a tea. We both also made a quid of them that we chewed.

The result of this third diet was further insight into The Shepherdess, how she teaches, and into myself.

She reminded me, for example, of an image she had shown me before, which seemed insignificant then: a street scene where I was being led as a child along a road by my mother who was pulling me by the hand toward an unknown destination. I had not understood the message at the time because the image itself seemed trivial. Now it seemed like the most important of Salvia's messages, especially in light of my life since then, and I remembered something else from my teenage years later, when I got into trouble at school, and my father was called to a conference with the head teacher who wanted to expel me. Explaining my behavior to him, my father had described me as "easily led" by others.

It seemed to be a theme of my life—perhaps the very first and most important theme—but one I had missed when Salvia first showed it to me, probably because it was so central to my identity and who I *thought* I was that it had become an unnoticed and unquestioned habit. It goes like this: I have often thrown myself into the dreams of others, wanting not just to help them realize their potential but doing much of the work for them. Josephine had wanted excitement, for example, travel, and adventure so I gave her Iquitos and the jungle, Cusco and the mountains, Spain, the plants, and a home she loved. She went back instead to all that she said she *didn't* want.

> *I gave you everything you ever wanted.*
> *It wasn't what you wanted*
>
> PAUL HEWSON

By trying too hard to create the dreams of others for them (and so, paradoxically, serving my needs rather than theirs) I had left them nothing to dream. I had also assumed that they *wanted* their dreams to come true but maybe a dream should just stay a dream for some people.

With what I know now, however, and all that Salvia has taught me I had a new commitment to myself that I would never again get involved in the same way with others, and, furthermore, I watch myself now whenever I sense this motif arising in me of being "easily led" into new situations, so I understand what my own motivations are and what needs in me they are signaling. It is evidence again that the messages of Salvia are never without meaning and, no matter how seemingly slight or unimportant, they have value for us; we just need to hear them.

A DICTIONARY OF SALVIA SYMBOLS

Salvia speaks in the language of dreams. It is a language that I and others (e.g., J. D. Arthur) have described as rather oblique: where *bowl* means "name" and *brick* means "worthiness," for example, just as a symbol in a dream often means more (or at least something different) from the thing that is actually seen.

I also suspect that the richness and content of Salvia symbols deepen with exposure to them and that we learn new and more involved symbology as our apprenticeship continues. During our first weeks of kindergarten, for example, we may start with the letter *A* as we learn to read and write but the teacher is more likely to instruct us on the meanings of the word *and* than *atrophy* or *antidisestablishmentarianism*. A scientist told me that the study of physics is a deepening in the same way. At introductory level we learn Newton's laws; at intermediate level we throw that away and hear what Einstein had to say; at degree and postgraduate level we sideline Einstein and enter the quantum world. As our understanding increases, and we have a new platform to build from, we learn something deeper and more relevant to what we consider to be the "real world" and how it operates and all that precedes it becomes an initiation only into the "Way of Science." I imagine that Salvia teaches in the same way, taking us from the basics to greater knowledge and fluency as our immersion in it continues.

The dictionary below should not be regarded as the final word on Salvia, therefore, but rather the first, kindergarten stuff. But at least it is a beginning. It was assembled by Lilly and me during the diet we took together, by listing common symbols (i.e., those experienced during journeys by a number of independent travelers) and asking those who received these symbols not so much what they *saw* as what the things they saw *meant* to them since a bowl may not be a bowl or a brick a brick; it may only look that way. It was also informed by Lilly and me dreaming ourselves back into the feelings we had when we received certain personal symbols and interpreting their meanings from that. Finally, for what it was worth (often not much) we also consulted a few dream dictionaries to see what a more standard interpretation might provide. The latter was less useful since Salvia has a vocabulary of its own, and while it may be related to human dreaming it is more than that and often very personal and extra-personal at the same time. That said, this is our first attempt at a dictionary of symbols and meanings.

(alien) abduction: Lack of control over life or allowing others to take control from you. (See, for example, Marla's account of being on board an alien spacecraft.)

alien(s): Isolation, (emotional) disconnection, feeling outside of things. (See, for example, Josephine's descriptions of a "blue god" at the controls of her annihilation machine.) More positively, new influences and forces of a potentially healing nature.

baby: Initiation; the true self; vulnerability; fear of weakness before others and revelation of true strengths. A new direction, realization, or project. (See, for example, Lela's account.)

baggage (suitcases, etc.): Identity. The past that has shaped, holds, or burdens you.

baptism: Return to a time with no worries or responsibilities. Where baptized (and in what) may signify the first pattern (e.g., the baptism of The Shepherdess in permafrost = coldness and distance; a clinical nature). Renewal. New approaches. Freedom or absolution from "sin" (old and/or unhealthy patterns of behavior). Cleansing, purification, release.

basement: The unconscious; a truth that is hidden.

bowl: Name (according to J. D. Arthur).

brick: Self-worth, value, personal value. When in a wall, one's place in the world, community, family, relationships, and so forth.

childhood: New possibilities, reevaluations of what is felt to be "known"; revisiting one's life story. Innocence.

conveyor: Life; its futility and smallness. Inevitability. When the end of the conveyor belt is seen: (a propensity for) endings, death, or escape.

death: New beginnings (when arising from endings) or danger of being drawn back into old patterns of behavior and emotional engagement or disengagement with the world.

Earth (planet): Limitations to knowledge.

empty street: The falseness of the world; fear of rejection; the emptiness of the self ("Who am I?").

eyes: Universe(s); galaxies; dimensions. Perception: how we view the world.

films: Old patterns; artificiality. The veneer of "reality." The games we play with others (roles, scenarios, etc.). (See, for example, John's account of old and new films.)

fingers: Confirmation; a sure thing (e.g., that you have met The Shepherdess when she interlaces her fingers with yours). Initiation, communication.

fire: Purification. Protection. Passion. Inspiration. Action. The body. Sex.

girlfriend (or wife): Insight into your waking relationship of what she means to you as a symbol of yourself in daily life. (May also be true if a boyfriend or husband appears in the journey but this is unconfirmed from the research.)

half (being half of something or cut in half): Incompletion. (John: "Half is worth half and nothing more.")

hand (holding by Salvia): Acceptance, connection, a fresh start.

hexagon: As a single form, insight from Salvia as to where our lives have become "closed" and old patterns are repeating themselves. In multiple form, a reminder that the universe is infinite and built on choices, that new possibilities are open to us.

ice: Being (emotionally or otherwise) frozen; inability to progress, being stuck.

idols (e.g., the "blue god," nuns, godly entities, and the altar before which Salvia was born): True reality and the falseness or limitations of human gods/beliefs.

immaculate conception (e.g., the birth of Salvia): Opening to a new level of consciousness. The seemingly impossible becoming seemingly possible.

jewelry: Personal value, status, or self-knowledge. (Psychological or unconscious) riches. Self-image.

journeys: Self-discovery; progress; change.

jungle (rain forest, perhaps also forests in general): Potential for growth; aspects of the self that are hidden or chaotic.

karma (sense of): The tendency to attract others (people, things, events) into our lives in line with our identity and actions; necessity for reevaluation or change. (Lilly: "Where your karma runs over your dogma.")

kitchen: (Need for) healing, security, or nourishment (the heart or soul of the "house").

lake (still): Receptivity.

lake (stormy): Emotional blocks; things bubbling to the surface.

landscapes (changing or various forms of): Emotional progress. But where these landscapes come to an end, therefore (for example, on an "annihilation conveyor") emotional blockages or lack of progress; things lost or being given away. Reflections of inner and outer landscapes. (See, for example, Josephine's accounts.)

laughter: Need to lighten up and not subscribe to "reality" as in any way serious or real. Being laughed at: insecurity and/or feeling unaccepted or unappreciated. (See, for example, Rob's accounts.)

moon: The Shepherdess.

neighborhood: Belonging and acceptance, power and identity (or their opposites, according to mood and feelings).

night: Death-rebirth; reflection; new beginnings; the shadow-self.

nun: "None" or "nothing" (meaning all or everything; potential and possibilities). Purity, chastity, and obedience but not to a traditional order or way of being, more to one's self, which now begins to manifest as knowledge and power. The union of opposites: virgin and whore.

owl: The Shepherdess. Life and death; (need for) healing; magic; occult knowledge; initiation.

parents: (Your) relationship to power, security, and love. (See, for example, Alex's account of being wallpaper in her parents' house.)

passenger: Control (or lack of it) in your personal life. (See, for example, Marla's description of being a passenger on a spaceship and Michael's vision of being on an airplane where an alien experiment was taking place.)

past (events, etc.): The current situation parallels an earlier one; old patterns and unresolved issues. Need to learn from the past, undo what was done, and/or not repeat the same mistakes.

pattern(s) (on fabric, clothes, etc.): Patterns in life, relationships, and emotions, ways of thinking and behaving and so forth.

pavement: Confirmation; a clear grasp of the situation. An exclamation mark; "Yes!"

pendulum: Confusion, chaos, being in the midst of change; a situation coming to the surface as part of a process to be worked through. "There is no time."

quarantine (e.g., being in a pod on a spaceship as part of an intergalactic or interdimensional journey): The sense that life is not under one's own control, that you are being manipulated or not fully present in the world; limitations to personal creativity; issues with power. (Again, see Marla's accounts.)

radiance (light): Wisdom, truth.

silver: The moon (Salvia).

skull(s): Birth; time; transience; consciousness; awakening.

space: Possibility (of breakthroughs); openness; expansion.

triangles: Time; protection; boundaries. (See, for example, Darryl's account.)

UFO: Alienation. Or a new force entering your life.

underwater: The womb; the unconscious.

Universe: Infinite possibilities; new knowledge or wisdom; new direction.

upside down (inversion, e.g., the hanged man in the tarot deck): Looking at things from a new perspective; a reversal.

veil: The hidden; mystery; secret knowledge; the occult.

void: Potential; the possibility of or need for change.

wallpaper: A shield; a secret. (See, for example, Alex's vision.)

wardrobe: Identity or self-image; transition or change.

web: Fate; choice; karma. Ability with self-knowledge to build one's own web of attraction. Without self-knowledge the possibility of creating and becoming part of a web of illusions. The senses. Divinatory potential. (Based on Lilly's account of her visions during her Christmas diet.)

wheel(s) (cogs, circles, etc.): (Need for) completion and love.

x-ray vision: Seeing beyond the surface (what is presented) to the deeper (emotional, etc.) reality from which things arise.

yearning (for someone other than yourself): Realization that part of oneself is missing and the person in your vision was or is a projection of this.

Zen: Union of opposites; realization that the everyday world, built on causalities, is limited and false. Cutting through the (or your own) bullshit.

NOTES

INTRODUCTION. BEFORE WE START DREAMING TOGETHER . . .

1. For some of the other controversies surrounding the *Codex Alimentarius* see, for example, Shepherd, "Nil by Mouth," www.guardian .co.uk/society/2004/feb/29/health.shopping.
2. Arthur, *Salvia Divinorum.*
3. In an interview with Joerg Auf dem Hoevel published in *Hanfblatt* [117: 46–49 (2009)], which can be read in full at www.aufdemhoevel .de/int_siebert_en.html.

I. SALVIA DIVINORUM, THE SHEPHERDESS

1. Wasson, *Maria Sabina and Her Mushroom Velada.*
2. Siebert, "Daniel Siebert Speaks."
3. Roth, "Popularity of a Hallucinogen May Thwart Its Medical Uses," www.nytimes.com/2008/09/09/us/09Salvia.html.
4. Ibid.
5. See www.sagewisdom.org.
6. See my books *The Hummingbird's Journey to God* (2009), *Cactus of Mystery* (2012) for more information on San Pedro, and *Plant Spirit Shamanism* (2006) for a discussion of ayahausca.
7. Valdes III, Diaz, and Paul, "Early History of Salvia," at www .a1b2c3.com/drugs/Salvia2.htm.

8. Ibid.

9. Rätsch, *Encyclopedia of Psychoactive Plants.*

10. Mayer, "Salvia divinorum."

11. Rätsch, *Encyclopedia of Psychoactive Plants.*

12. Ibid.

13. Heaven and Charing, *Plant Spirit Shamanism.*

14. Heaven, *Hummingbird's Journey to God.*

15. Turner, *Salvinorin.*

16. Heaven, *Cactus of Mystery.*

17. Turner, *Salvinorin.*

18. Ibid.

2. THE QUEST IN PERU

1. Rätsch, *Encyclopedia of Psychoactive Plants.*

2. Turner, *Salvinorin.*

3. Pendell, *Phamako/Poeia.*

4. Pendell, "On the Nature of the Ally" in *Pharmakopoeia.*

5. Arthur, *Salvia Divinorum.*

6. Turner, *Salvinorin.*

7. Andreas, "Mind Shattering."

8. Roadhouse, www.erowid.org.

9. Somatzu, www.erowid.org.

10. Dennis McKenna, from the documentary, *Vine of the Soul.*

11. Trendal, www.erowid.org.

12. Eliade, *Shamanism.*

3. THE QUEST IN SPAIN

1. Sharon, *Wizard of the Four Winds.*

2. Valdes III, Diaz, and Paul, "Early History of Salvia."

3. Trendal, www.erowid.org.

4. Glassalchemist, "How the Machine Works."

5. Ibid.

6. Somatzu, www.erowid.org.

7. Jodorowsky, *The Way of Tarot.*

8. Glassalchemist, "How the Machine Works."

9. See www.sagewisdom.org/danielsiebert.html.

10. Arthur, *Salvia Divinorum.*

11. Talbot, *Holographic Universe.*

12. Crystallinesheen, www.erowid.org.

4. CONTINUING THE QUEST IN SPAIN

1. Eliade, *Shamanism.*

2. Ibid.

3. www.aufdemhoevel.de/int_siebert_en.html.

4. Pendell, *Phamako/Poeia.*

5. www.sagewisdom.org/braidaetal3.pdf.

6. Hanes, "Antidepressant Effects of the Herb Salvia Divinorum," 634–35.

7. Michaels and Holtzman, "Early Postnatal Stress."

8. Hasebe, et al. "Possible Pharmacotherapy."

9. Beardsley, Howard, Shelton, and Carroll, "Differential Effects."

10. Xuei, et al., "Association of the Kappa Opioid System."

11. Walker and Koob, "Pharmacological Evidence."

12. Hofmann, *LSD: My Problem Child.*

7. THE TEACHINGS OF THE SHEPHERDESS

1. Pendell, from the correspondences in the Salvia section of *Pharmako/Poeia.*

2. Arthur, *Salvia Divinorum.*

3. Shulgin and Bennett, "Dr. Ecstasy."

4. Sharon, *Wizard of the Four Winds.*

5. Talbot, *Holographic Universe.*

6. Arthur, *Salvia Divinorum.*

7. Ibid.

8. DIETING THE SHEPHERDESS: A DNA FANTASY

1. Shanon, "Talking Trash."

2. Carter, *Mapping the Mind.*

3. Terence McKenna, *Food of the Gods.*

4. Ibid.

5. Schultes and Winkelman, "Principle American Hallucinogenic Plants."

6. Neihardt, *Black Elk Speaks.*

7. Harner, *Jivaro.*

8. Wasson, *Maria Sabina and Her Mazatec Mushroom Velada.*

10. LOOSE ENDS

1. Arthur, *Salvia Divinorum.*

2. Ibid.

GLOSSARY

ally: According to Carlos Castaneda in *The Teachings of Don Juan*, his first book about his apprenticeship within the shamanic traditions of Mexico, "An ally is a power capable of transporting a man beyond the boundaries of himself; that is to say, an ally is a power which allows one to transcend the realm of ordinary reality."

The concept is similar in Amazonian shamanism. A plant may become an ally by dieting it so that its spirit enters the shaman and becomes part of his own, giving him power, strength, and the ability to transmit healing to others by passing on the qualities and essence of the plant through touch, intention, and the use of sacred songs called *icaros*. These are taught to the shaman by the spirit of the plant and are a form of energy that may be directed into a patient via the voice in order to create a positive change in him or her.

ayahuasca: The visionary vine of souls plays a central role in the spiritual and cultural traditions of the Amazon and in 2008 was recognized by the Peruvian government as a National Treasure. Its ceremonial use is ancient. One of the earliest objects related to it is a specially engraved cup, now a museum piece, which was found in the Amazon around 500 BC, and shows that it has been used as a sacrament for at least 2,500 years.

The brew is made from two plants, the ayahuasca vine (*Banisteriopsis caapi*) and the leaves of the chacruna bush (*Psychotria viridis*). The mixture is prepared by cleaning the vines and adding them and the leaves to water. This is then boiled and reduced for several hours.

Via visions and spirit connections, the brew provides healing to the patient by offering him a new sense of understanding about what is happening in his life, allowing feelings to unblock so that sadness, anger, and other unhelpful energies are transmuted to ecstasy and love. During a ceremony, for example, a patient might make a healing connection between a negative event from the past and a pattern of *saladera* (bad luck) he is experiencing now. The brew releases this negative energy so that new positive energies can flow. This is a purification of the soul so that luck can change for the better, and old attachments and limitations are released. For more information on ayahuasca see my book *Plant Spirit Shamanism* (Inner Traditions, 2006).

curandero (curandera, if female): "One who heals" (from the Spanish *curar:* to cure or heal). A curandero is a plant spirit shaman who normally works with medicine plants as well as teacher plants such as Salvia, San Pedro, or ayahuasca. He performs his healings in collaboration with his spirit helpers and allies.

diet: A special shamanic regime followed in order to absorb the spirit of a plant and make an ally of it. The diet involves purification, abstention from some foodstuffs, alcohol, and sexual activity, as well as ritual seclusion, meditation, and cleansings. At the end of the diet, if successful and no taboos have been broken, the patient will have a new energy and strength that comes directly from the plant.

entheogen: "That which reveals the God within." A teacher plant such as Salvia, San Pedro, or ayahuasca that is taken in a strict ceremonial context for the purposes of shamanic seeing, vision questing, connection to spirit, or the attainment of healing and power

limpia: A ritual cleansing, which may take many forms. In Mazatec shamanism, prayer and tobacco smoke are used, the latter blown over the patient to purify him. In the Andes the patient may be bathed in the smoke of palo santo, a fragrant wood with spiritual powers. In the Amazon flower baths are prepared using particular plants that have the ability to heal, cleanse, or balance the patient's energies. The waters are poured over the patient, and he washes in them.

Mazatec: The indigenous people of the Sierra Mazateca in northern Oaxaca, Mexico. Mazatec shamans use psilocybin ("magic") mushrooms, *Salvia divinorum,* and morning glory seeds to facilitate special states of shamanic consciousness in themselves and their patients through which they contact the spirit world and perform healings, divinations, and cleansings. Several researchers have commented on the difficulty in obtaining detailed information on these ritual practices, however, as Mazatec shamans are secretive and protective of their knowledge.

mesa: A decorated ritual cloth used as an altar, holding power objects (called *artes*), which are used for healing during shamanic ceremonies.

moloka: In Peru, the shamanic temple in which ceremonies are held. Normally round and open sided. The word *moloka* translates from the Quechuan simply as "place" but the meaning is "an area for sacred gatherings."

San Pedro (Mexico): Dried tobacco leaf mixed with lime to form a powder that is worn in charms and amulets as a protection against diseases and witchcraft. It is also used in *limpias* (ritual cleansings) and carried by participants in Salvia ceremonies for assistance and security during their spirit journeys.

San Pedro (Peru): *Trichocereus pachanoi,* the "cactus of vision" is a sacred teacher plant of South America. Its name refers to Saint Peter who holds the keys to heaven and speaks of its ability to "open the gates" for us into a world where we can heal, discover our divinity, and find our purpose on Earth.

Its use as a sacrament and in healing rituals is ancient. The earliest archaeological evidence so far discovered is a stone carving found at the Jaguar Temple of Chavín de Huantar in northern Peru, which is almost 3,500 years old. Textiles from the same region and period of history depict the cactus with jaguars and hummingbirds, two of its guardian spirits, and with stylized spirals representing the visionary experience.

The ethnobotanist Richard Evans Schultes wrote of San Pedro in his book *Plants of the Gods* that it is "always in tune with the powers of animals and beings that have supernatural powers. . . . Participants [in ceremonies] are 'set free from matter' and engage in flight through cosmic regions . . . transported across time and distance in a rapid and safe fashion." The author Aldous Huxley wrote of his experiences in *The Doors of Perception* that "I was seeing what Adam had seen on the morning of his creation—the miracle—moment by moment, of naked existence . . . flowers shining with their own inner light and all but quivering under the pressure of the significance with which they were charged . . . a transience that was yet eternal life . . . the divine source of all existence . . . a repeated flow from beauty to heightened beauty, from deeper to ever deeper meaning." For more information on San Pedro see my books *Cactus of Mystery* (Park Street Press, 2012) and *The Hummingbird's Journey to God* (O Books, 2009).

BIBLIOGRAPHY

Andreas. "Mind Shattering: Experience with Salvia Divinorum." www.erowid .org.

Arthur, J. D. *Salvia Divinorum*. Rochester, Vt.: Park Street Press, 2009.

Ball, Martin. *Sage Spirit*. Ashland, Ore.: Kyandara, 2007.

Beardsley, Patrick M., James L. Howard, Keith L. Shelton, and F. Ivy Carroll. "Differential Effects of the Novel Kappa Opioid Receptor Antagonist, JDTic, on Reinstatement of Cocaine-Seeking Induced by Footshock Stressors vs. Cocaine Primes and Its Antidepressant-Like Effects in Rats." *Psychopharmacology*, November 2005.

Braida, Daniela. www. sagewisdom.org/braidaetal3.pdf.

Carter, Rita. *Mapping the Mind*. London: Phoenix Books, 1998.

Castaneda, Carlos. *The Teachings of Don Juan: A Yaqui Way of Knowledge*. New York: Washington Square Press, 1998.

Crystallinesheen. www.erowid.org.

DoOr. www.erowid.org.

Eliade, Mircea. *Shamanism: Archaic Techniques of Ecstasy*. Princeton, N.J.: Princeton University Press, 2004.

Glassalchemist. "How the Machine Works: Experience with DMT and *Salvia divinorum*." www.erowid.org. November 6, 2009.

Hanes, Karl. "Antidepressant Effects of the Herb Salvia Divinorum: A Case Report." *Journal of Clinical Psychopharmacology*, December 2001.

Harner, Michael. *The Jivaro: People of the Sacred Waterfalls*. Berkeley: University of California Press, 1984.

Hasebe, Ko, Koji Kawai, Tomohiko Suzuki, Kuniaki Kawamura, Toshiaki Tanaka, Minoru Narita, Hiroshi Nagase, and Tsutomi Suzuki. "Possible

Pharmacotherapy of the Opioid Kappa Receptor Agonist for Drug Dependence." *Annals of the New York Academy of Sciences,* October 2004.

Heaven, Ross. *The Hummingbird's Journey to God.* London: O Books, 2009.

———. *Cactus of Mystery.* Rochester, Vt.: Park Street Press, 2012.

Heaven, Ross, and Howard G. Charing. *Plant Spirit Shamanism: Traditional Techniques for Healing the Soul.* Rochester, Vt.: Destiny Books, 2006.

Hofmann, Albert. *LSD: My Problem Child.* New York: McGraw Hill, 1980.

Huxley, Aldous. *The Doors of Perception.* New York: HarperCollins, 2004.

Jansen, Karl. *Ketamine: Dreams and Realities.* MAPS, 2004.

Jodorowsky, Alejandro, and Marianne Costa. *The Way of Tarot: The Spiritual Teacher in the Cards.* Rochester, Vermont: Destiny Books, 2009.

Mayer, Karl. "Salvia divinorum: Ein Halluzinogen der Mazatteken von Oaxaca." *Ethnologia Americana* 14, 1977.

McKenna, Dennis. *Vine of the Soul.* (Documentary film) www.vineofthesoul.com.

McKenna, Terence. *Food of the Gods: The Search for the Original Tree of Knowledge: A Radical History of Plants, Drugs, and Human Evolution.* New York: Bantam, 1993.

Michaels, Clifford C., and Stephen G. Holtzman. "Early Postnatal Stress Alters Place Conditioning to Both Mu and Kappa-Opioid Agonists." *The Journal of Pharmacology and Experimental Therapeutics,* April 2008.

Michell, John. *Confessions of a Radical Traditionalist.* Waterbury Center, Vt.: Dominion Press, 2005.

Morrison, Jim. *The Lords: The New Creature Poems.* London: Omnibus Press, 1985.

Neihardt, John G. *Black Elk Speaks: Being the Life Story of a Holy Man of the Oglala Sioux.* Lincoln, Neb.: University of Nebraska Press, 1932.

Pendell, Dale. *Pharmako/Poeia: Plant Powers, Poisons, and Herbcraft.* San Francisco: Mercury House, 1995.

Rätsch, Christian. *The Encyclopedia of Psychoactive Plants.* Rochester, Vt.: Park Street Press, 2005.

Roadhouse. www.erowid.org.

Sack, Kevin, and Brent McDonald. "Popularity of a Hallucinogen May Thwart Its Medical Uses." *New York Times,* September 8, 2008. www.nytimes.com/2008/09/09/us/09Salvia.html.

Schultes, Richard Evans, Albert Hofmann, and Christian Rätsch. *Plants of the Gods: Origins of Hallucinogenic Use.* Rochester, Vt.: Healing Arts Press, 2001.

Schultes, Richard Evans, and Michael Winkelman. "The Principle American Hallucinogenic Plants and Their Bioactive and Therapeutic Properties." In *Yearbook of Cross-Cultural Medicine and Psychotherapy*. Edited by Michael Winkelman and Walter Andritzky. Berlin: Verlag fur Wissenschaft und Bildung, 1995.

Shanon, Claude E. "Talking Trash: What's in a Word?" *Scientific American,* March 1995.

Sharon, Douglas. *Wizard of the Four Winds: A Shaman's Story.* New York: Free Press, 1979.

Shepard, Paul. *Men in the Landscape: A Historic View of the Esthetics of Nature.* Athens, Ga.: University of Georgia Press, 2002.

Shepherd, Rose. "Nil by Mouth." *The Observer,* February 29, 2004.

Shulgin, Alexander, and Drake Bennett. "Dr. Ecstasy." *New York Times Magazine,* January 30, 2005. www.nytimes.com/2005/01/30/magazine/30ECSTASY .html.

Siebert, Daniel. "Daniel Siebert Speaks." *The Entheogen Review,* no. 4: (1994).

———. www.aufdemhoevel.de/int_siebert_en.html.

Somatzu. www.erowid.org.

Talbot, Michael. *The Holographic Universe: The Revolutionary Theory of Reality.* London: HarperCollins, 1996.

Trendal. www.erowid.org.

Turner, D. M. (Joseph Vivian). *Salvinorin: The Psychedelic Essence of Salvia Divinorum.* San Francisco: Panther Books, 1996.

Valdes, Leander J. III, Jose Luis Diaz, and Ara G. Paul. "The Early History of Salvia." *Entheogen Review* 10 no. 3. www.a1b2c3.com/drugs/Salvia2.htm.

Walker, Brendan M., and George F. Koob. "Pharmacological Evidence for a Motivational Role of Kappa Opioid Systems in Ethanol Dependence." *Neuropsychopharmacology,* February 2008.

Wasson, R. Gordon. *Maria Sabina and Her Mushroom Velada.* New York: Houghton Mifflin Harcourt, 1974.

Xuei, X., D. Dick, L. Flury-Wetherill, H. J. Tian, A. Agrawal, L. Bierut, A. Goate, K. Bucholz, M. Schuckit, J. Nurnberger, J. Tischfield, S. Kuperman, B. Porjesz, H. Begleiter, T. Foroud, and H. J. Edenberg. "Association of the Kappa Opioid System with Alcohol Dependence." *Molecular Psychiatry,* November 2006.

INDEX

ABOUT THE AUTHOR

Ross Heaven is the author of several books on shamanism and healing and runs workshops on these themes in Europe and Peru, including Shamanic Practitioner training programs; Shamanic Healing and Soul Retrieval courses; plant medicine retreats with San Pedro, Salvia, and ayahuasca; and journeys to Peru to work with indigenous shamans. He is also a shamanic healer and therapist and offers counseling, soul retrieval, and healing in the United Kingdom

He has a website at www.thefourgates.org where you can read more about his work as well as forthcoming books and other items of interest. He also provides a monthly newsletter by e-mail, which you can receive free of charge at ross@thefourgates.org.

Other books on plant teachers and medicines include *Cactus of Mystery* and *The Hummingbird's Journey to God,* about San Pedro, *Plant Spirit Shamanism,* about ayahuasca and Amazonian plant healing, and *Plant Spirit Wisdom* and *The Sin Eater's Last Confessions,* about Celtic methods of soul healing with herbs and plants. His full book list can be viewed at Amazon Books.

BOOKS OF RELATED INTEREST

Plant Spirit Shamanism
Traditional Techniques for Healing the Soul
by Ross Heaven and Howard G. Charing

Cactus of Mystery
The Shamanic Powers of the Peruvian San Pedro Cactus
by Ross Heaven

Salvia Divinorum
Doorway to Thought-Free Awareness
by J. D. Arthur

Plants of the Gods
Their Sacred, Healing, and Hallucinogenic Powers
by Richard Evans Schultes, Albert Hofmann, and Christian Rätsch

The Encyclopedia of Psychoactive Plants
Ethnopharmacology and Its Applications
by Christian Rätsch

DMT: The Spirit Molecule
A Doctor's Revolutionary Research into the Biology of
Near-Death and Mystical Experiences
by Rick Strassman, M.D.

The Psychedelic Explorer's Guide
Safe, Therapeutic, and Sacred Journeys
by James Fadiman, Ph.D.

The Secret Teachings of Plants
The Intelligence of the Heart in the Direct Perception of Nature
by Stephen Harrod Buhner

INNER TRADITIONS • BEAR & COMPANY
P.O. Box 388
Rochester, VT 05767
1-800-246-8648
www.InnerTraditions.com

Or contact your local bookseller